SOCIAL DISCOURSE AND MORAL JUDGMENT

SOCIAL DISCOURSE AND MORAL JUDGMENT

Edited by
Daniel N. Robinson
Department of Psychology
Georgetown University
Washington, D.C.

ACADEMIC PRESS, INC.
Harcourt Brace Jovanovich, Publishers
San Diego   New York   Boston
London   Sydney   Tokyo   Toronto

This book is printed on acid-free paper. ∞

Academic Press, Inc.
1250 Sixth Avenue, San Diego, California 92101-4311

United Kingdom Edition published by
Academic Press Limited
24–28 Oval Road, London NW1 7DX

Library of Congress Cataloging-in-Publication Data

Social discourse and moral judgment / edited by Daniel N. Robinson.
    p. cm.
    Includes index.
    ISBN 0-12-590155-0
    1. Social ethics.   2. Social psychology–Moral and ethical
aspects.   3. Discourse analysis.   I. Robinson, Daniel, date
HM216.S5495   1992
303.3'72–dc20   92-15214
                                                       CIP

73799

PRINTED IN THE UNITED STATES OF AMERICA
92 93 94 95 96 97   QW   9 8 7 6 5 4 3 2 1

CONTENTS

15 MORAL PHILOSOPHY AND SOCIAL SCIENCE: A CRITIQUE OF CONSTRUCTIONIST REASON

W. Gerrod Parrott

16 EPILOGUE

CONTRIBUTORS

Numbers in parentheses indicate the pages on which the authors' contributions begin.

JEROME BRUNER (99), 200 Mercer Street, New York, New York 10012

ROBERT P. GEORGE (123), Department of Politics, Princeton University, Princeton, New Jersey 08544

KENNETH J. GERGEN (9), Department of Psychology, Swarthmore College, Swarthmore, Pennsylvania 19081

ROM HARRÉ (61), Linacre College, Oxford, and Department of Psychology, Georgetown University, Washington, D.C. 20057

GEORGE S. HOWARD (151), Department of Psychology, University of Notre Dame, Notre Dame, Indiana 46556

JAMES T. LAMIELL (29), Department of Psychology, Georgetown University, Washington, D.C. 20057

FATHALI MOGHADDAM (167), Department of Psychology, Georgetown University, Washington, D.C. 20057

NANCY C. MUCH (133), Department of Psychology, Georgetown University, Washington, D.C. 20057

DANIEL C. O'CONNELL (113), Department of Psychology, Georgetown University, Washington, D.C. 20057

W. GERROD PARROTT (207), Department of Psychology, Georgetown University, Washington, D.C. 20057

DANIEL N. ROBINSON (1, 87), Department of Psychology, Georgetown University, Washington, D.C. 20057

JOSEPH F. RYCHLAK (43), Department of Psychology, Loyola University in Chicago, Chicago, Illinois 60626

JOHN SABINI (75), Department of Psychology, University of Pennsylvania, Philadelphia, Pennsylvania 19104

JOHN SHOTTER (181), Department of Communications, University of New Hampshire, Durham, New Hampshire 03824

MAURY SILVER (75), Department of Psychology, St. Francis College, Brooklyn, New York 11201

1 INTRODUCTION

Daniel N. Robinson

Moral science *or* social science? Moral science *as* social science? Moral science *is* social science. Here are imponderables that engaged the energies of ancient philosophers and have enlisted armies of able thinkers ever since, right up to our own "post-modernist" epoch.

In Book II of the *Republic* the myth of Gyges is introduced by Glaucon to remind Socrates that conduct is guided by impulsive desire and fear of punishment, and certainly not by timeless, universal principles of virtue. By turning his newly acquired and magical ring, Gyges is able to render himself invisible. It is not long before we find him killing the King, seducing the Queen, and taking control of the realm. What Socrates is urged to do in light of this is surrender his attachment to abstractions and address the moral dimensions of life in the idiom of daily *practices* as these unfold in real societies populated by actual beings.

Socrates is fairly successful in turning around the arguments of Glaucon and the others and establishing that the satisfaction of sensual desire cannot provide enduring happiness or any form of happiness compatible with human nature. By Book VII the realms of thought have been partitioned into the fruits of intellect and those of mere opinion, the latter nothing more than the residue of habitual modes of thought conditioned by custom. Only through the lifelong cultivation of intellect are the terms of a reasonable and virtuous life discovered, and only those who have made progress in this are fit to rule others. Only one who knows the good can lead others toward it.

What is rejected finally in Plato's *Republic* is the proposition that the sanctions

SOCIAL DISCOURSE AND MORAL JUDGMENT
Copyright © 1992 by Academic Press, Inc. All rights of reproduction in any form reserved.

of morality are grounded in nothing firmer than social conventions or the habits of the tribe. To insist that one *ought* to do only what is authorized by custom or prefigured in the very language of moral tuition is to invoke the concept of *duty* and thus to add something to the anthropological account; something that cannot be yielded within it. In the end, the moral realm is discovered only by one who takes counsel with conscience, and who does so chiefly by turning away from the tinsel of the market and the fellowship of the mob. Life within this realm is difficult and, as Socrates learned, perilous.

The Socratic conception of morality—or that state of *moral excellence* not fully rendered by the Latin *virtūs,* less by the English *virtue*—is grounded in the irreducible moral unit, the *person,* and is defended by arguments at once dialectical and transcendental. The dialectical character imposes the requirement that moral assertions submit to tests of reasonableness. This is a turning away from older forms of moral teaching embodied in the Wise Man or worked out in epic narratives and drama. The adoption of dialectic itself acknowledges that there are moral problems to be solved and that the solutions must pass the test of rational assessment. The ritual dance, the parable, the fable—in a word, the *liturgy*—will serve as little more than ornamentation. All *ipse dixits* are put on notice. Also ruled out is any total moral scepticism. Once sceptics grant that their utterances are meant to be taken seriously, or regarded as true, or not intended to deceive or cajole, they have joined the debate. Only after they have (if only implicitly) accepted the moral canons by which disputation itself (becomes possible) can their sceptical position even be advanced. The dialectic also admits only those who are not in the sleep-walking or brain-washed state of the automaton; those who can rise above the level of the merely habitual and, from a greater height, see what *ought* to be beyond the flotsam of what *is*.

The transcendental character of Socratic moral theory is warranted by the requirement that genuinely moral actions are *chosen,* and chosen because they are right. Were the choice to be governed by the consideration exemplified by Gyges, morality would be no more than a species of lust or some other condition of the body—or condition of a soul that had not liberated itself from the body-prison. It is in virtue of this transcendental feature that moral theories inspired by the Socratic dialogues are generally indifferent or even hostile to "biosocial" considerations. If such theories are not other-worldly, they are assuredly not worldly.

Rather more worldly, however, is the moral philosophy developed by Aristotle, partly to complete and partly to correct the teachings of the Academy. The moral domain for Aristotle is the domain of actual practices engaged in by real persons functioning within a larger social and political context. Absent such contexts, there would be little occasion for moral excellence. As for such excellence, it cannot be identified except through a developed *psychology*. But this psychology must itself be informed by the larger ethological, social, and historical records that provide an accurate account of the needs and propensities of the animal under consideration. If it can be said (as Socrates himself said) that Socratic moral teaching prepares one for death, Aristotle's might be regarded as preparing one not only for life, but for a rich and varied social life within a complex and demanding political environment.

For his own part, Aristotle seems finally to vote for the contemplative life pursued for no sake other than itself. But the social science developed in his ethical and political writings is not addressed to this reflective and contemplative being whose serenity excites images of "the Isle of the Blest." Rather, we are given a thoroughly *social* animal who must be able to carve a principled form of life out of the possibilities actually given. Yet, even on this understanding, Aristotle is persuaded that there are rational and moral powers existing apart from the social context and necessary for such contexts to be established and preserved.

In the *Rhetoric* Aristotle distinguishes between two kinds of law, one that he calls particular and the other universal. He then goes on to say that, whereas specific laws arise within a given community and pertain to its own members,

> Universal law is the law of nature. For there really is, as everyone to some extent divines, a natural justice and injustice that is common to all, even to those who have no association or covenant with each other. It is this that Sophocles' Antigone clearly means when she says that the burial of Polyneices was a just act in spite of the prohibition: she means that it was just by nature.
> "Not of today or yesterday it is,
> But lives eternal: none can date its birth." (*Rhetoric,* Book I, 1373^b 1–14)

Antigone is well aware of the customs of her world and of the fact that within this world the will of the Prince is the law of the land. King Creon has ordered that the body of Polyneices not be touched, but left for the dogs. The words Sophocles gives to Antigone are intended not to illuminate the customary foundations of law but to challenge them by pointing to something more fundamental and abiding; something on which custom itself must depend lest it be powerless to summon our fidelity.

Later in the same essay Aristotle considers the concept and function of *equity* within a legal context, taking it to be "the sort of justice which goes beyond the written law," compensating for the legislative impossibility of anticipating *every* species of infraction or injury (*Rhetoric,* 1374^a 25–1374^b 23). Again, the very existence of equity discloses that intuitive or native sense of justice that is wider than any collection of statutes and that finally must be assumed if such statutes are to be intelligible to those who would be ruled by them. What is contrasted here is the *lex scripta,* with its unavoidable ambiguities and incompleteness, and a pervasive *ius naturale* that makes it possible for at least one species to organize itself around the rule of law. The attribute or power or faculty by which this comes about is then taken to be part of the very definition of humanity and not something grafted on, taught, or imposed.

Plato and Aristotle are the authoritative ancient sources for most of the moral discourse that has animated Western intellectual history for the past two millenia. Absorbed first into Christian teaching and then more diffusely into secular political and moral philosophies, Platonic and Aristotelian conceptions would become objects of tireless revisions and interpretations between the extremes of reverence and contempt. Every age of intellectual energy has, as it were, earned its stripes by clarifying, criticizing, or stridently dismissing Plato or Aristotle, or by choosing one over the other. Thus does the Long Debate go on, our own epoch making additions that will have to be assessed by a still later age.

What sort of additions might Psychology and the social sciences make to this debate? For much of the present century no answer was possible if only because the discipline itself had essentially left the field! The so-called moral realm, on a behavioristic account, is the setting in which significant personal or social objectives are reached by the proper "scientific" management of reinforcing contingencies. Morality is just another and rather delphic term for the shaping of complex chains of behavior. If it is something else, it must be another instance of mere talk. "No praise; no blame" was the watchword of behavioristic moralists.

The psychoanalytic perspective, though taking moral issues seriously, tends to treat them as the unavoidable consequence of psychological conflicts raging at levels often beyond the awareness of the participants. Whatever might be said in behalf of such a view, it does not really look over the same domain of concerns occupied by the important treatises in moral philosophy and jurisprudence. Thus, neither the Skinnerian nor the Freudian conception of human nature provided a framework within which the admittedly central issues in moral discourse might be honored in their own terms.

Might more recent developments within Psychology offer more? And why should one expect as much from this quarter? If we are in fact in a position to do more than either echo or ignore older views it may be because centuries of scholarship have explained them more fully, and because we now may lay claim to a far broader and deeper body of anthropological and psychological evidence than any available to scholars of the past. It was Aristotle, we should recall, who attempted to craft a moral philosophy conditioned by what he took to be the essentials of human nature. An age claiming a more valid and complete set of human sciences might therefore be expected to develop a moral science more fully.

Similarly, the Socratic and the Aristotelian conceptions of morality are beholden to even more fundamental theories of rationality itself and those structured forms of thought that make principled conduct possible. If neither behaviorism nor psychoanalytic theory offers anything informing on these matters, the same cannot be said of the most influential recent developments. I shall note two of these, one of them being the focus of the present volume.

In the most recent decade the discipline has turned away from both behavioristic and psychoanalytic orientations, in at least two and diverging directions. The "cognitive revolution" has now more or less settled down into a number of interesting collaborative programs combining the special skills and perspectives of the neural sciences, computational linguistics, philosophy of mind, and computer science. The direction of research and theory in this domain is away from the behavioristic and descriptive psychologies that marked the boundaries of the discipline since the 1950s and toward more abstract and theoretical models of implicit processes and functions. A new or at least revived and highly technical "Faculty Psychology" is being refined in these busy kilns and, even if the promises made in behalf of this Psychology are never redeemed, many will agree that the programs have been liberating.

A less spectacular but perhaps more significant development has been taking place at the same time, similar to the "cognitive revolution" in the richness of interdisciplinary collaborations and in its impatience with the "Block Universes" of behavioristic and psychoanalytic psychologies. I refer to *social constructionism* specifically and, more generally, to an enlarged philosophy of social science fully incompatible with any and every positivistic scheme for psychological inquiry. The psychological facts of the world, on this construal, are cultural and linguistic products. They are grounded in practices calling not for description but interpretation. They become intelligible only within the broad context of local and more remote histories; within the context of lives as actually lived and their bequests.

In the dialogue *Cratylus* and elsewhere Plato recognizes the subtle and pervasive manner in which the conventions of language shape and color thought, but neither Plato nor Aristotle anticipated the importance attached to these conventions by recent works in social constructionism in the patrimony of Wittgenstein and Vygotsky. These same works consider ethnic and historio-cultural patterns of thought conditioned by and also shaping these linguistic conventions. The human "mind" that arises from this web of ethno-linguistic influences is no longer the inner resource of a moral individual, but the shared resource of a community of moral practitioners. This conception of morality, of which there are any number of historical heralds in the history of ideas, has now become influential partly because of the fuller anthropological and psychological record and also as a result of its application to wider fields of inquiry, for example, politics, law, education, literature, and the arts.

These developments are momentous and still unsettled. Yet even at this early stage the marks of earlier loyalties are visible. At least when judged from one perspective, social constructionism seems finally unable to embrace or explicate the *moral* dimensions of life any more fully than the psychologies it would replace. The perspective supporting this conclusion is not strictly "Kantian"— though Kantian moral theorists would surely find both of these new psychologies to be outside the moral realm—and not necessarily "absolutistic." It is, however, *individualistic* in taking the *person* to be the irreducible subject of moral regard and, to this extent, the collective as something of an abstraction or social science "construct."

As with other influential movements in the domain of moral discourse, the room for misunderstanding is great. Also great is the tendency for like-minded theorists to spend much of their time in each other's intellectual company and less time in the presence of critics no less admiring for their persistence. The present collection of essays is offered to reduce misunderstandings chiefly by directing sharp criticism toward these current conceptions of morality in relation to the psychological and social aspects of human nature.

The essays themselves were written for a symposium convened at Georgetown University in March of 1991. Target-articles were requested from five scholars strongly advocating social constructionism and two scholars likely to have strong reservations about it. Members of the Psychology Department at Georgetown then took on the burden of criticism, either in defense of or in opposition to constructionist theory, depending on the contents of the target-article. With all essays and replies assembled, every contributor received the full set before the symposium was held. Then an evening, a full day, and a morning were devoted to clarifying positions, to considering avenues of productive inquiry, and to marking those points on which more general agreement is likely to be elusive. Chapter 16, "Epilogue," presents some of the more fruitful colloquies and summary positions developed on these days.

If two "contenders" can be discerned at all in so complex a collection of theories, findings, and assumptions, they would be versions of the traditional "intuitionist" and "empiricistic" schools, but with great reservations surrounding these terms. The defenders of one or another version of social constructionism in the present collection (Bruner, Gergen, Harré, Howard, Much, Moghaddam, Sabini and Silver, and Shotter) are not in lockstep agreement with one another; consider the essays by Gergen and Harré and the essay by Howard and Moghaddam's critique of it. Nor are their critics all critical on the same grounds. The essays by George and Rychlak, and Robinson's critique of Sabini and Silver, are rooted in more or less classical moral theories of the "intuitionist" stripe (Plato, Aristotle, Kant) but there are differences even here.

What permits the constructionists to be located in the empiricistic tradition is their appeal to *external* sources of morality; to a moral ontology outside the person and located in the public duchies of language and culture. They are "empiricists" in the strictly literal sense (*observers*) if no other. As for intuitionism—a term that finds at least one "intuitionist" bridle—one can take it to mean no more than the locus of moral origins, this being the deliberating agent capable of excluding from the arena of deliberation all that is solely conventional.

REFERENCE

Aristotle. (1984). *Rhetoric*. In Jonathan Barnes (Ed.), *The Complete Works of Aristotle*, Vol. 2. Princeton: Princeton University Press.

2 SOCIAL CONSTRUCTION AND MORAL ACTION

Kenneth J. Gergen

In the Western tradition it is the single individual who serves as the atom of moral concern—that essence without which matters of ethical debate would have little point and without whose commitment indeed the society might revert to chaos. Thus philosophers seek to establish essential criteria for moral decision making, religious institutions are concerned with states of individual conscience, courts of law establish criteria for judging individual guilt, educational institutions are motivated to instill good personal values, and parents are concerned with the moral education and character of their offspring. Or to put it otherwise, in matters of ethics, morality, and ultimately the good society, the Western peoples are *psychologists*. It is the virtuous mind that propels meritorious conduct, and with sufficient numbers of individuals performing worthy acts, we achieve the good society. Professional psychologists thus come to play a pivotal role in the culture's concerns with moral action, for as it seems, they have the means by which the secrets of the virtuous mind (and more cogently, the iniquitous mind) might be disclosed. Thus, from Freud's early work on the formation of the Super-Ego, through social learning formulations of modeling, and contemporary theories of moral decision making, psychology has played (and continues to play) an important role in describing the basis of moral action and furnishing insights into its genesis.

Yet, the relationship between the psychologist and the culture is a precarious one. For moral discourse within the society at large, along with its conceptions of human functioning, reflects a number of ancient traditions—Hebraic, classic

Greek, and Christian among them—whereas psychological conceptions of human functioning (along with research methods designed around these conceptions) are largely products of the twentieth century. As we shall find during the course of this chapter, there are certain ways in which mainstream psychology threatens the very concept of moral action, and indeed all of moral discourse. However, the more general point is that discourse about moral action within the society stands in a dialogic relationship to the shared understandings within the psychological profession. The profession must thus be sensitive to the broader concerns of the culture, for without such sensitivity they fail to communicate. And most importantly for present purposes, the profession should be deeply sensitive to the implications of its formulations for cultural life more generally. To define the nature of individual functioning within the profession is to inform public understanding of the good and to fashion policies for treatment of the less than good.

It is within this context that I wish to consider two major views of moral action emerging within recent history, both in terms of what they say about individual functioning and what they offer to society more generally. These views, which I shall call the romanticist and the modernist, have figured within various psychological formulations, and both have multiple implications for societal action. However, as I shall argue, both the romanticist and modernist conceptions of moral action are flawed in important ways. Neither can deliver what is promised in terms of a viable conception of human functioning or ethical foundations for a viable society. It is in this context that I shall introduce an alternative orientation to human functioning, the social constructionist. It is an orientation that throws into question the psychologistic framing of moral issues. And, while it refuses to furnish an alternative foundation for moral action, it is this very refusal that may hold the greatest promise for human well-being.

ROMANTICISM AND INHERENT MORALITY

While there are many stories to be told about the romanticist movement in nineteenth-century arts, literature, philosophy, and music, I shall offer here only a brief condensation of existing treatments of romanticist presumptions of moral being. For the romanticist, the most significant domain of human functioning was beyond the immediate grasp of consciousness—a domain I have characterized elsewhere (Gergen, 1991) as a "deep interior." At the center of the deep interior was the human spirit or soul, related on the one hand to God (and thus touched with a divine element), but at the same time rooted in nature (thus possessing instinctive force). It was this energic force, fed by both divine and natural energies, that gave rise to passion, inspiration, and works of genius.

Most important for present purposes, within the deep interior were to be found inherent values or moral sentiments—guidance for a worthy life, inspiration for virtuous works, resources for resisting temptation, and foundations for philosophic and religious formulations of the good. As Shelley put the case, "the essence, the vitality of [moral] actions, derives its color from what is no way contributed to from any external source. . . . The benevolent propensities are . . . inherent in the human mind. We are impelled to seek the happiness of others." The view echoes as well in G. E. Moore's turn of the century volume, *Principia Ethica*. Moore trusts to the individual's deeply nurtured intuitions as sources of moral action. "They are incapable of proof or disproof," he writes, "and indeed no evidence or reasoning whatever can be adduced in their favour or disfavour." For Moore, "personal affections" and "aesthetic enjoyments" were among the greatest goods imaginable. Various strands of the romanticist legacy are today spoken of in terms of "expressivism," "emotivism," and "intuitionism." And, while romanticism ceases to play a compelling role in the intellectual world, it is probably the central means by which persons presently justify their moral positions in daily life.

THE WANING OF ROMANTIC MORALITY

Neither the romanticist conception of the human being nor its allied view of moral direction remains broadly robust. They cease to be viable in large measure because of the advent of alternative discourses—arguments of stronger rational and rhetorical appeal. Three of these lines of argument deserve attention:

1. *The Darwinian Thesis.* One can scarcely overestimate the impact of Darwin's *The Origin of the Species* on intellectual life at the turn of the century. For present purposes, however, Darwin's view was deeply inimical to the romanticist views of morality. For Darwin the various species of life were essentially locked into a Hobbesian struggle of all against all. The survival of the human species thus demanded that humans hold an adaptive edge over their competitors in the animal kingdom. And, if adaptation required an acute understanding of the environment and a systematic assessment of various courses of action, favored was a view of human functioning that would grant to the human just these capacities. The optimally functioning human being, in the Darwinian view, would be one who relied most heavily on powers of observation and reason. Such a conception of human functioning was not only at odds with the romanticist view of the individual, but as well with its companionate view of moral principles. An individual driven by sentiments, passions, or raptures would simply be nonadaptive; the romanticist is not ideally fitted for survival. And because moral sentiments do not operate on the basis of the real, but the ideal—because they are not tied to contingencies but to conscience—then moral sentiments are also suspect as guides to action.

2. *The Rise of Science*. Coupled with and congenial to the hegemony of Darwinism was the blossoming of the scientific perspective. During the nineteenth century impressive strides had been made in the medical sciences, chemistry, and physics and the technological results were becoming widely evident. Science thus came to be seen as the institution par excellence, fitted for survival. In effect, scientism served as a choral accompaniment to the Darwinian perspective. At the same time, science traced its origins to the Enlightenment, and to the significance of individual observation and rationality. Moral sentiments were, by definition, nonrational (or by implication irrational). Effective action in life, as in science, demanded astute observation and logical reasoning. To ground one's action in moral sentiments was no better than proclaiming one's affections or tastes.

3. *Cultural Consciousness*. As both Darwinism and scientism gained increasing voice, so were scholarly interests increasingly turned toward the objective study of the human species, both historically and cross-culturally. The publication of Edward Burnett Tylor's *Primitive Culture* in 1871 set the stage, in particular, for inquiry into various systems of ethical or religious belief. Such studies served in many ways as a means of replacing religious with scientific authority. For as such work attempted to demonstrate, the range and variety of religious and moral commitments were enormous. And given this variety there was little means by which Christianity could proclaim superiority. Claims to religious truth were thus reduced to little more than rhetoric. By implication, attempts to establish systems of value or ethics based on moral sentiments or intuitions now seemed to be Western prejudice in disguise.

MODERNISM AND MORALITY

As Western culture moved into the twentieth century, the romantic conception of the moral being was essentially losing its grasp on the intellectual imagination. Not only was it difficult to reconcile the romantic view of the deep interior with Darwinism, scientism, and the spread of cultural consciousness, but the romantic conception of fundamental or universal moral sentiments also proved unconvincing. Perhaps the death knell for romanticism in ethics was saved for later in the twentieth century. Of those various movements claiming transcendental probity in matters of human good, or moral superiority, two of the most outspoken were Communism and Nazism. While the former demonstrated the enormous oppression that could be rationalized by claims to superior insight into the good, the latter enabled the world to glimpse the apocalyptic potential inherent in such claims. This is hardly to say that the rhetoric of moral sentiments is dead. There are many and significant movements to demonstrate that the discourses of justice, equality, rights, and so on retain a powerful capacity to move human action.

However, little remains of the justification for such movements, and with closer inspection one worries about the imperious threat of the various movements involved.

It is thus that the romanticist view of the moral individual has grown weak within the present century. Its replacement, at least within the world of science and letters, is prefigured by the critiques of romanticism outlined earlier. To fault the romanticist conception of the moral being on the grounds of species survival and rationality, in particular, is to presuppose that there is a form of human being who, by virtue of observation and reason, is maximally equipped for building the good society. It is this conception of the human being—rational, observant, and thus capable of enhancing the human condition—that has become dominant within the present century. As Habermas (1982) views it, this modernist conception of the human being is a reinstantiation of the Enlightenment view. It is a view that has played a major role in shaping the discourse of empiricist philosophy of science, theories of economic man, discourse on liberty and democracy within political science, and socio-biological formulations, among others. It is this same view that has been normalized by most psychological theory and research during the present century. While learning theory formulations constituted the person as an adaptive organism, tuned to the contingencies of the environment, the cognitive revolution succeeds in establishing rational processes at the center of human functioning. In effect, both of these endeavors served to objectify the modernist (or neo-Enlightenment) conception of human functioning.

What is the place of moral (ethical, ideological) action in the modernist conception of the human as rational-instrumental being? An answer to this question must distinguish between two major influences of the Enlightenment on modernist views of the person. On the one side is that domain of modernist discourse informed by the empiricist tradition from Locke, Hume, and the Mills through Comte in the nineteenth century. In its emphasis on the environmental antecedents of mental functioning, the empiricist tradition laid the groundwork for a twentieth-century conception of the individual as a cog in the one great and universal machine. The individual, on this account, is little more than the result of systematic inputs. And, if all human activity is understood as a function of environmental antecedents—a view substantiated by much logical empiricist philosophy along with the behavioral view in the social sciences—then issues of "moral choice" are subverted. To the extent that people act morally, their behavior must be traced to preceding conditions, for example, family socialization, religious education, and character-building programs such as the Boy Scouts and the YMCA. Yet, precisely what constitutes *moral* action is not a matter that most philosophers of science, behavioral scientists, and others within the empiricist tradition wish to confront. For empiricist philosophers and scientists, the only important and answerable questions are matters of "what *is* the case." Concerns with "what *ought* to be" are beyond answer—mere metaphysics or worse. Adequate functioning within the sciences, just as in daily life, requires observation, reason, planning, and testing hypotheses in the world. Personal values, ethics, and political passions simply obfuscate the process. They act as biases that interfere with the kinds of impartial judgments necessary for effective action. In effect, questions of the good are obfuscating intrusions into both science and successful living.

It is largely for these reasons that many scholars today find the modernist conception of human functioning morally vacuous. The view of the ideal individual as scientist is one that leaves the individual with no sense of direction, no means of evaluating right and wrong, and no reason for seeking to alter the status quo. As scientists we may have knowledge of sophisticated weapons systems and their devastating effects, but there is nothing in such knowledge that admonishes (or invites) their use. The only means by which good actions may be guaranteed, from this standpoint, is through practices of socialization and education—essentially by stamping them in. Thus, questions of value are always solved at one step removed from the individual actor. The single individual is destined to act as others have designed, and they in turn as others have dictated. At no point is reflexive consideration of "the good" in itself made possible. In effect, questions of value are abnegated.

A second line of modernist thought can be traced to a rationalist tradition (Descartes, Kant). In this vein, modernist philosophers have attempted to provide rational foundations for moral action. John Rawls' *Theory of Justice* (1971) and Alan Gewirth's *Reason and Morality* (1987) are among the most celebrated exemplars. At the same time psychologists of rationalist stripe have reconstituted the problem of morality as a technical one. That is, rather than attempting to solve the abstract problem of the good, they have presumed the natural capacities of individuals for moral action. The question is then to explore empirically the nature of moral decisions—how, by whom, and in what circumstances do persons act morally. The most ambitious attempt of this variety is embodied by Lawrence Kohlberg's (1969) theory of moral development. Kohlberg posits a nativist theory of moral reasoning—in this way drawing from the romanticist presumptions of inherent capacities for moral direction, but now substituting "rational capacities" for the "sentiments." The ontogenetic unfolding of the individual mind will, argues Kohlberg, necessarily lead in the direction of abstract moral reasoning. At the early stages of development the individual will simply make those decisions that are rewarded by the social environment, or that he/she has absorbed from the social group. (In effect, the empiricist account is given credence, but only at the more rudimentary stages of development.) At the most mature stages of cognitive development, proposes Kohlberg, the individual will come to generate his/her own abstract principles of ethics.

Kohlberg's theory has been widely attacked for its androcentric and ethnocentric biases, along with its array of shaky premises. However, my concern in this case is yet another. For there is a general question at stake that Kohlberg's theory brings to light, a question that is relevant to virtually any attempt to rest a theory of moral action on the individual's possession of moral principles (whether inherent or environmentally induced). If we grant to individuals the capacity for abstract moral thought, a commitment let's say to principles of justice, equality, and individual freedom, would such persons form a reasonable basis for a moral society? Would increasing the number of such persons enhance the quality of cultural life? I think not. The chief problem of abstract principles of morality is that they are empty of significant content. Within themselves they contain no rules of instantiation; they fail to determine when and where they apply. One may thus be committed to the principle "Thou shall not kill." But the principle itself stands empty of implications for action. The words "shall not" and "kill" contain no information as to how they apply. Let us suppose, however, that the individual seeks, within his/her mental compendium, a precise definition of the kind from which action could be derived. "To kill," one concludes, means "to deprive of life." Such a definition might seem to furnish directive implications, but in fact this more precise definition is itself in the abstract. What, after all, does "deprive of life" mean over an array of concrete settings? As is quickly surmised, when abstract principles are defined, their definitions are also in the abstract—themselves failing to indicate when, where, and how they apply in particular circumstances. When one consults abstract principles, their explications are also in the abstract, and as well the explications of the explications in an infinite regress—from which there is no exit to action.

One may opt at this point for a social or communal determination of definition. Thus, the abstract proposition may not dictate action, but after extensive immersion in the culture one comes to learn (in practice) what the proposition demands. One learns, for example, that "Thou shall not kill" has little to do with "killer cakes," persons "dressed to kill," or smiles "that skill softly," that it does forbid certain actions toward one's kith and kin, but that it applies contingently to those of other religious, political, or racial persuasions. However, to rescue moral principles in this way from the shoals of infinite regress is to remove the psyche from the center of moral action. Any abstract principle may be linked to virtually any action—lethal or loving—depending on the cultural conventions operative at the time. Cultural conventions thus replace cognition as the fulcrum of moral action.

I further submit that it is precisely this conventional character of moral principledness that enables courts, governments, and religions to maintain laws, constitutional bases, and theological principles over the centuries, but simultaneously allows such institutions to act in highly divergent (if not incoherent) ways as conditions change over time. Constitutional guarantees were of little protection to Japanese Americans during World War II, and their implications for blacks, women, homosexuals, or pregnant teenagers is in continuous contention today. It is not the principles that are at stake in such cases, but the question of how and when they apply. It is not that cultural conventions stand in opposition to transcendental principles; rather, without this social determination of meaning such principles cease to be significant.

TOWARD A CONSTRUCTIONIST THEORY OF MORAL ACTION

Thus far I have attempted to outline the contours of both the romanticist and modernist perspectives on moral being, and to demonstrate major shortcomings in both—for psychology and society. To open consideration on a social constructionist alternative to these perspectives, it is useful to consider a line of argument developed by Alisdair MacIntyre in his volume *After Virtue* (1981). MacIntyre lends strong voice to those who find both romanticist and modernist attempts at generating moral precepts failed enterprises. Contemporary moral debate, for MacIntyre, is both "interminable and unsettlable" (p. 210). It suffers in particular in its attempt to establish principles or values that transcend the contexts of their usage. Without a context of usage, they lose both practical consequence and susceptibility to assessment. In place of these attempts MacIntyre traces moral action to lived narratives of identity. It is when individuals are embedded in community life, and develop life stories that account for their past, present, and future, that moral action is generated. The individual is accountable to these narratives of identity—both to himself and to others. "To be the subject of a narrative that runs from one's birth to one's death is . . . to be accountable for the actions and experiences which compose a narratable life" (p. 202). From this standpoint, what we take to be virtues are inseparable from the tissue of social relations.

> The virtues find their point and purpose not only in sustaining those relationships necessary if the variety of goods internal to practices are to be achieved and not only in sustaining the form of an individual life in which that individual may seek out his or her good as the good of his or her whole life, but also in sustaining those traditions which provide both practices and individual lives with their necessary historical context. (MacIntyre, 1981, p. 207)

With these arguments MacIntyre succeeds in moving the fulcrum of moral action from the individual mind to relations among persons. It is only persons within relationship who can sustain forms of moral action. Yet, in my view MacIntyre does not extend the case to its full potential. For if the narratives (along with the related forms of intelligibility) in which we are embedded are products of ongoing interaction, then we can move on to separate problems of moral action from issues of mental state. This is to say that participating in a moral society is not fundamentally a private act—within the psyche—but a public act, inseparable from the relationships in which one has been or is embedded. Morality is not on this account something one possesses *within,* but is a participatory action that gains its meaning only within the arena of cultural intelligibility. One participates in the cultural forms of action as in a game or a dance; questions of why one is moral or immoral do not require a specifically psychological answer any more than questions of why one moves in three-quarter time when waltzing or plays tennis with balls as opposed to shuttlecocks. A moral life, then, is not an issue of individual sentiment or rationality but of communal participation.

What are we to make, from the constructionist vantage point, of what has traditionally been taken as sentiment, reasons, deliberations, values, intentions, and the like? Are we wholly to abandon concern with such states? Although this question is complex, let me propose for now that for the constructionist these various terms—so prominent in traditional discourse on moral action—are not abandoned so much as reconstituted. At least one aspect of this reconstitution requires both an ontological deconstruction and a discursive reconstruction. Again to extend MacIntyre's thesis, if the narratives by which we understand ourselves and our relationships are forms of social accounting, then so are their contents. These contents would include what we take to be states of mind— matters of "intuition," "sentiment," "values," and "reason." To narrate about one's mental life is thus to join in a form of cultural story telling, in relating acceptable and intelligible tales. And, for theorists to speak of the necessary psychological ingredients for a moral life is simultaneously a form of cultural narration. The psychological ingredients—the major locus of concern for romanticists and modernists—are thus de-ontologized. The language of moral sentiments and moral deliberation, on this account, does not refer to (describe or reveal) mental events located within the minds of single individuals and directing their actions. Rather, they are reconstituted as linguistic (poetic, rhetorical) forms of social practice.

If mental language does not acquire its meaning and significance from mental states, how does it function? What is its bearing on issues of moral action? From the present perspective, accounts such as "I feel this is right," "That would violate my principles," or "I think this is immoral" are in their very saying constitutive features of everyday life. Such sentences are used by people in carrying out various social rituals, patterns of interchange, or cultural projects. They are, in an Austinian sense, social performatives and carry with them a range of illocutionary implications. They operate within relationships to prevent, to admonish, to praise, and to invite various forms of action; they may also establish one's public identity, furnish others with a guide to one's future conduct, and achieve unity within a group. In effect, moral and ethical languages are among the resources available for playing the games and participating in the dances of cultural life. They are moves or positionings that enable persons to construct the culture in what we take to be a moral or ethical way.

To clarify the arguments to this point it is instructive to compare them with the thesis developed in Charles Taylor's magnificent volume *Sources of the Self* (1989). Taylor's major attempt is to resuscitate the assumptions underlying the Western conception of self, and which serve as the implicit basis for moral action. These implicit "frameworks provide the background . . . for our moral judgments, intuitions or reactions. . . . To articulate a framework is to explicate what makes sense of our moral responses" (p. 26). It is not simply that this attempt to lay out the "moral topography" of Western culture may "counteract the layers of suppression of modern moral consciousness" (p. 90). Rather, as Taylor sees it, the languages of self-understanding—and thus moral action—serve as "moral sources." They are "constitutive of human agency," such that "stepping outside these limits would be tantamount to stepping outside what we would recognize as integral, that is, undamaged human personhood" (p. 27). In these respects Taylor's position is congenial to the form of constructionism being developed here. Moral language is essentially a resource for generating and sustaining actions that we hold to be moral within the culture. To resuscitate the language is thus to "open us to our moral sources, to release their force in our lives."

Yet, Taylor's worthy project is set within a broader context of assumptions that run counter to the constructionist thesis. For, as he sets the course he falls back on the romanticist view of natural or instinctive good. "Moral reactions," as he sees it, "are almost like instincts, comparable to our love of sweet things, or our aversion to nauseous substances, or our fear of falling" (p. 5). Moral language of the kind he attempts to restore to consciousness is, from his perspective, an expression of these instinctive moral urges. "Ontological accounts offer themselves as correct articulations of our 'gut' reactions" (p. 6). "Moral ontology . . . articulates these intuitions" (p. 8). Further, the means by which these languages gain their life within the culture is not, for Taylor, primarily social but psychological. Failing to possess these moral orientations, argues Taylor, "is not to know who one is" (p. 29). They also elicit natural desires. "Moral sources empower. To come closer to them, to have a clearer view of them, to come to grasp what they involve, is for those who recognize them to be moved to love or respect them, and through this love/respect to be better enabled to live up to them" (p. 96).

From a constructionist standpoint, this latter array of assumptions are not only difficult to justify, but run counter to the argument for moral language as socially constitutive. For if moral language has the function of generating ontologies within a culture, so it should follow that the romanticist beliefs in intuition, love, and respect are also products of the cultural language. The very processes that Taylor uses to explain the formation of moral articulations are found to be reified forms of these articulations. They are not generative of the articulations; rather the articulations generate the sense of palpable psychological processes. For the constructionist the linguistic articulations so valued by Taylor are not to be traced to the mental processes of single individuals. Rather, language is taken to be a byproduct of human relatedness. Thus, with Taylor, attention is drawn to the historical emergence of moral language; however, the attempt in this case is not thereby to valorize such languages, but to comprehend the conditions and circumstances in which such linguistic conventions came to play a functional role in social (and intellectual) life. In this case the languages of moral reasoning would be resuscitated, not because they are foundational to a moral life, but because they may open up or remind us of modes of speaking (and acting) that may otherwise be lost or destroyed in the hurly-burly of contemporary life. Before exploring positive implications of a constructionist standpoint, further attention is required to the place of moral discourse.

MORAL DISCOURSE: NECESSARY AND DESIRABLE?

Although moral injunctives now play a significant role in the organization and coherence of social life, and the revitalizing of traditional moral languages may enrich the range and potential of our interchanges, we should be wary of the conclusion that moral language is both essential and desirable for what we take to be a morally structured society. Such discourse may figure prominently both in our daily actions and in the rationalization of national policy (as in "fighting a *just* war"). However, this is not to say either that the terms of morality (ethics, values, rights) are necessary for the "good society" or that human interests are best served by these sorts of performatives.

In the first instance, why should we conclude that languages of "ought," "duty," "rights," "principles," and the like are essential to agreeable (if not laudatory) forms of social life? The parent–child relationship is instructive in this regard, for in such relationships a fully satisfying symbiosis may be achieved without the benefit of specifically moral discourse. In the same way, most friendships, colleagial relationships, and business proceedings take place unproblematically, and without recourse to a vocabulary of moral necessity. In effect, persons are fully capable of mutually satisfying relationships without moral performatives.

More speculatively, I propose that such languages owe their development primarily to instances in which there is a *breach* in the acceptable patterns of interchange. Should one or more members of a relationship violate acceptable patterns, moral language may be employed as a means of correcting, rechaneling, or transforming the offending action. In effect moral language largely functions as a means of sustaining patterns of social interchange in danger of erosion. Such languages are not so much *responsible* for the generation of agreeable forms of society as they are rhetorical means for sustaining lines of action already embraced. Satisfactory cultural conditions require neither persons with moral states within their heads nor social institutions with moral credos.

Yet, if moral language largely serves pragmatic functions—and largely those of sustaining particular courses of action—the question may further be raised as to whether it is the most useful or effective means of enhancing the quality of cultural life. If moral language is not essential, how does it function in comparison to other possible means of achieving the same ends? Findings from Felson's (1984) research on convicted criminals is informative at this juncture. As he found, among ex-offenders who had been convicted for crimes of aggressive assault, the majority traced their actions to incidents in which someone (often the victim) was seen as acting immorally (breaking a proper rule), there was verbal admonishment, and the putative rule breaker attempted to save face by a hostile reaction. Such exchanges culminated in physical assault, essentially traceable to the attempt to correct the iniquitous. In effect, when the language of rights and wrongs was introduced into the situation there was not an enhancement of the human condition but deterioration.

In my view this deterioration is intensified by that very tradition seeking so steadfastly to establish moral foundations for society—from early theology and romanticist intuitionism to modernist attempts at rational foundations. And here I am speaking of a tradition that has attempted to locate universal standards of the good—principles of right and wrong, codes of ethics, constitutional principles, bills of universal rights, and so on that aspire to speak beyond time and place. The critical shortcoming of such approaches is revealed in Alan Gewirth's volume cited earlier. In his preface he first attacks conventionalist forms of morality, that is, attempts to establish principles or rules that capture or express one's cultural tradition. As he points out

> This approach . . . incurs a severe difficulty. For so long as the rightness or correctness of the principle itself . . . is not established, such a procedure still leaves the system without any warrant of its rightness or correctness. Partisans of *opposed* cultures, traditions, or social systems may each claim self-evidence for their own moral principles, and they hold that their respective rules and judgments are the morally right ones. Hence a moral principle's success in justifying . . . any one culture, ideology, or tradition does nothing, of itself, to *prove* [*its*] *superiority* over the moral rules or judgments of *opposed* cultures or traditions. (Gewirth, 1987, p. x)

Gewirth then goes on to point out that

> this fact has supplied one of the strongest intellectual motivations for the various ancient modern thinkers who have tried to provide a firm nonrelativist foundation for ethics. By giving a rational justification to one or another supreme moral principle, they have hoped to *disprove or establish the wrongness of rival principles.* (p. x)

As Gewirth then notes, no attempt to establish a superior system has been successful; in each case critics have located serious flaws. His attempt, thus, will be to "present a new version of rational justification," which will give precedence to one moral system over all others.

I have italicized several key words and phrases in these passages that reveal the central metaphor underlying much work within the universalist tradition. In effect, it is a metaphor of conflict—of opposition, of rivalry, and the ultimate quest for one system or culture achieving superiority over all. Or, to put it more bluntly, it is a quest for ultimate hegemony, of cultural dominion and domination.

In the less dramatic cases, such tendencies toward universalism can act so as to disrupt otherwise satisfactory forms of interchange—forms of longstanding often having reached a state of highly nuanced and finely balanced sophistication. As we have seen, moral or ethical precepts do not themselves dictate any specific form of action. Most frequently they are used as rhetorical sanctioning devices for preferred ways of life. Thus, as the precepts of any group strive toward universality, they operate so as to discredit ways of life in other groups, and to champion as their replacement the home customs and mores. Thus, as Christian missionaries carry the gospel to other lands, the teachings themselves are of little significance. Through local hermeneutical procedures they may typically be made compatible with existing customs. It is the way in which the precepts are used to discredit and to justify that alters local patterns in often disruptive ways—damaging cultural patterns of longstanding utility within the local setting. As Westerners concerned with the liberation of women we may decry the masking of the female face in the Arab world: Are the masks not oppressive to women, and thus both unjust and inhumane? Yet, within traditional Arab culture the masks play an important role in constituting and sustaining a large number of interrelated customs and rituals. To remove them on Western ideological grounds would be to threaten cultural identity itself. To estimate the effects of removing the masks, consider the results on an expansionary Muslim movement that sought to place such masks on the faces of contemporary Western women. It is not ultimately a matter of ideology or morality that is at stake here, for there is nothing about desiring gender equality that necessarily speaks to matters of facial masking. Rather, moral precepts become the justification for undermining otherwise congenial and satisfying ways of life.

More extreme than the deterioration of cultural traditions are the destructive hostilities invited by the language of ethical superiority. When preferred ways of life are labeled as universally moral and right, and deviations as immoral, evil, and inferior, the stage is set for the most brutalizing of conflicts. The major problem of arrogating preferences to the status of universal principles is that the latter brook no compromise, and deviants take on an inhuman demeanor. The number of human deaths resulting from claims to superior values is, I suspect, beyond calculation.

FROM THE MORASS TO THE MORALITY OF RELATIVISM

We now find ourselves sinking into "the morass of moral relativism," or so the condition is oft characterized. And, to bury ourselves deeper within the mire, we find ourselves unable to account for the very processes traditionally held responsible for moral action—or more radically, rejecting the very psychologistic orientation that has so long served as the mainstay of moral accountability. Yet, rather than bemoaning this sorry state, and using it as the catalyst to yet another hegemonic entry into the two thousand-year-old parade of failures, I think it is an auspicious time to open consideration on the positive potentials of relativism. I am not claiming here that all forms of relativism are equal in implication. There are many means to a relativistic end, and each should be considered separately and comparatively. However, in the preceding I have outlined the rudiments of a social constructionist orientation that brings us to the present juncture. The major questions, then, concern the positive potential of such a view for what we might take to be a morally acceptable society.

Perhaps the most effective opening in this case is to return to linguistic considerations. As we have seen, through a focus on the social pragmatics of language use the discourse of both morality and self are de-ontologized. Such discourses, I have proposed, do not inherently describe worlds outside themselves but are used by persons in carrying out their various relationships. In effect, both moral ideals as levels of real world attainment and selves as intentional agents are thereby removed from the center of concern. They cease to be the center of questions about which deliberation and study should reveal useful or necessary answers. Yet, such a move does not thereby leave us without means to proceed. For this analysis has required that we take seriously the process of linguistic construction itself. If moral principles and psychological selves are objectified forms of language, we may then inquire into the processes by which such objectifications take place. That is, we may raise significant questions concerning the origin and sustenance of meaning.

As implied in the preceding, the constructionist turns critical attention to processes of relationship. Following Wittgenstein, the constructionist agrees that there are no "private languages." Rather, language gains its status as such through social participation. A sentence does not acquire meaning through its isolated existence. It achieves its significance through the reactions of others—their assent that indeed meaning has been achieved. In this sense, virtually any utterance from a simple cough to Shakespeare's *Othello* may be fraught with meaning, or reduced to nonsense—depending on the reactions of others. And these "reactions," in turn, lack significance until rejoined by others. In this sense I cannot mean until you allow me to do so, and your allowances cannot mean until I accept them as such. In Shotter's terms, linguistic meaning is the achievement of "joint action."

Through this analysis we reach the stage at which *relationship* becomes focal. It is out of *interdependence* that the very conceptions of self and moral principles become possible. In effect, human relatedness becomes an originary source, the terrain upon which concerns with human well-being should be rooted. I propose that this site is far more fruitful in implication than that offered by its psychologistic predecessor. Let us briefly consider four of these implications:

1. From Imperialism to Collectivism

As we find, the impetus toward universal standards of right and wrong is blunted by the present arguments. Such standards not only serve to disrupt established and smoothly coordinated relationships of long-standing, but lead as well to a needless obliteration of human life. Constructionist relativism replaces the absolutist claims of ethical imperialism with a collective search for meaning. Disquisitions on right and wrong are replaced with communal considerations of consequence. Carol Gilligan's (1982) reply to Kohlberg's formulations of ethical decision making furnishes a useful illustration in this respect. As we have seen, Kohlberg viewed the highest form of ethical decision making as emanating from the cognitive capacities of the single individual. Ideally each individual should reach conclusions of universal proportions. Less ideal by several degrees, for Kohlberg, was a form of decision making in which individuals took into account the approval of others, what others would judge to be normal or right on the occasion. As Gilligan responds, a more socially centered form of decision making is favored by women as opposed to men. In her research on abortion decisions, she found women to be highly concerned with their responsibilities to others, and a sense of caring for others' well-being. The sense of self could not be disconnected from what they perceived as a web of relations in which they were engaged.

Yet, there is little reason to see this form of collective activity as uniquely feminine. It is a means by which any problem of human conflict, whether or not designated a problem of morality, can be approached. In the constructionist frame it is a means of expanding the number of voices that speak to issues of interdependence. It enables "the moral problem" to be refracted through multiple lenses, thus enriching the range of understandings and broadening sensitivity to the manifold consequences. To be sure, such a process of broadened interchange will seldom move toward a clear and necessary conclusion. But such conclusions—even if fortified by the rhetoric righteousness—are in the end simplistic and insensitive.

2. From Retribution to Reorganization

As we have seen, in the traditional orientation, instances of immoral action are traced to the mental processes of individual actors. As much research has demonstrated, there is a strong tendency to presume that evil acts derive from evil origins; those who engage in immoral actions are thus presumed to be lacking common human characteristics (e.g., a sense of decency, conscience, a sense of right and wrong, willpower), to be suffering from the ill workings of their minds (e.g., reason overcome by emotion, temporary insanity), or to be something less than human (e.g., monstrous, bestial, satanic). From the constructionist standpoint, all such attributions are de-ontologized and reconstructed as illocutionary acts. Thus questions of just recrimination, retribution, moral instruction, and the like become secondary. More important, individual psychology is removed from central consideration and replaced by concern with the organization of relationships.

On both a scholarly level and the level of daily life this means exploring the domain of relationships in which any putative act of immorality takes place. The legal system moves slowly in this direction. In a recent Philadelphia case a woman dressed in Army fatigues entered a shopping mall with an automatic rifle and began firing at the customers. Several were killed and many wounded. From the traditional standpoint, prime attention would be paid to the psychological state of the criminal: was the woman emotionally deranged, did she know right from wrong, etc. However, the victims of the crime subsequently generated a suit against an extended array of individuals and institutions: the local police who were aware of the woman's dangerous condition, the owner of the firearms store where she purchased the weapon, the shopping mall for its lack of protection, and so on. Yet, even this expansion in the range of complicity does not go far enough, and it too retains a retributive edge. One can only lament in reviewing the vast and collective complicity that engendered what we now take to be "the evil Saddam Hussein." The arms sellers, the oil guzzlers, the Arab League, the Iraqi people, a belligerent Israeli government, supportive Palestinians, and a long indifferent U.S. government are only a few of the contributors to establishing the conditions under which "foul play" was invited.

Invited as well by a constructionist standpoint are explorations into the historical roots of developing problems and to patterns of otherwise unnoticed interdependence. Rather than seeking to establish who is right and wrong, who are to play the roles of the just and the blameworthy, attention is drawn to the way in which certain problems are historically prepared. By viewing issues in a diachronic mode it is often possible to demonstrate that today's taken for granted truths, or palpable rights and wrongs, have only become so by virtue of long and unexamined usage. By exploring their historical contingencies, these truths and justices may often be relativized, and unbridled commitment defused. Further, inquiry may reveal ways in which otherwise acrimonious groups are locked together in mutually supportive relationships. I think here of the abortion controversy in which each of the participant parties claims universal right—compromise within these mutually exclusive frames becomes impossible. Yet, the roots of both pro-life and pro-choice ideology have a long and complex history within the Christian religion, and pro-choice commitments can scarcely be separated from feminist politics. Neither history will reveal grounds for universal claims.

Further, both parties draw sustenance from the American tradition of individual liberty; in this way they are both dependent on the same source for their activities. Or to put it otherwise, without the support of the "opponent" in the source ideology the clash could not take place. And, this interdependence is but one of a broad number. In many matters—from local policies on building codes to international policies in the Gulf—pro-life and pro-choice advocates may walk arm in arm. As history and interdependence are increasingly revealed, so may absolutist claims be softened.

3. From Archaeology to Anthropology

Let us consider as well the role of psychological inquiry from the present standpoint. Where moral action has traditionally been concerned the psychologist has, in a metaphoric sense, played the role of the archaeologist, using shards of behavior to draw conclusions about a mysterious and inaccessible world. As the preceding makes clear, this form of inquiry is deeply problematic, not only in terms of its justificatory basis but as well in terms of its applications to human well-being. A replacement is needed for the traditional metaphor and its associated activities.

At least one metaphor useful for guiding future undertakings is that of cultural anthropology. If it is not the individual's interior to which moral action is traced, but to relational interchange, then a chief focus of scholars concerned with the human good should be on these processes of interchange. That is, like the cultural anthropologist, the major emphasis should be on rituals, patterns, and practices of cultural life. If we are concerned with the ways in which human suffering is brought about, attention should be directed to those cultural processes in which suffering is a typical outcome. Drawing from the work of Felson (1984), Averill (1982), and Pearce and Cronen (1980), I have attempted with colleagues Linda Harris and Jack Lannamann to document a common pattern of spiraling hostility. In this form of interchange it is customary for one hostility to trigger another of greater intensity until either the relationship is terminated or physical aggression is invited (Harris, Lannamann, and Gergen, 1986). Thus, physical violence in this context is not traced to the deteriorated psychological conditions of the individual but to a cultural ritual—which could be otherwise. Congenial with such undertakings are studies of the social and linguistic conditions under which actions become defined as aggressive or hostile (Mummendey, Lenneweber, and Loschper, 1984; Bornewasser, 1990), of violence at football matches (Marsh, Rosser, and Harré, 1978), and the emergence of deceit (Gergen, 1989). In each case the interest moves from the individual's interior to the collusions, negotiations, collaborations, and other interpersonal processes in which our actions are embedded. I hardly view work of this kind as exhaustive of scholarly possibilities.

4. From Principles to Practices

Traditional approaches to moral action have attempted to establish an abstract and universal canon of virtues, and then to worry about their installation in the minds of individuals. From the constructionist perspective, such endeavors are flawed. No amount of debate over the nature of the good and no amount of moral instruction will ensure good acts. For principles of the good do not and cannot dictate concrete actions, and any action at any time may be constructed as good or evil from some vantage point. In a broader sense this is to say that hopes for the good society should not ultimately be lodged in formulations of principle. The Word will not provide "the way, the truth and the light." This does not mean an abandonment of moral discourse so much as a reconstituting of such concerns and a broadening of the field of relevance.

Within the domain of language the focus shifts from the axiological to the practical. Under conditions of conflict or distress, what linguistic forms may be employed to bring about a more satisfactory coordination of participants? What linguistic resources do people have at their disposal under such conditions? Can the available range of resources be expanded? It is in this regard that Taylor's (1989) attempt to resuscitate the moral languages of the past are to be appreciated. However, inasmuch as moral discourse is only one means of achieving satisfactory coordination, exploration is required into new ranges of rhetoric. Most inviting is the possibility of developing new forms of relationship, fresh rituals for reconciling differences among persons. For example, communications theorists and family therapists have been highly successful in developing new techniques for dealing with interpersonal conflicts. Techniques of reframing, reconstituting narrative understandings, and shifting from conflict to meta-reflective postures all contribute importantly to the repository of cultural resources. We find, then, an invitation to the creative expansion of the language.

Yet, the task of locating practical means of enhancing coordination is scarcely exhausted by a focus on language. Means are required for a comingling not only of perspectives, ways of seeing things, and talk about values, but of life patterns. There is an important sense in which traditional moral discourse is divisive. When committed to an absolutist language, those who fail to share become "the other." This may be so even when the preponderance of one's daily activities are virtually synonymous with those of "the infidel." Thus there is substantial similarity in the quotidian activities of various Middle Easterners, Irish Protestants and Catholics, Pakistanis and Indians, and Greeks and Turks. Yet, commitments to differing absolutes—to alternative formations of sounds and markings—has contributed to enormous conflict and suffering. Coupled with a suppression of such languages, constructionism invites consideration of ways of synchronizing activities at the level of practical, daily interchange.

REFERENCES

Averill, J. R. (1982). *Anger and aggression: An essay on emotion.* New York: Springer-Verlag.

Bornewasser, M. (1990). *Aggression als Interpretationskonstrukt.* Habilitationsschrift, Universitat Munster.

Darwin, C. (1859). *The origin of the species.* London: Oxford University Press.

Felson, R. (1984). Patterns of aggressive social interaction. In A. Mummenday (Ed.), *Social psychology of aggression.* Heidelberg: Springer-Verlag.

Gergen, K. J. (1989). Invitciones al engano: An analisis micro-social. *Bulletin de Psicologia, 22,* 7–40.

Gergen, K. (1991). *The saturated self.* New York: Basic Books.

Gewirth, A. (1987). *Reason and morality.* Chicago: University of Chicago Press.

Gilligan, C. (1982). *In a different voice.* Cambridge, MA: Harvard University Press.

Habermas, J. (1982). Modernity—An incomplete project. In H. Foster (Ed.), *The anti-aesthetic, essays on postmodern culture.* Port Townsend, WA: Bay Press.

Harris, L. M., Lannamann, J. & Gergen, K. J. (1980). Aggression rituals. *Communication Monographs, 53,* 252–265.

Kohlberg, L. (1969). Stages and sequences: The cognitive-developmental approach to socialization. In D. A. Goslin (Ed.), *Handbook of socialization theory and research.* Chicago: Rand-McNally.

MacIntyre, A. (1981). *After virtue.* Notre Dame, IN: University of Notre Dame Press.

Marsh, P., Rosser, E., and Harré, R. (1978). *Rules of disorder.* London: Routledge and Kegan Paul.

Moore, G. E. (1903). *Principia ethica.* Cambridge, MA: Cambridge University Press.

Mummendey, A., Lenneweber, V., and Loschper, G. (1984). Aggression: From act to interaction. In A. Mummenday (Ed.), *Social psychology of aggression.* Heidelberg: Springer-Verlag.

Pearce, W. B., & Cronen, V. E. (1980). *Communication, action, and meaning.* New York: Praeger.

Rawls, J. (1971). *Theory of justice.* Cambridge, MA: Harvard University Press.

Shelley, P. B. (1976). On love. Shelley's literary and philosophical criticism. (J. Shawcross, Ed.) London: Frowde.

Taylor, C. (1989). *Sources of the self.* Cambridge, MA: Harvard University Press.

3 PERSONS, SELVES, AND AGENCY

James T. Lamiell

In the first half of Chapter 2 (this volume) Professor Gergen argues that previous systematic attempts to handle the problem of moral action from a psychological perspective—attempts subsumable under the intellectual traditions of romanticism and modernism, respectively—have proven unsatisfactory. On Gergen's view, modernism fails because, owing to its fundamentally mechanistic conception of the psychological functioning of the human individual, questions concerning the moral worth of one's actions are ultimately subverted entirely. Lacking the equivalent of an autonomous will, the individual can never properly be said to *choose* one course of action over another, and hence can never properly be held accountable for his/her actions. The question of morality thus simply vanishes.

Romanticism, on the other hand, Gergen finds equally wanting as the basis for a psychological theory of moral action. Romanticism does posit what Gergen calls a "deep interior" and what many others would call an autonomous *self,* and via this postulation provides the theoretical wherewithal necessary even to discuss the moral worth of an individual's actions. Questions then arise, however, concerning the *grounds* for an individual's willful selection of one course of action over another, and it is here where Gergen finds romanticism unsatisfactory. It leaves us, as Gergen says, not with *concrete* guidelines for moral action, but instead with mere absolute principles of morality (e.g., 'thou shall not kill') empty of significant content (Chapter 2, this volume).

It thus appears to Gergen that one of the two major forks in the road to a viable psychological theory of moral action leads into a vast desert, where discussion of moral action simply dries up, whereas the other leads into an equally vast fog bank, where one can grope about in discussions of abstract moral principles, but where no unambiguous guides to moral action can be discerned. Gergen's solution to this dilemma is to abandon the quest for a *psychological* conception of moral action altogether in favor of a social constructionist orientation. This orientation, Gergen states, is one "that throws into question the psychologistic framing of moral issues. And, while it refuses to furnish an alternative foundation for moral action, it is this very refusal that may hold the greatest promise for human well-being" (Chapter 2, this volume).

This promise, it turns out, finds its final redemption in what Gergen calls *the morality of relativism*. Social constructionism thus quits the desert of modernism by simple virtue of the fact that, under the terms of the former, he claims, moral action is a legitimate topic of discourse. At the same time, social constructionism cuts through the fog of romanticism by its refusal to appeal to any "deep interior" or autonomous self within individual persons as the seat of abstract moral principles from which moral action would issue. Since in practice one cannot know if, when, or how to apply an abstract principle in any given concrete case, Gergen finds it not only unnecessary but actually undesirable to leave a "seat" for such principles in an individually autonomous self, and since such nonabstract principles as are worked out to handle the particulars of any given concrete instance are of necessity grounded in the more or less "local" values and customs of the community or social unit in question, the seat for *those* principles could only be that community or social unit itself. To quote Gergen:

> This is to say that to participate in a moral society is not fundamentally a private act—within the psyche—but a public act, inseparable from the relationships in which one has been or is embedded. Morality is not on this account something one possesses *within*, but is a participatory action that gains its meaning only within the arena of cultural intelligibility. . . . The psychological ingredients—the major locus of concern for romanticists and modernists—are thus de-ontologized. (Gergen, Chapter 2, this volume)

To provide us with at least a glimpse of the direction in which a social constructionist conception of moral action would move us, Gergen cites a case involving a woman who, dressed in army fatigues, fired on, killed several, and injured many customers in a Philadelphia shopping mall. Gergen comments as follows:

> From the traditional standpoint, prime attention would be paid to the psychological state of the criminal: was the woman emotionally deranged, did she know right from wrong, etc. However, the victims of the crime subsequently generated a suit against an extended array of individuals and institutions: the local police who were aware of the woman's dangerous condition, the owner of the firearms store where she purchased the weapon, the shopping mall for its lack of protection, and so on. Yet, even this

expansion in the range of complicity does not go far enough, and it too retains a
retributive edge. (Chapter 2, this volume)

At this point, the reader is given to wonder whether, under the terms of social
constructionism, all vestiges of a "retributive edge" are to be eliminated. Gergen
does state that "questions of just recrimination, retribution, moral instruction,
and the like become *secondary*" (Chapter 2, this volume; my emphasis), but that
really does not much clarify matters for me. One is also given to wonder why the
social constructionist would regard the expanded range of complicity described
by Gergen as not going far enough, and, perhaps most importantly of all, what
"going far enough" would entail. With specific reference to this last point, I do
not see where Gergen's exposition offers us any answers to the following questions: (1) What is it about the social constructionist perspective that entitled the
so-called "victims" of the shooter's outburst to regard themselves as *victims?* (2)
Why, if we can regard as in some measure culpable for this crime not only (if at
all!) the shooter but also the local police, the owner of the firearms store where
the shooter purchased the gun, and officials of the shopping mall, can we not
regard as equally culpable the "victims" themselves? After all, they, too, were
part of the larger social constellation within which the event took place, and had
they not been present at the shopping mall to begin with, then of course the
woman in question could not have shot them.

Pending some clarification of these and a host of other matters (see the
following), I am not sure that the social constructionist perspective on moral
action leads to anywhere I would want to be. And yet, I would not wish to leave
my own readers with the impression that I find nothing of merit at all in the social
constructionist view. On the contrary, and as I argued nearly two years ago
(Lamiell, 1989), I have no doubt whatsoever that thoroughgoing analyses of the
role played by the historical-cultural-social-linguistic milieu in the development
of persons and in the nature of their social interactions have been and will
continue to prove illuminating. We *do,* after all, live in a social world, and, as I
argued at Oxford, a great deal of what we do in that social world is nothing if not
massive testimony to the importance we attach to it. In the domain of child-
rearing and education, for example, we simply could not do what we do with the
seriousness we do it did we not believe that the sort of world we present to our
children *matters;* that as concerns their development as persons and as citizens of
the community it *matters* how we act toward them, what we say to them, what
we permit and do not permit them to say to us and to each other, what they may
and may not do with their time, what they may, should, may not, and should not
read, and so forth. Moreover, that the decisions we make in these regards are
themselves constrained in some fashion by the historical-cultural-social-
linguistic milieu in which each of us has him- or herself developed seems to me
beyond reasonable doubt. Of course, conceding this point in the abstract is one

thing; pursuing it in its concrete particulars, through systematic empirical inquiry and careful scholarly analysis is quite another, and this is why social constructionists have important work to do. I would point to Gergen's discussion of the untoward consequences of moral discourse as illustrative of the possibilities here, even though I am not ready to concur with the conclusions Gergen would have us draw from that work.

I shall return to this last point later. First, however, I think it useful to point out that, if I have understood Gergen's argument properly, he would object to the very language I have used in my bow to social constructionism. As paradoxical as this may seem, I feel certain that Professor Gergen would reject the notion that the merits of social constructionism are to be judged in terms of the light it sheds on the social-psychological development of persons. In Gergen's view, I suspect, this perspective would only re-install the psychologically functioning individual as the center of discourse, and his entire analysis proceeds from the conviction that this is the one thing we must *not* do if we would escape both the desert of modernism and the fog of romanticism. It is around just this point, then, that the battle must finally be joined.

To this end, let us begin with a consideration of the very first sentence of Gergen's essay: "In the Western tradition it is the single individual who serves as the atom of moral concern—that essence without which matters of ethical debate would have little point and without whose commitment indeed the society might revert to chaos" (Chapter 2, this volume). Now there is certainly a sense in which this is true: without persons to author the actions that in turn become the subject of moral discourse, there simply is no moral discourse. If, to pursue Professor Gergen's example, no person fires on shoppers to begin with, then there is no action there to appraise for its moral worth, from a romanticist, modernist, social constructionist, or any other perspective.

At this point, however, I feel certain that Professor Gergen would wish to interject that it is also true that, without an irreducibly *social* unit of one sort or another—a couple, a family, a neighborhood, a community, a state, a nation, etc.—there is no *venue* for the moral discourse referred to here, and hence, again, no moral *discourse* at all. Strictly speaking, one can act neither morally *nor* immorally toward oneself; one can act morally or immorally only vis-à-vis one or more others.

The notion that this tenet must be rejected by one whose views are situated somewhere within the rationalist tradition (my preferred label for what Gergen calls the "romanticist" view) is, as I see it, the most basic problem with Professor Gergen's analysis. Thus when he contrasts the social constructionist view with the rationalist view by saying that, under the terms of the former in contrast to the latter, "to participate in a moral society is not fundamentally a private act within the psyche, . . . not, on this account, something one possesses *within*," Gergen is taking aim at a straw man. There is simply nothing in the rationalist thesis, that is, in the thesis that a coherent discussion of moral action must be grounded in a coherent conception of individual persons, that either (a) makes participation in a moral society a "fundamentally private act" or (b) gainsays the contention that moral *action* is an irreducibly *inter*-personal affair. We have no problem at all conceiving of hydrogen and oxygen as entities indispensable to discussions of the chemistry of water, without fancying that water is therefore somehow a fundamentally "hydrogen" or "oxygen affair." We would, however, have a rather formidable problem trying to discuss the chemistry of water within a framework where hydrogen and oxygen had been "de-ontologized." Similarly, rationalism has no problem at all conceiving of individual persons as entities indispensable to discussions of moral action without thereby fancying that participation in a moral society is a fundamentally private act (indeed, this very phrase strikes me as oxymoronic). Rationalism does recognize, however, that a very serious problem indeed would arise in a discussion of moral action as a phenomenon emerging from the relationship between two or more individual persons were that discussion to proceed within a framework where individual persons had already been "de-ontologized." Stated otherwise, rationalism recognizes what social constructionism seems all too prepared to look past, namely, that lacking some way of talking about individual persons, there is no conceivable way of talking about any relationship between "them," and hence no way of talking about moral action as one kind of relationship *between* "them-s."

In my view, Professor Gergen's own writing clearly illustrates the futility of attempting to frame a conception of moral action within which the individual person is thoroughly "de-ontologized." Having pointed to the chief problem of abstract principles of morality, that is, that they are empty of significant content, Gergen notes that "*one* may opt at this point for a social or communal designation or definition." He says that "*one* may not be able to consult the abstract proposition directly, but after extensive immersion in the culture comes to learn (in practice) the range of appropriate actions." He explains that "*one* learns . . . that 'Thou shall not kill' has little to do with 'killer cakes,' persons 'dressed to kill,' or smiles 'that kill softly,' that it does forbid certain actions toward *one's* kith and kin, and that it applies contingently to those of other religious, political, or racial persuasions" (Chapter 2, this volume; my emphasis). It is via considerations of this sort that Gergen arrives at the conclusion that "[c]ultural conventions . . . replace cognition as the fulcrum of moral action."

Now, granting Gergen's altogether reasonable thesis that one does learn, through extensive immersion in the culture, "the range of appropriate actions"— and, here again, I find nothing in the tenets of rationalism that would require or even encourage one to deny this—an important question remains as to the identity of the *one* to whom Gergen refers. In a system where individual persons are de-ontologized, what would ever license any reference at all to "one"? "One" *what?* And while we are at it: What is the nature of the "learning" that this "one" undergoes, or is learning, whatever it might in fact be, a phenomenon that social constructivism is not called upon to discuss? Further: If, with Professor Gergen, we are now going to speak of cultural conventions as the *fulcrum* of moral action—a metaphor that, at least by certain lights, strikes me as harmless in and of itself—will the rules of this language game also permit us to speak of the *lever* of moral action? If not, why not? If so, who or what assumes the "role" of lever? Who or what shall be thought of as exerting force upon that lever, and to what end?

All of these questions, and many more like them that might be raised in response to various other phrases sprinkled throughout Professor Gergen's text, serve here only to underscore the point that not even social constructionists can speak coherently about moral action without some way of referring to individual persons. Just what it is we will wish to say about individual persons remains, at this point, very much open to question. But that we must have *something* to say in this regard seems to me unarguable, and I find myself thus forced to conclude that any version of social constructionism that would require us to "deontologize" persons as a prerequisite for discussing moral action must be rejected.

As suggested previously, this does *not* mean, so far as I am concerned, that all of what the social constructionist perspective would offer us in this domain must be rejected. The question thus becomes: How might we proceed in a way that redresses what I have argued is social constructionism's excesses but at the same time preserves its salutary features? As is the case with many other issues of concern to me these days, I find the thinking of the German philosopher/psychologist William Stern instructive in this regard. Working within a decidedly rationalistic framework, Stern began his *Die menschliche Persönlichkeit* (1923) with the following observation (my translation):

> Here will the critical personalism [the name given by Stern to his theoretical outlook] have to prove, that it is equally distant from a one-sided individualism, which understands only the right and happiness of single individuals, as it is from a socialism, in which individuality [*individuelle Eigenart*] and personal freedom is entirely choked by the pressure of supra-personal demands. (From the foreword to the first edition of the second volume of *Person und Sache*, p. x[1])

On page 63 of the same text, Stern observes the following:

> Right and law are without doubt supra-individual forces, to which the individual must accommodate him/herself. . . . A right exists only insofar as it maintains its sanction through a "supra-person" (a people, a humanity), the preservation of which

---

[1] The original German from which this passage has been translated reads as follows: "Hier wird der kritische Personalismus zu erweisen haben, daß er gleich weit entfernt ist von einem einseitigen Individualismus, der nur das Recht und das Glück der Einzelindividuen kennt wie von einem Sozialismus, in dem die individuelle Eigenart und persönliche Freiheit ganz von dem Druck Überpersönlicher Forderungen erwürgt wird."

should thereby be secured. But were there only this "supra-person"; were the individual within nothing but a thing, then likewise there would be no such thing as a right. Where there is a sanctioning-of-right "supra-person" there must also be a capable-of-right [competent; *rechsfähige*] individual person. The latter must relate his/her self-directed personal sphere [*Eigensphäre*] and personal action [*Eigentat*] to the personal spheres and personal actions of other equal and higher personal unities. The person must, therefore, incorporate the ends of others into his/her self ends.[2]

There are several points warranting our careful attention here. The first is that Stern finds it entirely conceivable that a system of thought can preserve a basic commitment to the notions of human individuality and personal freedom without lapsing into an uncritical celebration of individual*ism*. I think that this is a terribly important idea, and I rather suspect that most if not all social constructionists would agree.

Second, despite the rationalistic moorings of his critical personalism, Stern has no difficulty at all conceiving of rights and laws as supra-individual forces. He maintains, quite properly, that where there is no people (society, culture) of which to speak, nor can there be coherent talk of rights and laws, or, by extension, moral action. This is perhaps as explicit a recognition as one could reasonably hope for, within Stern's critical personalism in particular or within rationalist thought more generally, of the inherently *inter*-personal nature of moral discourse.

Third, none of the foregoing considerations blinded Stern to the fact that any discussion of the inter-personal would have to bring with it a treatment of the personal, and indeed, one according to which individuals would have to be regarded as something other than mere things. For if, as Stern says, rights and laws (and, by implication, moral action) cannot be realized outside consideration of the supra-personal, nor can they be realized within a framework where the supra-personal is regarded as constituted only of things. For Stern, a thing is an "existence" (*ein Existierendes*) that neither fashions any unity of self nor executes, in purposive fashion, goal-directed activity, whereas a person is an "existence" that does both.[3] For Stern, therefore, the notions of *self* and of *agency* are

---

[2] The original German from which this passage has been translated reads as follows: Recht und Gesetz sind weifellos überindividuelle Mächte, denen der Einzelne sich zu sügen hat. . . . Ein Recht gibt es nur insofern, als es durch eine Überperson (Volk, Menschheit), deren Selbsterhaltung dadurch gewahrt werden soll, seine Sanktion erhält. Aber gäbe es nur diese Überperson, wäre der Einzelne in ihr nichts als Sache, dann gäbe es gleichfalls kein Recht. Zur rechtssanktionierenden Überperson muß die rechtsfähige Einzelperson treten. Diese muß ihre selbstzweckliche Eigensphäre und Eigentat in Beziehung setzen zur Eigensphäre und Eigentat neben- und übergeordneter Personaleinheiten, also die Heterotelie in ihre Autotelie übernehmen."

[3] "Unter 'Person' wird verstanden 'ein solches Existierendes, das trotz der Vielheit der Teile eine reale eigenartige und eigenwerige Einheit bildet und als solche, trotz der Vielheit der Teilfunktionen, eine einheitliche zielstrebige Selbsttätigkeit vollbringt.' . . . Der Gegenbegriff der Person ist die 'Sache.' 'Sie ist ein solches Existierendes, das, aus vielen Teilen bestehend, keine reale eigenartige und eigenwertige Einheit bildet, und das, in vielen Teilfunktionen funktionierend, keine einheitliche zielstrebege Slebsttätigkeit vollbringt.' " (pp. 4–5 of *Die menschliche Persönlichkeit*)

built into his conception of persons. It is by means of the former concept that Stern is able to speak of an "existence" capable of appropriating socio-cultural (supra-personal) ends as his/her *own,* and by means of the latter concept that he is able to speak of that same "existence" as acting *with purpose* in accordance with, in opposition to, or without regard for those supra-personal ends.

As sketchy as this introduction to Stern's thought is, it will perhaps suffice for my present purpose, which is to suggest how critical personalism both *explicitly* incorporates certain features of the social constructionist perspective on moral action and yet also succeeds at certain key points where, in my view, social constructionism fails.

Regarding these latter points, I would note first that critical personalism makes moral action a legitimate topic of discourse in a way that social construc-tionism really does not, Professor Gergen's protestations to the contrary notwith-standing. As we have just seen, the tenets of critical personalism imply (in my view quite properly) that questions concerning the moral worth of an action cannot even surface outside of a system of thought that (a) grants ontological status to individual persons and (b) does so in a way that requires one to regard those individual persons as something other than mere things. Since social con-structionism professes to "de-ontologize" persons, it would appear that, under its terms, the first of these two provisos is flatly rejected. Moreover, even if at this point social constructionists were prepared to concede that there really can-not be any talk of "collectives" (Gergen, Chapter 2, this volume), without there also being at least whispered references to whatever it is that a collective is a collective *of,* this would not, in and of itself, meet critical personalism's proviso (b). In either case, it seems to me, we really are forced to conclude that, whatever else it might be, social constructivism is, finally, *not* a framework well suited to a discussion of moral action.

Perhaps Professor Gergen would rejoin here by pointing out that my argument only appears to undermine social constructionism's claim to a voice in moral discourse by dubious virtue of my stubborn recourse to those very rationalistic assumptions that he has already found wanting, and that social constructionism has thus called into question. I might find myself bowing to such a rejoinder if and when it trails a much clearer exposition than has yet been provided of the "one-s" that pepper Gergen's discussion of how "cultural conventions" replace cognition as the "fulcrum" of moral action (see the foregoing). Pending some such exposition, and providing that if and when it comes it does not itself incorporate rationalistic assumptions, I find it best to just acknowledge that those assumptions are simply the price of admission into the arena of moral discourse. One can pay this price "in cash," as it were, by making those assumptions an explicit feature of one's systematic thought (as Stern and many other thinkers within the rationalist tradition have done), or one can pay the price "on credit," so to speak, with language the bill for which one day comes due. Sooner or later, however, the price must be paid.

Now the social constructionists might well remind us here that, in the final analysis, what most troubles them about this transaction is not the price of admission into the arena of moral discourse based on rationalistic assumptions, but the atmosphere within the arena itself. Here, Professor Gergen really points to two problems. One is the fog of "abstract moral principles empty of significant content" that sent him groping for the exits in the first place. The other has to do with the untoward consequences of moral discourse itself. Given these problems, the question arises as to why one should want to reenter the rationalist arena of moral discourse anyway. The short answer to this question is: because it's the only arena in town. But as a somewhat longer answer is in order here, let us consider, in turn, each of the two problems cited by Gergen.

As regards the first, the question I would raise is: From the social constructionist perspective, what, precisely, is so problematic about abstract moral principles empty of significant content? In Chapter 2, Gergen states that "it is not that cultural conventions stand in opposition to transcendental principles; rather, without this social determination of meaning such principles cease to be significant." Perhaps so, but is this social constructionism's justification for rejecting (or trying to reject) a system of thought geared toward the articulation of such principles? Should we reject mathematics on the same grounds? If it is social constructionism's business (within the arena of moral discourse) to determine if, how, and when some abstract moral principle served up by rationalism applies in a given particular case, what would social constructionists do in a world where there were no longer any abstract principles over which to puzzle in this regard?

By raising these questions, I am attempting to suggest to my social constructionist colleagues that rationalism's gift of abstract moral principles empty of specific content might really *not* be all that problematic after all. To be sure, they leave unfinished much of the often hard work involved in appraising the moral worth of some given specific action, but this, it seems to me, is merely to say that within a rationalistic framework the point is never reached where we humans, individually and collectively, can simply give ourselves over uncritically to a set of algorithms guaranteed to cover any conceivable eventuality. Moreover, though for their abstractness such principles *do* leave unfinished business, they also provide the wherewithal for *conducting* that business, and I am not in the least persuaded that social constructionism can provide that wherewithal for itself. For example, where Gergen notes, in the context of his discussion of the untoward consequences of at least some forms of moral discourse, that "when the language of rights and wrongs was introduced into the situation there was not an enhancement of the human condition but deterioration" (Chapter 2, this volume), one wonders about the provenance of his notion about *the human condition*. Is there something within social constructionism itself that provides the standard against which we are able to discern when the human condition has been enhanced and when it has been deteriorated, or is this an(other) instance in which some thinly disguised vestige of the rationalist quest for abstract principles has slipped into the discussion? I rather suspect the latter when I read that "human relatedness becomes an originary source, the terrain upon which concerns with human well-being should be rooted."[4]

Still, even if the social constructionism train runs off from the rationalist tradition on a circular track, it does traverse some consequential territory along the way. I have in mind here that previously alluded to portion of Gergen's text where he treats of the potentially untoward consequences of moral discourse. In this connection, Gergen refers to work by Felson (1984), who found, in the words of Gergen, that

> among ex-offenders who had been convicted for crimes of aggressive assault, the majority traced their actions to incidents in which someone (often the victim) was seen as acting immorally (breaking a proper rule), there was verbal admonishment, and the putative rule breaker attempted to save face by a hostile reaction. Such exchanges culminated in physical assault, essentially traceable to the attempt to correct the iniquitous. (Chapter 2, this volume)

It is here where, in the quotation cited, Gergen speaks of the deterioration of the human condition that followed upon an introduction of the language of rights and wrongs into the situation, a point he reinforces by reference to "the destructive hostilities invited by the language of ethical superiority."

As Gergen himself notes, the lesson to be drawn from observations of this sort is that "we should be wary of the conclusion that moral language is both essential and desirable for what we take to be a morally structured society." The thesis is that, in practice, moral discourse that incorporates references to abstract and allegedly universal principles somehow sparks the "conflict, . . . opposition, . . . rivalry, and the ultimate quest for . . . superiority" that is in turn destructive rather than enhancing of human well-being. I am appreciative of Professor Gergen's concerns in this regard largely because I have little doubt that the empirical phenomenon he describes is very real and very serious.

However, I do not believe that the use of moral language per se is the true source of the problem here. Nor do I believe that the banishment of moral language would do much to solve that problem. I believe instead that the problem we are dealing with here is essentially the problem of individual*ism*, that is, a problem rooted in the two-pronged personal conviction that (a) to be *recognized by* others as an individual is, finally, more important than anything else and (b) to insure such recognition, one must somehow distinguish oneself or set oneself apart *from* those others, preferably in a "socially desirable" (read: "on average approved") way, but even in a socially *un*desirable ("on average disapproved")

---

[4] Gergen's idea here is, by the way, strikingly reminiscent of the concept of *das Gemeinschaftsgefühl* so very central to Alfred Adler's *individual psychology*, and the affinity between Adler's thinking and that of Stern is, in turn, something explicitly acknowledged by Stern in *Die menschliche Persönlichkeit*.

way if necessary. I believe that at least within our own present socio-cultural-historical circumstances, and perhaps within others as well, a great many persons have given these individualistic convictions top priority, to the point where moral discourse of the sort described by Professor Gergen is *not* really *moral discourse* at all, even where it involves language with a moral "ring."

An example of my own design might help to further clarify matters here. I arrive home two hours later than I had led my wife to believe I would, without having notified her, in the interim, of the fact of and reasons for my delay. On the basis of the abstract principle that one ought not leave one's spouse waiting, wondering, and worrying in this fashion, she is furious with me and makes that fact known. "You have no right to do this to me!" she exclaims. I retort, "Hey, what's so bad about this? Last month you went off shopping and came home *three* hours late! You're worse than I am!" She responds: "OK, if what you did was so good, you just *wait* 'til the *next* time! I'll show you!"

For the presence in this hypothetical interchange of such expressions as "you have no *right* . . . ," "what's so *bad* . . . ," "you're *worse* . . . ," and "if what you did was so *good,*" it certainly appears, on its surface, as homey sort of debate over moral principles. I would submit, however, that it really is not. It is nothing more than an individualistic struggle for high ground—it is a debate about who is a better person—and certain expressions often found within genuine moral discourse are serving, in this instance, only as pretext. The object of this game is *not* to reach, through rational dialogue, a position on the *moral* worthiness of my *action,* but to salvage a misguided sense of the *personal* worthiness of my *self.*

Now since terms like "personal" and "self" are veritable staples of rationalist language, it seems warranted to conclude here, as Gergen apparently has, that it is in that language, and in the philosophy that spawns it, where the problem lies. I, on the other hand, would redirect our attention to the foregoing phrase "misguided sense," for I believe it is *there* where the real problem lies. More specifically, I think that what we want to attack here is not the language of genuine moral discourse, but the rampant individualistic notion—perhaps *the* cultural phenomenon of our time—that in order to be anybody at all, one must be a somebody different from (and preferably if not absolutely necessarily more socially desirable than) others. It is when a sense of self is rooted in such thinking, and when the task of realizing that particular sense of self is assigned top priority, that we end up with interchanges of the sort described here, and of the sort mentioned by Professor Gergen.

What is the alternative? It would take more space and time than has been allotted to me here to treat thoroughly of this question, but the key, I believe, is to realize that an entirely viable sense of self, and of personal worthiness, can be pursued, realized, and maintained wholly apart from the purposive attempt to set oneself apart from others that is the very lifeblood of individualism. One does this via appraisals of one's own actions over against some ideal. This ideal might or might not itself be articulated through social or inter-personal dialogue, and it might or might not be realized or realize-able in practice. While it is thus beholden in a sense to what is *reason*-able, it is at no time and in no way *beholden* to considerations about what is *norm*-al, even if in certain specific instances it *happens* to *correspond* with such considerations.

What this view recognizes above all else is that there most certainly can be individual*ity* without individual*ism*. One's status appraised over against some ideal remains what it is no matter how it compares with the status of others, and, indeed, whether it is compared with the status of others or not. I believe that, armed with this basic idea, it will be possible to advance the vision of Stern's critical personalism beyond the point where Stern himself seems to have been able to take it. Further, and of more immediate relevance in the present context, I believe that this basic idea points the way out of the important problem brought to our attention by Professor Gergen in his discussion of the hazards of moral language. To illustrate this point, and by way of conclusion, I return to the hypothetical scenario sketched earlier.

In the interest of adhering to the *moral* agenda set by my wife's comment "You have no right to do this to me!" in protest against my tardy and theretofore unexplained arrival home, the proper response would have been words to the effect "Your complaint is well-founded, and I am sorry. Here is what happened." At this point, I might or might not be able to provide an honest and reasonable explanation for the transgression (e.g., flat tire on country road, no phone nearby). The point is that both the apology for *and* the explanation of the transgression bow to some transgressed principle, and in the process acknowledge not only the validity of that particular principle, but the validity of principled social interaction more generally. In the process, the interpersonally destructive features of the previous dialogue are completely eliminated. The fact that it is I and not she who is guilty in this instance of transgressing a principle of our relationship does not, in and of itself, carry any implications for my sense of personal worthiness, because my status in that regard is not linked to her status in that regard to begin with. If my action in the circumstance has been reproachable, this is so because I have violated a principle of our relationship *period,* and not because I have done so *and she has not.* Moreover, an apology and explanation for having done so is due her whether she, too, has violated the very same principle in the past *or not,* and there is no listing of her transgression of this same or any other principle(s) that can exonerate me in this regard. Nor, of course, are her past, present, or future transgressions "out of bounds" as topics of discussion, so long as it is remembered that they are separate topics, each to be evaluated on its own merits over against the principle(s) in question, and never to be arrayed "side by side" to the specious end of determining "who's better." There is nothing in rationalism that insists that morality is a zero-sum "game."

Hence, it is not necessary to be *more* moral than someone else in order to be moral at all, and *being* more moral than someone else does not ensure the achievement of sufficient fidelity to some principle of moral action.

My belief, then, is that insofar as we can succeed—with the help of social constructionists—in dissolving what might be termed the cult(ure) of individualism, and in establishing in its place not a framework within which persons and selves as agents are "de-ontologized" but rather one built around a non-normative conception of human individuality generally and moral action specifically, we will have taken an important step toward the realization of a paradigm that recognizes the irreducibly social nature of moral action and yet at the same time preserves such key rationalistic concepts as persons, selves, and agency, without which moral discourse simply cannot proceed.

REFERENCES

Felson, R. (1984). Patterns of aggressive social interaction. In A. Mummenday (Ed.), *Social psychology of aggression*. Heidelberg: Springer-Verlag.

Lamiell, J. T. (1989). *On social constructivism as the basis for a psychological theory of personality development*. Unpublished paper, presented at the meeting of the Friends of Good Psychology, Oxford, England, 24 June, 1989.

Stern, W. (1923). *Person und Sache, II. Band: Die menschliche Persönlichkeit (Person and Thing, Vol. II: The Human Personality)*, 3rd unrevised edition. Leipzig: Verlag von Johann Ambrosius Barth.

4 MORALITY IN A MEDIATING MECHANISM? A LOGICAL LEARNING THEORIST LOOKS AT SOCIAL CONSTRUCTIONISM

Joseph F. Rychlak

As an undergraduate at the University of Wisconsin, I took a course from Hans Gerth on the sociology of knowledge. This was a graduate-level course in which we studied the two-volume set of Becker and Barnes (1952). It was a challenging and truly memorable course. I believe that the best psychology textbook that I studied from at Wisconsin was the first edition of Krech and Crutchfield's (1948) work on social psychology. In graduate school at The Ohio State University I minored in social psychology, and at one point took preliminary steps to switch into this area as my major. My master's thesis was a cross-cultural study of Japanese students in America (Rychlak, Mussen, and Bennett, 1957). My doctoral professor in clinical psychology, Julian Rotter, advanced a theory of behavior called Social Learning Theory. Shortly after taking the Ph.D. I published one of my best experiments to date on a speculation derived from Festinger's social-comparison process (Rychlak, 1960). I mention these biographical facts at the outset to emphasize that I have always been and still am very drawn to sociocultural considerations in human behavior.

When I attended The Ohio State University in the 1950s the term "construction" or "constructivism" was pretty much limited to the theorizing of another one of my professors, George A. Kelly (1955). Whereas Rotter's (1954) theorizing followed a neo-Hullian path, Kelly's approach raised fundamental questions about the learning process per se. He challenged traditional learning-theory explanations of human behavior. Kelly's focus, therefore, was *not* social but individual (see Rychlak, 1990, for an elaboration of this point). He was looking at the *person* as construer or conceptualizer. Kelly therefore turned my attention to the responsibility that we in psychology have to delineate and elaborate the actual way in which people "work" as psychological beings—interpersonally, intrapersonally, while asleep, while awake, and so forth. He fought a pitched battle with the behaviorists over their mechanistic theories of human cognition. Construction had a teleological meaning for Kelly. It suggested that people are active agents, framing or conceptualizing their environment rather than being passively shaped by their environment.

Today, reference is made to a constructivist or constructionist "movement" taking place in psychology, and a major flank of this supposed movement embraces what is termed a "social constructionism" (Gergen, 1985). We are gathered here at Georgetown University to ferret out some of the suggestions and implications of constructionism in general and social constructionism in particular. As we are fortunate to have Professors Gergen and Harré in attendance (I am informed that the latter will be commenting on this paper), I will focus primarily on their writings—although I would like to refer to Berger (1963; with Luckmann, 1966) as well. Both Professors Harré and Gergen have mentioned the importance of values, the moral order, and so on, in their social-constructionist writings. An additional aim of our conference is to address this moral aspect of life as it pertains to the constructivist outlook.

Let me say at the outset that I am willing to consider myself a "constructivist" theoretician if this means what Kelly meant by the term. Whether I am a "social constructionist" or not depends upon what we are likely to work out at this conference. I can think of a way in which it could be correct to call me a social constructionist, but this requires some preliminary analysis and I am not at all certain that I will end up where Professors Gergen and Harré are situated following such analysis. Over the past 25 years I have worked out a view of human behavior and learning that I call Logical Learning Theory (Rychlak, 1988). I will not burden the conference members with a detailed presentation of this theory, but enough will emerge in the issues I address to convey a sense of what I am trying to accomplish in this teleological approach to human behavior. I begin with a discussion of the process versus content distinction, move to the difference between a mediational and a predicational model, and then take up the question of what "construction" can mean. I then close with some observations on the moral dimension of life.

PROCESS VERSUS CONTENT IN THEORETICAL DESCRIPTION

One of the first things I learned in doing research is that it is easy to confuse the empirical "findings" of an experiment with the activity or process that supposedly brought these findings about or made them happen. We all know that for any fact pattern observed taking place in an experiment there are, in principle, N potential explanations. This follows from the fact that in science we are always constrained by the "affirming the consequent" fallacy as we move from our theory to its experimental test, resulting in the possibility that an alternative theory can account for the experimental outcome (Rychlak, 1980). Empirical data do not speak for themselves, and we will always have "in principle" (not necessarily "in actuality") alternative ways of "construing" them. Gergen (1982) has explored this limitation in science with penetrating insight, though I would not concur with his recommendation that we should drop traditional validation in preference for a socio-rationalistic form of science (p. 207). I think it best simply to recognize that we cannot have logical certainty in science. We should applaud this fact rather than wring our hands over the supposed loss in predictive lawfulness, for what this limitation signifies is that human beings as conceptualizers will always be relevant factors in what can be known. And since the study of human beings as conceptualizers is what psychology is all about, we have a marvelous opportunity here for our profession to take the lead in important work.

When we look more carefully at disagreements between theories over the "observed findings," we appreciate that this invariably comes down to the nature of the process that produced the findings in the first place. I think there are various realms of theoretical interest that draw different theoreticians, and each of these realms seems to suggest its own distinctive process. By a *process* I mean some discernible, repeatable course of action. In physics/astronomy, for example, a central process is that of gravitation. Some presumed "action at a distance" holds the planets in their orbits as they fall through space within force fields. It is difficult to say precisely what gravitation "is," of course. Newton frankly admitted he did not know how gravity came about, even though he could point to its effects in holding things in place (Wightman, 1951, pp. 101–102). Einstein was later to interpret gravity as curved space, and he and Whitehead had a famous disagreement over their respective understandings of the "laws of gravitation" (Palter, 1956).

But the nature of the planets, with their observed and predicted patterns of action, is not what is at issue here. These patterns were observed, tracked, and predicted long before physical scientists appeared on the historical scene. The planets are therefore to be construed as "contents" working within or issuing from the field forces of a gravitational process. And it is in the precise nature of this process that we find our theoretical disagreements. Thus a *content* is an ingredient, element, or product of a process. What I now suggest is that when we observe the "findings" of an experiment, we are unfortunately limited to the content side of the scientific ledger. We can "see" the results of our experiment like we can "see" the orbiting of the planets. The trick is to explain the process that brought these results about. And we know right off that, in principle, any of

N potential processes can be advanced—though usually there are only a few such theoretical formulations vying for explanatory dominance.

To give another example of the process/content distinction, it has always been my belief that this is what separates the Kantian from the Lockean conception of "idea." Kant (1952) considered the idea to be an aspect of the very process known as "reason," which cannot be derived from the environmental products of nature but which helps to organize them a priori (pp. 150, 193–194, 200, 238). In opposition to this process conception of the idea we have Locke, who considered ideas to include just about anything that could be triggered by or otherwise found originating external to the person's mental process. Thus, he would say that we have "ideas" of sight, sound, taste, and even feelings. Ideas were akin to inborn structures molded and triggered biologically or environmentally shaped and placed into the mind as if into an "empty cabinet"—a metaphor he actually used (see Cranston, 1957, p. 266). Locke therefore made ideas into contents of—rather than aspects of—a cognitive process (See Rychlak, 1981, pp. 275–276). They were "objects" of the understanding, to be perceived and input "as given" biologically or environmentally rather than functioning innately from within to process and hence organize external experience. To claim such organizing capacities for the mind was to believe in "innate ideas," preformed "givens" rather than formative actions (Locke, 1952, p. 97).

MEDIATIONAL VERSUS PREDICATIONAL PROCESSES

Now that we have distinguished between a process and its content we can ask whether psychology has settled upon "a" process to explain human behavior. Actually, I think that there has always been a fundamental conflict over this question, a conflict that is presaged in the comparison of Kant and Locke on the interpretation of the "idea." Thus, I would suggest that we can distinguish between two models of a process in psychological explanation—the predicational and the mediational.

By *predication* I mean *a process involving the act of affirming, denying, or qualifying broader patterns of meaning in relation to narrower, targeted patterns of meaning.* When predication is taking place we always have a realm of meaning that is functioning as a wider or broader range, extending itself to a narrower and targeted item of meaning. Take, for example, the historical phrasing of the Aristotelian syllogism. The major premise is "All human beings are mortal." If we were to diagram this process through use of Euler circles, we would have a large circle labeled "mortal beings." Placed within this wider-ranging circle we would have a smaller, targeted circle labeled "humans." There could be other circles placed within the larger circle as well, labeled "fishes, insects, birds," and so forth. The "circles within circles" modeling here symbolizes the process under description of meanings extending from the wider "predicating" circles (mortality) "to" the smaller, targeted circles (with overlapping circles at times, etc.).

If we follow this process forward to the minor premise and say "This [single organism under our observation] is a human being," we would symbolize the latter by placing a dot within the small circle labeled "humans." Immediately as we align the meanings symbolized by our two circles and the dot we would have created our conclusion: "This [organism] is a mortal being." The broader realm of meaning termed the major premise instantaneously focuses upon and thereby enriches the minor premise, which in turn instantaneously focuses this meaning even more specifically on the single organism targeted, to create the conclusion: "This [specific organism] is a mortal." We witness here an outcome of logical ordering, a process that has nothing to do with time's passage. There is an *immediate* continuity in meaning-extension from the wider background to the successively narrowing focus. The *process* organizes, aligns, patterns, etc., the meanings that issue as its *content*.

It is always possible to reverse the order of items being patterned meaningfully in the major premise. We could reverse this alignment to say "All mortals are humans," and reason to the conclusion that any mortal organism under our immediate observation is therefore human. Some primitive groups actually frame things this way. The fact that a more civilized person would claim that we are making a logical error here, since we could be observing a "mortal" snake, is irrelevant to the fact that predication is a process that stands apart from the meaningful contents that it aligns, generates, produces, and so forth. Most disputes in human affairs occur over the major premises under framing, rather than the conclusions that follow from them. People rarely think as logicians or statisticians do, but there is nevertheless a discernible logic reflected in their "illogical" reasoning (Kahneman, Slovic, and Tversky, 1982).

The other process, and by far the more prevalent one employed in psychology, is mediation. By *mediation* I mean a form of explanation in which *a content formed outside a process is taken in and comes to play a directing role in that process that is not intrinsic to it*. The patterning into meaning of items processed in mediation is not intrinsic to this process. Mediational processing is akin to a conveyor belt, a taking-on or taking-in (inputing, encoding) from sources external to it, and then being directed in the kinds of meanings that will issue based upon what has been taken in. The meanings under conveyance by a mediational process are prepackaged. They enter with their form already delineated.

Time's passage is crucial in a mediational process, because an already formed antecedent meaning is united by a "mediator" to an already formed consequent meaning. The "mediator" is the first to enter from or be shaped by outside forces, and this externally derived item henceforth functions between the "earlier" and "later" flow of meaningful events. The meanings being related here with the assistance of the mediator are associated together strictly on the basis of their input order and prevalence. Mediators thus shape cognition into a pattern based upon the contiguity and frequency of the events that have been directed inward. This is a "mediate" process over time because it has no intrinsic direction, and hence it cannot arrange a pattern of "immediate" meaning in the way that the logical process of predication can. The mediational process is never an originating source of influence or control in the way that the predicational process is. Mediation waits on some other event to occur before it swings into action.

We can now see the parallel between predication and mediation in the Kantian–Lockean difference over the nature of an idea. Kant employed a predicational model of process whereas Locke relied on a mediational model of process. Literally all psychological theories can be divided into these two contrasting approaches, although it is also possible to find some theorists attempting to "mix" them together—a difficult and frequently clumsy effort leading to unsatisfactory results.

There is a feature of a predicational process that I have not yet addressed, one that is totally lacking in the mediational process. Following Kant, not to mention historical usages trailing back to 2500 B.C., I used to discuss this as *dialectical* reasoning (Rychlak, 1981/1968), and although I still use this term, over the years I have found that "dialectic" lugs too much historical baggage with it to be completely clear on how I want to use it. In recent years, I have been referring to and studying empirically the role of *oppositionality* in cognition, which provides me with roughly the same benefits that "dialectic" did. It is self-evident that oppositionality in human cognition is simply a further description of predication. Indeed, it involves a kind of duality within the predicational process. I offer the following definition: *oppositionality is a form of "double predication" in which one pole of a duality intrinsically delimits and hence frames the definition of the other pole, and vice versa. Psychological states of oppositionality include contrariety (the basic state), contradiction, negation, and contrast.*

The clearest manifestation of oppositionality in predication can be seen in the Euler circles model. When we settle on a wide-ranging realm of meaning within which to situate some target that will draw this meaning—as when we say "Marcia is responsible"—we sometimes forget that the wider circle labeled "responsibility" or "responsible people" has an implied meaning of "irresponsible people" surrounding it. This is a reflection of the "double predication" I refer to in oppositionality, for it is impossible to delineate a categorical assertion without thereby implying that it can be contradicted, negated, contrasted, and so on. The upshot here is that when the predicational process is under way it is best described as "taking a position" within a sea of opposite meaning-possibilities, rather than "taking in" or inputting singular "building blocks" that add up to this or that meaning based upon the frequency and contiguity of past contact with the items in question.

I might mention in passing that, in a recent effort (Rychlak, 1991), I have tried to show how the Boolean interpretation of disjunction on which computers rely—that is, "A or B, but not both"—carries out the aspect of mediational modeling we are now considering. Human beings, I argue, reason according to a non-Boolean disjunction involving "A or B, or both." It is in the uniting of the "both" that we can find this double predication of oppositionality taking place, and on the basis of which people derive their human agency. Oppositionality in meanings is what forces the human being to "take a position" on the ever-generating meanings of life (refer to the foregoing).

Indeed, I would suggest that Kant's (1952) reference to a "transcendental dialectic" (p. 109) is a reflection of predicational modeling because it suggests that the person has an intrinsic capacity to see to the opposite of the factually given or the sound predication and take flight thereby into illusion. I do not share Kant's concern with this human capacity to flee reality or disregard "proper" steps in reasoning. As a psychologist I must explain people as they are—thinking well, thinking poorly, "warts and all!" Besides, it is through such flights of illusory fancy that great innovations in thought can occur. Einstein's thought experiments undoubtedly made considerable use of this intrinsic human capacity to reason dialectically (i.e., oppositionally). This brings us to the issues confronting our conference.

THE MEANING OF INDIVIDUAL OR SOCIAL "CONSTRUCTION"

As I noted at the outset, Logical Learning Theory is a teleological explanation of human behavior. I am not arguing for a deity or a natural teleology; only for a human teleology. And, of course, I rely upon the predicational model as a reflection of the logical process that I believe all people on the face of the earth employ. To be human is to predicate experience. The word "predication" serves a double duty, which leads to some confusion at times. That is, it can refer to the process of predicating as well as to the content that issues from this process. As we noted earlier, we can say "Marcia is responsible" and consider this a description of the process in which the larger Euler circle (responsible people) engulfs the smaller circle (Marcia). But, we can also think of this statement as a "predication" that we hold concerning a person of our acquaintance. In this latter case we are dealing with a content, an item of belief that has been produced by the process and now can be pointed to, written down on paper, committed to memory, and so forth.

I derive my argument for human agency from the predicational process per se, *not* from the content resulting. There are formulations of agency or "free will" that rely on the "number of alternatives" programmed or input into a mediational process (e.g., Thoreson and Mahoney, 1974, p. 5; Dennett, 1984, pp. 37, 62, 169). We might theorize that enough innate mediators have been programmed into a person at birth so that he or she could not "expend" them in two lifetimes of enacting them overtly. Or, a theory might suggest that a person who had input (learned, etc.) more mediating "ways" of behaving (e.g., how to relate to other people) would therefore be freer—have "more" free will—than a person who lacked such facilitative mediators as cognitive contents. From my point of view, such formulations of agency or free will are erroneous. They are nonteleological or mechanical, making the person into a conveyor rather than an initiator of behavior. I find the human's agency in the process, not in the number of contents under conveyance or framed by the process.

I would define *agency* as *framing and behaving for the sake of predications that are in conformance with, in opposition to, or without regard for biological or social determinants.* Agency is made possible by the oppositionally generated, transcendent capacity for predication to rise above and thereby reflexively affirm (select, choose, decide, etc.) "this" course of action rather than "that" course of action. Sometimes this affirmation is harmful to the person doing the predicating. Standing against social pressures can lead to ostracism or worse. Ignoring certain physical promptings can result in biological collapse. But, people do indeed "take such positions" in life. They have a transcending, self-reflexive capacity to put their physical and social pressures to evaluation, negating them entirely, or furthering them all the more.

Now, so far as I am concerned "construction" is a synonym for predication. It has the same double-duty kind of role that can lead to confusion. We can think of a construction as a process, or as a content within that process. Social influence can be thought of as "individuals construing [predicating] in common" and the resultant beliefs can be termed a "construction [predication] held in common." Social norms, social stereotypes, and all manner of behaviors that differentiate one culture or subculture from another would therefore constitute *content* differences. However, the process that resulted in these contrasting contents would be identical. Just as certain cultures favor spicier foods than others without suggesting thereby that the digestive process is culturally determined, so too am I suggesting that people are marvelously different in the contents incorporated in and produced by a common predicational or constructional process.

Psychology has to date been pinning its hopes on mediation to explain such differences within and between cultural or social identities. This mediational style of explanation has cast our theories from an extraspective or third-person point of view. We have tended to account for human behavior as "that, over there," an efficiently caused succession of *mechanical* events. I would argue that all learning theories are at heart "social" learning theories because they must find some source of influence external to the individual to shape cognitive contents, since there is no intrinsic source of such patterning within the mediational process. Today's explanations based upon the computer analogue persist in this mechanistic vein (Rychlak, 1990). In contrast, I follow Kelly (refer to the foregoing) to suggest that people must be understood from an introspective or first-person ("I, me") point of view, which is where they always "take positions" on life in a formal-final cause fashion—that is, *for the sake of* the meanings they affirm, negate, ignore, misconstrue, etc. So, it is very difficult for me—as it was for Kelly—to give over the source of predication to something that is not firmly based in the individual qua predicator (Maher, 1969, p. 218). All of which takes me to the concept of "social construction."

When I read Peter L. Berger (1963; with Luckmann, 1966), whom I understand is sometimes referred to as one of the "fathers" of social constructionism, I find myself agreeing with his views on this topic. Berger (1963, pp. 91, 125) likes to point to the differences between Durkheim and Weber regarding the study of society. Durkheim, a so-called "objectivist," thought of society as a "phenomenon *sui generis*" (ibid., p. 91). Durkheim wanted to avoid "reducing" the social to the individual, because he feared this would permit psychology to swallow up sociology. He maintained the extraspective perspective in construing society as a distinctive, supra-individual process. The individual becomes a content of the social process on this view. Weber, on the other hand, was considered a "subjectivist," trying to understand the collective from the introspective perspective of the individuals who formed it (Berger and Luckmann, 1966, p. 18). As a consequence, Weber's theory stressed that social actions embodied people's intentions—a fact that is not lost on a teleological theorist like myself.

Berger tried to bring the objectivist and subjectivist views of society together, claiming both that "*Society is a human product*" and also that "*Man is a social product*" (ibid., p. 61; italics in original). This would imply to me that there are separate processes for the social and the individual, and each in turn is a product or content of the other. But Berger does not really work things out in this manner. I am not so sure Durkheim would be pleased with his resolution, for when he comes right down to it, again and again Berger places the initiating *process* in the individual and the institutionalized *contents* of this process in the social structure.

Thus, Berger essentially defines social construction as follows: "all social phenomena are *constructions* produced historically through human activity" (ibid., p. 106). There is an interaction between the individual and the society, depicted as dialectical in nature. I take this to mean that at any one historical point of time there is an ongoing social content of belief available to the person, who in turn modifies and contributes to it so that it also changes its meaning(s) in due course. Invariably, the initiating source is the individual, for at no point is there a "group mind" or supra-individual process suggested to frame things or "construe" events over and beyond the person's externalized ideas, which are objectified and then subsequently internalized by others (ibid., p. 183). The person is never simply a pawn (content) in the group process.

In fact, Berger (1963) specifically refers at one point to "rebellious constructions of the mind" that can "liberate the individual to a considerable extent from the definitory system of his society" (p. 133). People can "say 'no' to society, and often have done so" (ibid., p. 142). This suggests to me that an individual can transcend, self-reflect, and negate a social belief in precisely the way that I have construed agency (refer to the foregoing). In one highly interesting passage Berger and Luckmann (1966) show how a religious genius might concoct a "new mythology" that will become part of the cultural lore (objectified) and then be used as a grounds for social action (internalized) by succeeding generations (p. 83). I like this kind of constructivism, because it provides me with work. As a psychologist, I can study this individual process and hopefully convince my sociological colleagues that it is predicational in nature. This kind of psychological study does not "reduce" the social to the individual, for there are supra-individual patterns of institutionalization that require study in their own right. Social pressure, or the logical weight of influence that the collective has upon the individual, is also something that requires study in its own right. Of course, I am not too pleased with Berger's frequent use of "mechanism" to describe social behavior (ibid., pp. 55, 109). There are also many references to the mediation of this or that social structure (e.g., social roles; ibid., p. 76). But I think such terminological problems could be dealt with to everyone's satisfaction.

Thus, a Logical Learning Theory analysis of social constructionism would have the basic learning *process* rooted in the predicational capacities of the individual, who is not shaped into accepting but literally needs or wants to accept various socially institutionalized *contents* (mores, beliefs, norms, myths, etc.) in a continuing effort to make sense of and enrich life. The contents taken over from the socio-cultural context would represent the standing "social constructions." Invariably, when social theorists caution us about culturally relative beliefs they point to such contrasting contents. We are told that Western Europeans believe one thing and Northern Native Americans believe another. Who is to say which cultural content is "the" better rendering of reality? These content-beliefs are best understood as guides for the persons concerned in these social identities to live somewhat different lives. As Berger and Luckmann (1966) phrase it: "The social stock of knowledge . . . supplies me [i.e., a person] with the typificatory schemes required for the major routines of everyday life" (p. 43). We are socialized by taking over this stock of knowledge predicationally, and behaving for its sake. We require this structure, particularly when it involves interpersonal considerations. I readily accept their definition of socialization: "Primary socialization involves learning sequences that are socially defined" (ibid., p. 136). What we need to do now is clarify the nature of this learning process. We must show that it involves predication qua construction-as-a-process.

When I now turn to the writings of Gergen and Harré, I find them departing from Berger in the direction of Durkheim and hence I am unable to call myself a social constructionist of their ilk. Both Harré (1989, p. 440) and Gergen (1989, p. 466) believe that psychological theoreticians have fallen prey to a Cartesian dualism in which there is a "knowing subject" on the one hand and an "object of knowledge" on the other. But if one believes, as I do, in a construing qua predicating organism then this "object of knowledge" is not separated from the organism who literally frames it into existence! In a predicational process, the content or object of knowledge is not "reflected" or "mirrored" (ibid., p. 446) from the outside. It is structured from the inside. Rather than taking this predicational approach, both Harré (1989, p. 442) and Gergen (1989, p. 472) rely upon the views of Wittgenstein concerning the use of language terms, which pattern into "games" of representation to create a social reality for the individual.

Here is where we see Gergen (ibid.) clearly following Durkheim's path: "It seems essential that we avoid reducing the social world to the psychological" (p. 479). Knowledge issues from a supra-individual process of relatedness, as follows: "what we take to be knowledgeable propositions about the world are essentially the outcome of social relatedness. What we take to be knowledge bearing propositions are not achievements of the individual mind, but social achievements" (ibid., p. 472). Contrast this with Berger and Luckmann's (1966) view that "all social constructed universes change, and the change is brought about by the concrete actions of human beings. . . . Reality is socially defined. But the definitions are always *embodied,* that is, concrete individuals and groups of individuals serve as definers of reality" (p. 116).

Harré (1987a) also places the origin of social definitions in a nonembodied, supra-individual collectivity, as follows: "We should begin with the assumption that the primary location (in both a temporal and a logical sense) of psychological processes is collective rather than individual" (pp. 4, 5). There is a certain equivocation in his view, however, since he almost seems to be referring to individual embodiment when he states that: "People should be thought of as constructing a permanent and continuous conversation, in which such acts as promising, avowing, disavowing, lying, denying, and so on, are going on. In the course of that conversation, they construct all kinds of public matters, including decisions, scientific theories, football matches, and so on" (Harré, 1984a, p. 128). It appears here that people are constructing (process) things in a social nexus, a position which would not necessarily contradict a predicational model of such interaction. Thus, though Harré (1987b, p. 5) speaks of the "myth" of individualism, this belief could be seen as a content that had issued from the embodiment of individual "predicators" (process) engaged in conversation.

But I am afraid this predicational bubble bursts as we look deeper into the origins of social constructions. For here it is quite clear that both Gergen and Harré rely upon language to account for how it is that social constructions arise.

Such constructions will become the "effects" (contents, products) and not the "causes" (process) of linguistic usage. I have always had a problem with this theoretical position since it seems to me that there can be no language without a predicating logical process, one that at the bare minimum has the prelingual individual presuming—*not* "knowing" verbally—that words make "sense" before any language terms can be acquired (see Polanyi, 1964, p. 151, for a discussion of this point). We are back to that "double-duty" issue again, for language can stand as a content bearing meanings, or it can be thought of as a process that brings such meanings into existence. If the latter, how does this construction process take place? We find Gergen and Harré relying upon descriptive terms like "linguistic convention" (Gergen, 1982, p. 92) and "learning" (Harré, 1984b, p. 174) to describe how it is that people presumably acquire their views of social reality. And, of course, the conveyor of such views is language. So, the question for the psychologist becomes "how is language learned?"

If we go to Wittgenstein at this point, the prospects for a teleological account of human learning are nil. According to his view, children are "trained" into their so-called language games by examples, rewards, and punishments. The success of the child's training depends upon his or her instinctive capacities to react properly. Wittgenstein (1969) minced no words in referring to this training process as follows: "I am using the word 'trained' in a way strictly analogous to that in which we talk of an animal being trained to do certain things" (p. 77). Wittgenstein is obviously prepared to see the person as a mediating mechanism of some type, moved along by material—and efficient—causation. It is therefore not surprising to find his interpreters such as Bloor (1983) drawing direct parallels between Wittgenstein and the theories of B. F. Skinner (pp. 52–54).

Gergen (1985) criticizes the "endogenic" theorizing of cognitive psychology (p. 269), because this internal processing of information takes the focus off "exogenic" processes of social construction. He believes that cognitive psychologists have only a secondary interest in the cognitive styles of other cultures and historical periods:

> In contrast [to the cognitivists], for the social constructionist, there is an acute sensitivity to the perspectives of other peoples and times. For, as the investigator demonstrates variations in perspectives, the effect is to break the hold of the common sense realities of contemporary culture. It is to deconstruct local ontologies, and thereby free the individual from the constraints of existing convention. (Gergen, 1989, p. 476)

Indeed, the cognitivists' very belief in an endogenous process is rooted in the exogenous linguistic realm of social influence, "the metatheoretical basis of the science itself" (Gergen, 1985, p. 269).

I have been unable to pinpoint what kind of learning process Gergen has in mind when he refers to people's use of linguistic conventions (Gergen, 1982, p. 92). He accepts "symbolization" (ibid., p. 161) as a human capacity, enabling alternatives to be framed, and even mentions "processes of self-reflexive activity" (ibid.). Yet, consistent with his Durkheimian leanings, he would like to see a flowering of the exogenic world view in philosophy and psychology (ibid., p. 184). Since I think of the "exogenic" as another way of referring to mediational modeling, I conclude that Gergen would have no problem with the Wittgensteinian mechanistic approach to training children in language games.

As for Harré, I can draw on personal experience to arrive at the same unhappy conclusion. At a conference on the "self" several years ago, Harré delivered a plenary address in which he advanced his views on what this concept could mean (published subsequently as Harré, 1987b). I was stunned by the fact that he explained selfhood away, referring to the notion of a self in the discussion following his address as a "linguistic convention." His theory held that people believe they have selves after they have first learned from their society the theory that "persons" exist. One theory feeds into the other. Additionally, even our sense of intentionality is transmitted by way of such linguistic acquisitions. Following his address, I pointed out to Harré that he had used the term "learning" several times, and therefore he must have had some learning theory in mind. What was it? Harré answered that he always thought Hull's (1952) learning theory was a suitable explanation! Hullian learning theory is, of course, a prime example of mechanistic, mediational explanation.

It seems that neither Harré (1987a, p. 10) nor Gergen (1987, p. 21) are believers in a human teleology, meaning by this the view that the individual is an originating source of influence on his or her behavior. I detect little concern on his part when Gergen (1982) writes approvingly that "the individual may be 'programmed' to process information in an infinity of ways. Such programming is clearly susceptible to exogenous influences" (p. 56). Since all information, all knowledge is believed to be carried by language, our role as psychologists is to study the contents carried along by this social process, becoming thereby increasingly cognizant of human diversity. Agency, intentionality, purposivity, identity, free will, etc., are all tossed into the same mediating hopper as "linguistic conventions." What is more, even morality can be so understood. As Harré (1984b) tells us: "I hope to show that moral responsibility comes into being in a society by way of the people coming to believe that they are agents" (p. 85).

MORALITY AS PROCESS OR CONTENT?

Here is where I find myself clearly rejecting the social constructionism advanced by Harré and Gergen. I believe that morality begins in the very *process* of a moralizing organism. Morality requires an organism that is fundamentally an evaluator, functioning according to an active process in which a "position" must continually be taken (framed, affirmed, believed in, hoped for, etc.) precedent to the actions that follow. This organism must have the intrinsic capacity to see that avenues *might be* taken other than the one opted for even as this is being enacted. The one opted for would be evaluated on some predicating basis, of course, a basis we call in this context a "value." The value per se would represent a content statement of what the person has evaluated as a presumably "higher" end (telos) than has been manifested in his or her behavior—or the behavior of others—to that point in time. This, of course, is merely a further description of what I have referred to earlier as human agency. I cannot see how moral suasion could influence an organism that merely input and carried forward linguistic conventions as rank-ordered signals—some defined as "higher" in value by the culture than others. Without some personal evaluational effort by the organisms concerned, these orderings would represent an arbitrariness lacking in moral conviction.

I do not deny that we have such orderings of value contents in the culture, and seek thereby to convey them to all participants. These are, as Berger has taught us, embodied principles, "oughts," expressed by individuals and then objectified as cultural artifacts and introjected as "norms" by others in the society. Social *norms* are thus akin to *predications held in common* by a collective of individuals seeking meaning, identity, and a feeling of heightened morale in their lives. I think the reason such ethico-moral practices are accepted by others in the first place is because, as evaluating organisms, they see the great benefit in holding to the particular predications advocated—sometimes merely "in principle."

That is, I think anyone living in any culture on the globe knows that there are moral ideals, and then there are the realities of how people actually behave "most of the time." Hence, if there is such a thing as a moral order, it is surely very complex, including the orderings of various subcultures and minority groups within the broader society. But we all know the "highest" form of morality for the societal reference group to which we are conforming at the moment, even if we rarely come up to it in our behavior. It is difficult for me to see why an advanced society, if it really were the source of morality, has such an involved and often conflicting network of moralities. Better to "construct" people as robotic uniformities for smooth functioning.

On the other hand, if people band into social identities out of some *personal* need to create a meaningful existence, it is clear why we have so many different codes of ethics and religious beliefs in this world. There are many ways in which to embody such beliefs, and some groups are prompted into existence by counter- ing the moral claims of others—which means that influential leaders, models, myth-makers and the like find some reason to oppose one another. The very problem of communication among individuals doubtless focused such individual differences around those who could be directly informed, by word of mouth, concerning the predications under affirmation by their leaders. As communication is made more general in this electronic age we see people moving closer to a common value structure, although traditions still keep us apart on many counts.

So, from the point of view of Logical Learning Theory, morality begins in the very process of predication, which always demands that a position (choice, decision, point of view, belief, etc.) be taken by the human reasoner. And, one of the major positions taken is that of an affective assessment—a judgment of liking or disliking, which extends readily to such moral estimations such as "the good" and "the bad" or "the right way" and "the wrong way" in which human affairs are to be carried out (Rychlak, 1988, Chap. 9). The human being is at heart an evaluating organism. Social contents reflect this fundamental human capacity. It is no accident that moralistic rules of thumb such as the *Golden Rule* or the *Categorical Imperative* are written quite simply and directly at the level of the individual, for they represent a guide—encompassing the social!—by which the *person* can live. But the point in all this is that the predicating organism *requires* such guides, such assumptions, rules of thumb, "for the sake of which" he or she is to operate. A sense of "things could be different" that in turn implies "things could be better" is ever-present in the psychic processes of the human being, for this is how predication "works" (refer to the earlier discussion).

It seems to me that Harré's (1987a, p. 9) interpretation of the moral order is laden with contentlike prescriptions and proscriptions. He tells us that the moral order defines rights, duties, and obligations (ibid., pp. 10–11). The essentials of a moral order include categorizations, typologies, and warrants, all of which suggest to me a content approach to morality (Harré, 1984b, p. 245). If we view the society as bringing to bear such constructions qua contents by way of linguistic conventions, entered into the individual's mediating processes and carried forward mechanically (i.e., via efficient causation), then this is the *only* question open to us concerning morality. What are the specific rights, duties, and obligations stipulated by the society in question? As psychologists, we are not to ask why human beings "work" in this strange way to begin with, seeking to align an evaluative ordering to behaviors "for the good of the group," which can mean a delinquent gang, football team, United States citizenry, terrorist organization, and so forth.

I find it hard to believe that mediating mechanisms can "be" moral, since they cannot in principle ever evaluate their inputs "from the outset" of mental life. Such evaluations are simply earlier inputs mediating present inputs. The moral order is etched on the tabula rasa intellect just like any other mediating cue. It becomes a matter of "color this mediating cue moral" and "color this mediating cue nonmoral." There is no intrinsic judgment involved here by the person qua mediator whatsoever. I think that morality is trivialized by this account. But if we view the individual as a predicator, then the moral order follows from the person's implicit processing needs to render a continuing evaluation of what "ought" to take place in the henceforth. The "henceforth" is always under production by the resultant evaluations. The moral order is, in effect, an aspect of the "logos" that the predicational process is *always* addressing, framing, taking a position on, etc. Indeed, I believe it is impossible for a predicating intelligence to avoid ethico-moral issues. The duality of what "is" and "is not" the case at any point in time necessarily drives home (suggests, implies, etc.) the logical possibility of "improvement" to the predicating intelligence.

I am not quite certain how Gergen would differ, if at all, from Harré's position on a moral order. As I understand his socio-rationalist position (Gergen, 1982, pp. 207–208), he argues that since all psychological research is a "rhetorical implement," its chief function is to lend persuasive appeal to the theoretical language being advanced by the researcher in question (ibid., pp. 102–103). He would like to see knowledge removed "from the data-driven and/or the cognitively necessitated domains and place it in the hands of people in relationship" (Gergen, 1985, p. 272). His form of social constructionism offers no "truth through method" (ibid.). Rather than follow the myth that rigorous methods will yield sound fact, independent of the intentions of the researcher, Gergen believes that "virtually any methodology can be employed so long as it enables the analyst to develop a more compelling case" (ibid., p. 273). It follows from all of this that what the scientist is involved in is morality, since what is studied and how it is studied is determined by the values he or she brings to the scientific quest: "To the extent that psychological theory (and related practices) enter into the life of the culture, sustaining certain patterns of conduct and destroying others, such work must be evaluated in terms of good and ill" (ibid.). The scientist of the future can no longer claim to be a "victim of the facts," but must consider the "pragmatic implications of such conclusions within society more generally" (ibid.). Since all is language, Gergen places his hopes on dialogue for the future of a morally responsible science (ibid.).

Others have pointed to the possibility of political power plays in Gergen's socio-rationalism (e.g., Stroebe and Kruglanski, 1989, p. 486), so I will not take up this issue. I have only two brief comments to make on Gergen, as I bring this chapter to its end. The first is that he, quite brilliantly, points out the foibles of the scientist as a human being. Scientists most certainly do engage in rhetoric and polemics, and this does not stop at the door leading to their laboratories. But, how can Gergen now overlook the very same human foibles when he comes to values and morals? Talk about rhetorical implements! It seems to me that, as a "language game," the experimental design has a far clearer "scoring" procedure than does the dialogue made contingent upon ethico-moral ascriptions, debates over what would be good and what would be bad research topics, the effect on social relations (morality) of certain empirical findings, and so on.

My other point is that in his theoretical development I believe that Gergen actually makes my case for predication. That is, he insightfully appreciates that since the predicating scientist is a central player in the "research" language game, and there are disagreements over the rules, interpretation of findings, etc., in this game, it ultimately comes down to a dialogue or dispute among participants over the value-laden assumptions they are to make and follow. Facts do not speak for themselves because the human organisms framing experience bring them into "reality." Now, admittedly we need a social context within which to delineate and play out our game! But even this context can be understood as the wider realm of meaning, framed by a human intelligence searching for a position that is satisfactory to all. This formulation of psychological science encompasses the human image that I have constructed/predicated in this chapter, which is conveyed linguistically for all to read. I am hoping to objectify it enough so that it might eventually be introjected and thereby employed more generally by others whom I bump into in my social order.

Is this "I" I am referring to merely a linguistic convention, input years ago and currently mediating what is printed here? Or, is the "I" really predicating things, as I believe? Shall we dialogue? Is the "we" any more real than the "I"? Will there be any embodiments in our dialogue, or merely "freely floating" linguistic systems representing contrasting and conflicting social orders beyond our individual influence? Can we have a social order or a linguistic system without a predicating logos framing them in the first place? Might we actually be engaged in a dia-logos? Do we next construe a construction, or are we simply babbling the already constructed? Questions, questions. Let the dialogue begin. . . .

REFERENCES

Becker, H., and Barnes, H. E. (Eds.). (1952). *Social thought from lore to science* (2 vols.). Washington, DC: Harren Press.

Berger, P. L. (1963). *Invitation to sociology: A humanistic perspective.* New York: Doubleday Anchor Books.

Berger, P. L., and Luckmann, T. (1966). *The social construction of reality: A treatise in the sociology of knowledge.* New York: Doubleday Anchor Books.

Bloor, D. (1983). *Wittgenstein: A social theory of knowledge.* New York: Columbia University Press.

Cranston, M. (1957). *John Locke: A biography.* New York: Longmans, Green.

Dennett, D. C. (1984). *Elbow room: The varieties of free will worth wanting.* Cambridge, MA: Bradford Book of the MIT Press.

Gergen, K. J. (1982). *Toward transformation in social knowledge.* New York: Springer-Verlag.

Gergen, K. J. (1985). The social constructionist movement in modern psychology. *American Psychologist, 40,* 266–275.

Gergen, K. J. (1987). Warranting the new paradigm: A response to Harré. *New Ideas in Psychology, 5,* 19–24.

Gergen, K. J. (1989). Social psychology and the wrong revolution. *European Journal of Social Psychology, 19,* 463–484.

Harré, R. (1984a). Social elements as mind. *British Journal of Medical Psychology, 57,* 127–135.

Harré, R. (1984b). *Personal being: A theory for individual psychology.* Cambridge, MA: Harvard University Press.

Harré, R. (1987a). Enlarging the paradigm. *New Ideas in Psychology, 5,* 3–12.

Harré, R. (1987b). The social construction of selves. In K. Yardley and T. Honess (Eds.), *Self and identity: Psychosocial perspectives.* New York: Wiley.

Harré, R. (1989). Metaphysics and methodology: Some prescriptions for social psychological research. *European Journal of Social Psychology, 19,* 439–453.

Hull, C. L. (1952). *A behavior system.* New Haven, CT: Yale University Press.

Kahneman, D., Slovic, P., and Tversky, A. (Eds.). (1982). *Judgements under uncertainty: Heuristics and biases.* Cambridge, England: Cambridge University Press.

Kant, I. (1952). *The critique of pure reason.* In R. M. Hutchins (Ed.), *Great books of the western world,* Vol. 42, pp. 1–250. Chicago: Encyclopedia Britannica.

Kelly, G. A. (1955). *The psychology of personal constructs* (2 vols.). New York: W. W. Norton.

Krech, D., and Crutchfield, R. S. (1948). *Theory and problems of social psychology.* New York: McGraw–Hill.

Locke, J. (1952). *An essay concerning human understanding.* In R. M. Hutchins (Ed.), *Great books of the western world,* Vol. 35, pp. 85–395. Chicago: Encyclopedia Britannica.

Maher, B. (1969). *Clinical psychology and personality: The selected papers of George A. Kelly.* New York: Wiley.

Palter, R. (1956). Philosophic principles and scientific theory. *Philosophy of Science, 23,* 111–135.

Polanyi, M. (1964). *Personal knowledge: Towards a post-critical philosophy.* New York: Harper & Row.

Rotter, J. B. (1954). *Social learning and clinical psychology.* Englewood Cliffs, NJ: Prentice–Hall.

Rychlak, J. F. (1960). A socio-psychological theory of performance in competitive situations. *Human Relations, 13,* 157–166.

Rychlak, J. F. (1980). The false promise of falsification. *The Journal of Mind and Behavior, 1,* 183–195.

Rychlak, J. F. (1981). *A philosophy of science for personality theory,* 2nd ed. Malabar, FL: Robert E. Krieger Publishing Company. [First edition, 1968, Boston: Houghton Mifflin.]

Rychlak, J. F. (1988). *The psychology of rigorous humanism,* 2nd ed. New York: New York University Press.

Rychlak, J. F. (1990). George Kelly and the concept of construction. *International Journal of Personal Construct Psychology, 3,* 7–19.

Rychlak, J. F. (1991). *Artificial intelligence and human reason: A teleological critique.* New York; Columbia University Press.

Rychlak, J. F., Mussen, P. H., and Bennett, J. W. (1957). An example of the use of the incomplete sentence test in applied anthropological work. *Human Organization, 16,* 25–29.

Stroebe, W., and Kruglanski, A. W. (1989). Social psychology at epistemological cross-roads: On Gergen's choice. *European Journal of Social Psychology, 19,* 485–489.

Thoreson, C. E., and Mahoney, M. J. (1974). *Behavioral self-control.* New York: Holt, Rinehart & Winston.

Wightman, W. P. D. (1951). *The growth of scientific ideas.* New Haven, CT: Yale University Press.

Wittgenstein, L. (1969). *The blue and brown books.* Oxford, England: Blackwell.

5 ON BEING TAKEN UP BY OTHERS

Rom Harré

READING RYCHLAK

I would like to test my understanding of Joseph Rychlak's main theses and his proposals apropos of the moral element in psychology by trying to rephrase his remarks in my own terminology.

1. Rychlak reminds us that for any alleged fact there are indefinitely many explanations possible in principle. This point is familiar to philosophers of science as Clavius' paradox or the underdetermination of theory by data. But he omits the equally important reciprocal thesis—every human experience is capable of indefinitely many different construals in presenting it propositionally as fact. This is the principle of the theory-ladenness of observation. As Whewell remarked, "facts" and "theories" mutually determine one another. This need not be construed as radical relativism. I believe that it is possible to understand how the historical dialectic between theory and fact gives us a better "grip on reality" through progressive mutual refinement of our concepts and our percepts.

2. People are active agents, using whatever resources they have available to try to bring off their diverse projects successfully. We can find this thesis advocated in Aristotle. We can also find it, as Rychlak does, in the writings of George Kelly, and in the works of most wise people between.

3. People are capable of acting alone, as atomic individuals. I shall assume that this principle refers not to some native capability but to a being already

trained in the socially acceptable behavior through which he or she manifests him or herself as a person. This assumption may not be true to Rychlak's theory.

4. What sort of products do people create? The most general description of human artifacts would be that they are ordered structures, some synchronic, others diachronic.

5. Discourses are human products. Some are ordered by preexisting "templates," the rules of logic. Let us call these "syntactic" structures. Others are ordered pairwise, by virtue of certain relevant semantic properties of their elements. Let us call these "semantic" structures. I would add that most discourses are ordered in both ways. For instance, that an answer follows a question is, in a broad sense, syntactically required. That a query about the price of eggs should be followed by a statement of a sum of money is, in a broad sense, semantically required.

6. People act on the basis of their own and other people's evaluations of possible outcomes of their actions.

Where do Rychlak and I part company? I am not averse to any of the above theses. Indeed I think I could provide both empirical evidence and theoretical arguments in their favor. However, there are two areas of significant disagreement. These are disagreements not only between Rychlak and myself but also reflect matters that I think are contentious in the work of Kelly.

First, I think the individualism endorsed by Rychlak is largely an illusion. This contention will have to be spelled out in detail. Of course there are human individuals who act alone. But no person could have always existed alone—self-made. The individuality of people is not in question. Who would deny that there are selves? Not the author of *Personal Being* (Harré, 1985)! The question is how do they come to be individuals capable of autonomous conduct and so of action that in a Judeo-Christian culture is individually personally accountable?

Second, Rychlak seems to me to miss an important aspect of discourse, germane to the foundations of a moral psychology. This omission is very significant. What is said (and what is thought, felt, wished for, and so on) must not only be intelligible, that is, be constrained by local syntactical and semantic conventions; it must also be warrantable—be the right and proper thing to say, think, feel, want, or do, in the circumstances.

Discourses (and courses of action generally) must not only make sense to the actor and to any others who might be involved, they must also be defensible. There is not only a logical and semantic "order" that is used by people to shape their lives, there is also a locally valid cluster of moral orders. Just to point out that people evaluate possible outcomes is not enough to support the claim that moral matters are deeply rooted in the bases of human conduct. There are all kinds of evaluations. Only those that concern the good of others and our relations to them can count as moral evaluations. In the phenomenon of psychological symbiosis, whose central importance is, or ought to be, the leading "constructionist" principle, individual psychological activity is shown to be rooted in joint activity at the heart of which are interpersonal relations of trust and care.

To find myself bracketed with Gergen is a flattering conjunction but it hardly reflects my views in philosophy of psychology. I am no relativist, and insofar as I can make sense of post-modernism, I think it is seriously and dangerously in error. On the other hand, I do not believe in the stability and sempiternality of facts nor in the inductive method. Life is practice, and it is in the study of practice that our epistemologies must be grounded.

READING HARRÉ

Inevitably one reads a text or listens to a speech through frameworks of presuppositions and with the help of one's existing concepts. This is one of the reasons that have made it difficult for the advocates of social constructionism to be properly understood. If, as we believe, the main phenomena studied by traditional psychology, such as memory, reasoning, the emotions, and so on, are *locally* generated in certain discursive practices, then almost nothing of the old ways through which psychologists tackled these human phenomena remains intact in an adequate human science. Rychlak is reading me as if I was trying to do some more psychology, only differently. I am after something entirely other. If I were to write a book summing up all these years of work I would call it *Instead of Psychology*.

It is evident from Rychlak's paper that I have failed to get my thought across to him in several important respects. For instance, because there is development in one's agentive powers he thinks somewhere we must have or should have a "learning theory." But that is already to misunderstand the approach. It presupposes the thesis, which I vigorously deny, that psychological processes are essentially individual. Let us follow tradition and call this "individualism." As an enthusiast for idiographical studies in which $N = 1$ I am interested in how individuals are locally created in joint action with others. The exact status of individuals in psychology is a puzzle since it is *evident* that our agentive powers are jointly produced and jointly exercised. My attempt at a resolution of this apparent paradox is entirely Vygotskian/Wittgensteinian. If someone insists on the need for a learning theory, that is, an account of how a single specimen of *Homo sapiens* could acquire the wherewithal to accomplish a social act, one can only reply ironically "any one will do." Pavlov/Skinner or Hull—it does not matter because it is quite beside the point. As Wittgenstein (1953) demonstrated, rule observance cannot, in the end, be founded on rules. Somewhere in the analytical hierarchy one must come on natural regularities, the human "form of life" and/or trained responses, proper to the local tribal "form of life." But at that point we have left "psychology" in that we have left behind the matters of concern, namely, remembering, reasoning, planning, emotions, agentive action, and so on. Learning theories will be needed at the level at which Wittgenstein's "spade was turned"—but not for psychology.

SOCIAL CONSTRUCTIONISM

What do I mean by social constructionism? I think it is instructive to launch into an exposition through a series of contrasts in underlying assumptions between social constructionists and traditionalists.

1. Other students of the characteristic activities of human beings, be they behaviorists or those practicing cognitive "science," assume that people are automata whose behavior is caused by local contingencies acting on preexisting generative mechanisms. The apparently huge gap that separates behaviorists from cognitive "scientists" is really very narrow. Indeed all that separates them is an opinion about the substance of the mechanisms that supposedly bring about human action. The constructionist point of view must, of necessity, remain much closer to whatever are the local commonsense conceptions of human action than does the behaviorist or cognitive science outlook. If people are indeed artifacts then local methods of people making are bound to leave their mark on how people "work." There are great differences in the ways people are formed, so there are great differences in the practices through which people of this or that pattern manage their lives. Historical and anthropological studies, as well as revealing great differences, do find clusters of closely related cultures sharing conceptions of the genesis of action. Common to most of the ethnographies of the "European" tribes is the idea that people are, in principle, active agents who shape their conduct in accordance with local norms. Individuals who fail to do so risk various kinds of obloquy, and even, if their eccentricities become too tiresome, incarceration.

2. Older ways of conceiving of "what makes people tick" (we note the horological metaphor) model their picture of the genesis of human action on patterns of theory found in some of the physical sciences. We might call this the Hertzian pattern. Theorizing begins by assuming that behind the phenomena there lies another realm of entities, like those we can observe, whose interactions, though not observable, nevertheless generate the observable phenomena. For constructionists there are no such mechanisms, physiological or mental. There is no "language of thought" behind the uses of language. Nothing is hidden, to quote Wittgenstein. Dispositions must be grounded in some permanently existing state of the human being and the only states that appeal to me ontologically are neurological. There are no mental mechanisms—only discursive practices. Some are linguistic but some draw on other semantic systems and

use symbols other than words. The root ideas in our local conception of human agency, according to which we manage our lives, include the taking of responsibility, the displaying of one's actions as according with locally valid rules and norms and other accounting procedures, are discursive practices. Practices are skilled performances. As I argued extensively in *Personal Being* these skills are acquired in the course of social interactions in which they are first performed by someone else on behalf of the junior member of a symbiotic dyad. They are not native endowments. The basic concepts of constructionist psychology will be "discursive practice," "skill," and "ability," not "mental (or physiological) mechanism."

3. The constructionist is not supposing for a moment that human actions are socially *caused*. Rather the theses at the heart of the position have to do with the social *nature* both of people and of their acts. Human actions become determinate as acts only in the joint production of illocutionary force with the help of others. Secondly, what it is to be an individual, that is, a socially and psychologically independent being, is locally given and necessarily itself a product of social interaction of the generally symbiotic form.

4. My own research interest has been focused on the discursive conditions for the production of selves and on the discursive production of agency. In these cases, there is both a moral order presupposed and moral relations created in the social production of these psychological matters.

A reservation must be entered at this point, and let it function as a warning, too. Whatever form of enquiry with which we eventually replace psychology must be sensitive to the fact that the self may not be the unit of practical morality even in those (Western) cultures in which metamoral talk places such an emphasis on supposedly autonomous moral selves.

THE BASIC CONSTRUCTIONIST THESES

1. According to social constructionism, all significant action is jointly produced and thereby subject to the constraints of a local moral order. As Austin (1965) remarked, illocutionary force exists only in the mutual keying of speaker's intention with hearer's uptake. The relevant intentions and uptakes are, of course, those that interactors display—not their undisclosed attitudes to the action, whatever they might be. Much is yet to be learned about how the metaphor "keying in" is to be construed in particular cases.

2. It is particularly important to see that the moralizing of psychology (in contrast to a moralizing about psychology) is framed entirely within a Vygotskian/Wittgensteinian assumption of psychological symbiosis—we are forever in Vygotsky's "zone of proximal development."

3. Human beings are not people qua members of the biological species *Homo*

sapiens. People are made (constructed) by other people on occasions of joint action. In particular, the "self" is a social construction.

4. From a psychological point of view, the primary reality for people is conversation. Many psychological phenomena exist only in conversation, for example, emotions, decision making, remembering, and so on.

5. People, once constructed, can and do act individually by conversing reflexively.

MORALITY IN LANGUAGE

Taking the view that most of what has passed for aspects of human psychology is produced in the uses of language, we must surely try to discern how deeply certain moral assumptions are embedded in the conditions for the possibility of language in general as well as in the local linguistic practices. In this way we shall make good our escape from relativism.

Holiday (1988) has argued that a certain skeleton moral order must obtain for language to be possible. (This is not an etiological nor is it a historical observation—it concerns the logical conditions for language to exist.) He finds three conditions, or in his way of expressing it, three core language games—there must be personal trust; there must be a kind of distributive justice; there must be respect for ritual. Strange as the last may seem, it becomes clear why it should appear among the root conditions when we reflect on the way order is maintained among the symbolic users of systems. The system itself must be respected. It must be accorded a kind of sanctity. This thought is connected with Wittgenstein's thesis of the autonomy of grammar. In the absence of these core language games, there may be vocalizations, but they could *not* constitute the human use of language.

A second, more locally distinctive way that moral orders sustain language use appears in those rights and duties that can be looked on as conditions for conversational order to be sustained. There are rights and duties to speak and rights and duties to listen, to reply, and so on. These are enormously variable. Habermas tried to devise a moral order of speaking that would reflect a kind of ideal of interpersonal relations, but one can hardly imagine it being implemented.

LANGUAGE IN USE

According to my version of social constructionism, the basis of moral psychology is going to be found in the study of language in use. In recent years there has been a strong movement away from thinking of language as a formal system underlying the occasions of use of linguistic symbols in speaking and writing.

The idea that language in use, conversation, is the basic linguistic and psychological reality highlights concepts like speech act, indexicality, context-dependence, psychological symbiosis, cultural, ethnic, and gender specificity, etc., for central use in the study of language.

In psychology, the preceding contrast in attitudes toward language appears in the opposition between the idea that people are automata and language is a device for communicating subjective states from one to another (the old coding/decoding theory), and the idea of people as agents and language as a means of joint action itself continuously produced by joint action. But to avoid repeating some old errors, careful reassessment of what it means to say that language is a rule-governed activity must be undertaken. The temptation to reify rules comes, in part, from the thought that surely something must preexist the joint activities through which speech acts become determinate acts. This assumption must be brought into question because it is just the assumption that leads to problems. People have been trying to find a location for transcendent templates since Plato enthused over the forms.

Within this framework of concepts, there is a place for the idea of causation but it is invoked only in the exceptional cases. The "default" explanatory concept is something like "normative regularity." But both causal and normative regularities can be taken as mere Humean concomitances (motivating primitive methodologies such as the use of ANOVA on a large data base) or they can be taken as instances of the exercise of power. Under the latter option, an investigator must try to find out what are the powerful particulars at work in the genesis of the phenomena. In the psychology case, the question boils down to a choice between rules or people as the operative entities. According to my version of constructionism, one of the crucial things that culture provides for people is the local form of agency. People are empowered in various ways. Different cultures and different locations in the corresponding social (moral) order empower people with respect to different possibilities of rewriting the script, revising the rules, challenging the norms, and so on. This observation is behind the argument that Shotter and I have made much of, that psychology is essentially a moral science, no matter what its more crass practitioners may think. Writing out the norms immanent in a practice tends to legitimate them. By defining people psychologically as automata, we disempower them.

The label that has finally been attached to our point of view, not, I must say, to my entire contentment, and replacing Secord's and my neologism "ethogenics" (Harré and Secord, 1973), widely used in Spain and Italy, is "social constructionism." Some notion of "society" or better "community" is thereby invoked. One weasel word replaces another! It can sound as if there is some entity, "society," which acts upon human raw material to engender persons. The burden of our argument is that people engender people. But they perform this miracle in joint action and in the course of engaging in certain discursive practices. "Society" is not anything, not even a kind of abstract thing. It is the orchestration of individual speakings and doings. The question for a psychologist of social action is this: What are the means by which this orchestration is routinely accomplished? It might, for example, be rule following.

What is it in the individual tribal member that preexists intelligible activity, and makes it possible? In recent years, most academic and clinical psychologists would have answered "mechanisms." When challenged to produce one it turns out that these "mechanisms" are unfortunately not available to our inspection. Neither the information-processing modules dear to the AI crowd nor the forming and dissolving of complexes in the hidden realm of the Freudian unconscious are available. It looks as if both snarks are boojums! Oh for Ockham and his razor!

Our local tribal psychology is also ready with answers to our question. Knowledge and belief (that is, certified and uncertified opinions about what it is proper to do when and how to do it) are the grounding of many skills and abilities. As Ryle (1947) pointed out, if this way of putting the matter is adopted, we had better be clear that much of what counts as knowledge is "know how" rather than "know that" or "know what." The notion we need here (and that is implicit in ethnomethodology) is that of something being "immanent in a practice." The contrast is with whatever is transcendent to a practice. Looking for a transcendent source of immanent order is, as I argued earlier, as hopeless as looking for mental processes. Why don't we just get on with the fascinating task of describing what people do and of speculating on what they can and can't do, and why these limits exist? All we need to ascribe to individuals are skills and abilities to engage in joint action.

Briefly returning to the issue of how we are to develop a conceptual system for studying how we acquire skills, Vygotskians need only the idea of copying or imitation. In the zone of proximal development the senior partner is already performing skillfully in supplementing and complementing the junior partner's efforts. The junior partner copies what the senior is doing. Conditioning, be it classical or Skinnerian, no doubt sometimes goes on, but one does not see much of it in watching the young become competent.

THE AGENCY QUESTION

I shall now lay out a possible constructionist account of agency, the essential moral attribute of persons. Is constructionism committed to some form of the passivity doctrine? And is the alternative to acknowledge, after all, the existence of an active ego as substance? The concept of "self" is currently used by speakers of English for two quite different human identities. The self-1/self-2 distinction involves distinguishing the managing self from the self that is managed and publicly presented, expressed in the "self concept." An individual's "self concept" is a set of beliefs entertained by that person as to their own personal attributes. The former is manifested in the sense we have of our personal singularity, a sense the content of which is as culturally variable as the multitudes of social selves. It has long been realized that we cannot become acquainted with any occurrent properties of the self-1, the managing self. The constructionist thesis is this: There *are* only persons. A person may mistakenly attribute their sense of singularity to the existence of a substantial self—a Cartesian ego— under the influence of philosophy.

Now to the nativist question. Granted that the self-2 is socially constructed and culturally variable, is the self that manages (in another terminology the person = Mead's "I") a native endowment or is it also a social construction? I argue that in acquiring the ability to perform the local discursive practices, a person becomes an agent. But that is to have a unified cluster of certain powers and skills, not to incorporate a mysterious inner soul, the ego. How could this thesis be tested? One way would be to trace the way that agency is exercised and develops; the way that in certain pathological conditions it declines. There are people who believe that their every move and thought is determined from else- where. There are psychologists who treat human beings as automata whose actions are caused by something other than themselves. There are cultures in which agency is not valued and the skills for agentive accounting of one's actions and decisions are not trained in. (Julian Jaynes (1976) might have said something as a historian of the sense of agency and how it affects what people do and how they think about themselves.)

Could awareness, surely a native endowment, be enough to account for the managing powers of the self-1? Clearly not, since at least a synthesis of experi- ence into a centered structure is necessary so that what happens is understood as what happens to *me,* and what is done, is done by *me.*

Are Miss Beauchamp and other multiple personality sufferers relevant? One candidate for the source of the identity of the person as manager is that person's body. But in Miss Beauchamp's case there are more managing selves than there are bodies. There are three persons (in the sense of selves-1) and only one body. How did Morton Prince (1905) know this about Miss Beauchamp? It appeared in her agentive discourses, in particular the way pronouns were distributed in the talk that issued from what was indisputably one body. Miss Beauchamp's dis- course was multiply centered in that what she said she perceived, what she declared she remembered, and what she claimed responsibility for was split into three coherent groups, each separately indexed pronominally.

WHAT IS AGENCY?

In this final section I want to sharpen the discussion further by comparing and contrasting Rychlak's conception of human agency with mine. From Chapter 4 of this volume I take the following:

1. A definition of agency as "framing and behaving for the sake of predications that are in conformance with, in opposition to, or with regard for biological or social determinants."
2. A condition for agency specified as a capacity for "predication" to "rise above and thereby reflexively affirm" one course of action rather than another.

There are some puzzling aspects to this proposal, but they may be merely terminological. For instance, does "conformance"—a word I am not familiar with—mean "conformity"? It seems, too, that the term "predication" is used in some special sense since predication is an act of sentence/statement construction. Surely agency is more than a capacity to act for the sake of formulating certain sentences! In the course of his gloss of his account of agency, Rychlak seems to slip between language and action. He writes of an "affirmation" being harmful to a person when, for instance, they stand out against social pressures. But it is one thing to affirm that all property is theft and quite another to try to bring down capitalism by fomenting a strike. Both may be discursive practices that lead to trouble but there are great differences in their perlocutionary effects. It is also unclear whether he intends the condition I have set out as (2) to be necessary or sufficient or both. If it is, as the annexed phrase "makes possible" suggests, a necessary condition, then we need to be told what more is required for sufficiency.

"Predication" is also used by Rychlak to identify an alleged ambiguity in the concept of "construction." Couched in a more usual terminology I think he means that a construction might be the product or the process of making. I mean it just one way. I believe that the "agentive self" is a social construction, by which I mean the result of the inculcation of certain discursive skills in the course of a complex and long-lasting process of person making. But Rychlak seems to think that I mean that agentive acts are the upshots of exclusively social, that is, collective, processes. But that is to confuse social causation of action with social construction of actors. Once constructed, the homunculus (-a, but not -um) can act alone in whatever agentive manner its culture will allow. Mostly people make their decisions in community, but that too is a skill.

There is yet another difference between us to be detected in this passage. Not only is Rychlak a nativist about cognition, and an individualist about action, he is also a believer in the universality of the relevant aspects of human cognitive capacities. A nativist need not be a universalist but it is a natural conjunction of erroneous assumptions. He asserts in Chapter 4 (this volume) that while the contents of "predicational processes" are culturally various, they are managed by a common cognitive procedure. With all due respect I think that is not generally so. Even in observing our own community we can accumulate masses of evidence to show that the processes of moral cognition employed by women differ in significant ways from those used by men, and not just in content, but also in logical form. There are plenty of cultures where those who conformed, by Rychlak's account of agency, would be taken to be mad at best, possessed by hostile spirits at worst. What of the Christian doctrines of prayer and of grace? And so on and so on.

Nevertheless, I want to emphasize that in several respects my account is like Rychlak's. Agentive power for me is grounded in the capacity to construct hierarchical discourses. As I argued in *Personal Being,* the picture of a cognitive mechanism conjured up by the idea of means/ends hierarchies ought to be read as a schematic grammar. Agency is discursively produced in that:

1. What I do is shown to myself and others as chosen from among alternatives if I am a child of the Judeo-Christian tradition; Islamic moral psychology is rather different, with its own cluster of favored discursive practices.

2. What I do can be shown to be in accordance with some principle, rule, motive, or plan. The discursive character of "acting in accordance with motive, etc." has been clearly demonstrated by K. Burke and C. Wright Mills. The core of Wittgenstein's extensive study of rule following is the insight that people actively use rules to display the correctness of their actions. His study of the recalcitrant pupil (surely done from life! How those village children must have irritated him!) shows how utterly wrong it would be to treat people's actions as caused by the rules that define the correctness of the practice in which they are engaged. I cannot think where Rychlak got the idea (Chapter 4, this volume) that Wittgenstein is "obviously prepared to see the person as a mediating mechanism rather, moved along by material—and efficient—causation." The parallel with Skinner drawn by Bloor and Day is superficial and to do with Wittgenstein's endorsement of the principle that "nothing is hidden." It is a prescient criticism of the program of cognitive science.

3. Agency is a discursive skill. The managing self is, ontologically, just the person. But the people have a sense of self—a singularity in space and time—to which powers of decision and action are willingly attributed. But why? Because people are also, in our culture, brought to take themselves to be singularities in various manifolds of positions in moral universes.

4. To be an agent is, in part, to believe oneself to be an agent, with respect to this or that aspect of one's situation. Foreigners are amazed and amused to see how readily Americans conform to rules and conventions, including the convention of declaring themselves to be autonomous individuals. Other countries, other mores. But wherever we are, there are human beings who seem to lose the capacity to formulate alternative principles of action—who cease to believe in the conventional character of the ties that bind us—there are madmen and behaviorists everywhere.

As far as "learning" goes, I can only reiterate, *once again,* that all we have need of is Vygotsky's developmental psychology. In the "zone of proximal development" the junior partner in the symbiotic group is routinely and fully completed as a competent performer. How much of this joint action is taken over by the junior member is highly contingent. We do not need a learning theory. The universal human tendency to imitate the actions of others is quite enough.

SUMMARY OF THE CONSTRUCTIONIST VIEW OF PERSONS

The idea of a passive person whose actions are caused or forced by something else other than the person: this is the basic thought of psychologies as diverse as Skinnerism, AI/CS, and eliminative materialism. In none of these is the person the active agent or powerful particular, responsible for bringing off or bringing about the action. Only in a skills psychology can we raise serious questions about moral responsibility.

The idea of the active person: we think of people as skilled agents, bringing about wanted states of affairs according to or guided by certain norms. This introduces us to two kinds of issues.

1. The nature of skilled performance. It is something other than merely activated dispositions or tendencies, and involves the notion of a power.

2. What sort of performances are they that should interest us? One of great importance is the living and telling of narratives. So the main skill to study is that of active narration, in its two modes: living and telling, in accordance with the norms and conventions of narration current in that milieu. People guide their conduct in this way, use rules and conventions and so on, in order to produce conduct that is meaningful. Meaningless conduct presents people with a problem. We are inclined to fall back on a causal explanation—no fully competent person would allow themselves to produce such a mess. Something other than themselves must be at work in generating disorderly and seemingly random behavior.

To put finally to rest the suspicion of relativism, I would make a fundamental distinction between moralities that take the "substance" of the moral world to be actions (actions such as the basic particulars of moral discourse, if you like) and those that take that "substance" to be persons. MacIntyre (1981) seems to me, rightly, to have drawn attention to the drift from person-focused moral theorizing to action-focused moral theorizing that has occurred since the Renaissance. Utilitarianism, emotivism, hedonism, and deontologies of various hues have taken the action as the focus, not the person performing the action. One's morality has come to be defined through what one *does*, not through what one *is*. So moral philosophy has come to focus on the qualities of actions that are germane to their moral standing.

Let me sketch a priori some features of the person-centered view, at least as I take it. The "original" moral acts qualify as virtuous only insofar as they are person creating and person sustaining. Superogatory acts in this dimension are person enhancing—steps to eudaimonia. The philosophical analysis of the concept of person must, on this view, be at the root of an account of what identifies a moral domain. "A" domain at this point, rather than "domain," because we still have to confront gergenism. That confrontation is forced upon us because like Shotter (1984), Vygotsky (1978), and others, and unlike the genevans and their disciples, I take persons to be artifacts, not natural growths. They are artifacts of cultural processes, generated in joint actions, including if you like the telling of stories among many other ways of doing things together. (Cf. the underquoted book by Jeff Adams 1979!) If one believes in the artifactual genesis of persons, are the products of person making sufficiently locally diverse to justify gergenism?

This question, like all questions focused at this level of generality, can be embedded in an empirical enquiry or tackled conceptually. Like my supervisor, the late J. L. Austin, I do not think these domains of enquiry are radically disjoint. As Wittgenstein said, we must agree in a form of life, that is a language, but "queer as it may sound" we must also agree in judgments. Absent Catherine Lutz I revert to the a priori. Persons come in diverse species, but the universality of the genus is guaranteed by one condition, that one and all they be linguistic beings. (That qualification is in need of much development, but it would take a rerun of the *Philosophical Investigations* to spell it out adequately.) I share with Vygotsky, and I think Bruner, if I get the message of what possible worlds mean to him, the opinion that agency is possible only to a being that can represent to itself what is not yet or what has not been. And that is made possible only if the being is "linguistic." One can see how gergenism can arise if one pays attention only to moralities of action, and neglects the universal conditions in personhood for any such morality to be possible. Moralities of action as diverse as those of Christianity and of Islam rest on a common view of persons.

It follows that developmental psychology is in the moral domain in two ways—as a story about how people are made it sustains a generic moral order, but as a legitimizing discourse it also sustains particular ways of people making. And so seems to present this or that local way as universal. We were all "instructed" subtly to take on the person-making ways of upper-middle-class Francophone Swiss!

I think Shotter and I share the view that "person" is a comparative concept. One can be more or less of a person. Some ways of person making produce artifacts that are less persons than other ways. Here we return to the idea of practices that enhance personhood and those that demean or cripple it. This insight, if it is one, has an important ontological consequence. What is it that people have "by nature"? Not personhood—but certain potentialities and native powers to acquire the discursive skills that are constitutive of beings who are such.

If we look to our cultural roots we find person centered moralities in the writings of Aristotle, of Kant, and of Wittgenstein. According to the latter, there is nothing you can say or do that, of itself, constitutes your moral standing. Your moral worth is what you *are,* and that can be shown but it cannot be said. In Kant's moral scheme (Kant, 1783) the categorical imperative does not determine what one should do—it is a formal principle—it leads to the formulation of a prescription of a Kingdom of Ends. The point of Kant's morality is the preservation of persons. And of Aristotle's their enhancement?

REFERENCES

Adams, J. (1979). *The conspiracy of the text.* London: Routledge and Kegan Paul.

Austin, J. L. (1965). *How to do things with words.* New York: Oxford University Press.

Harré, R. (1985). *Personal being.* Cambridge, MA: Harvard University Press.

Harré, R., and Secord, P. F. (1973). *The explanation of social behaviour.* Oxford, England: Blackwell.

Holiday, A. (1988). *Moral powers.* London: Routledge.

Jaynes, J. (1976). *The origin of consciousness in the breakdown of the bicameral mind.* New York: Houghton Mifflin.

Kant, I. (1783/1956). *Groundwork of the metaphysic of morals,* translated by H. J. Paton. London: Hutchinson.

MacIntyre, A. C. (1981). *After virtue.* London: Duckworth.

Prince, M. (1905). *The disassociation of personality.* London: Kegan, Paul, Truscott and Schrubner.

Ryle, G. (1947). *The concept of mind.* London: Hutchinson.

Shotter, J. (1984). *Social accountability and selfhood.* Oxford, England: Blackwell.

Vygotsky, L. (1978). *Mind in society.* Cambridge, MA: Harvard University Press.

Wittgenstein, L. (1953). *Philosophical investigations.* Oxford, England: Blackwell.

6 THE MORAL DIMENSION IN SOCIAL PSYCHOLOGY

John Sabini and

Maury Silver

We don't know much about social science, so we thought we would take the unusual, at least for us, step of deciding that that was a reason not to write about it. We do know a bit about social psychology, so we thought we would write about that instead. We might as well register another cavil; we're not sure there is a moral dimension of things, either, but we won't fuss over that here.

This chapter has three sections. In the first we will discuss the moral dimension as it is represented in American social psychology. In the second section we want to contrast that position with morality as it emerges in the "social constructivist" position as articulated by Berger and Luckmann in *The Social Construction of Reality,* and as used—for good or ill—by us in *Moralities of Everyday Life.* (This happens to be the development of a social constructivist view of morality that we are most familiar with.) In the final section, we want to address explicitly why *Moralities of Everyday Life* paid so little attention to morality, and why one might pay attention to morality within a social constructivist framework.

THE MORAL DIMENSION IN CONTEMPORARY AMERICAN SOCIAL PSYCHOLOGY

So what is the status of the moral dimension in social psychology? The matrix for thinking about morality in social psychology was formed by the coming together

SOCIAL DISCOURSE AND MORAL JUDGMENT

in the 1930s and 1940s of two distinct traditions: psychoanalysis and animal learning theory. The question about morality that both traditions wanted to address was this: How does an organism that decides what to do based on its immediate hedonic calculus come to follow moral rules? Both traditions offered accounts of how moral considerations could become a part of the organism's current hedonics. The answers, to be sure, were in different languages—the psychoanalytic tradition spoke of "internalization" of the parents, the learning tradition spoke in terms of "higher order conditioned stimuli" of various fantastically complex sorts. The differences between the accounts are less striking than the similarity. But, to repeat, they were primarily interested in showing how moral concerns *could in principle* be elements in a hedonic calculus; to the degree that the programs accomplished this, they saw themselves as having solved the problem that their own programs set them: accounting for "moral behavior." I will make, briefly, several points about this—all of them are by now old chestnuts.

The first chestnut is that the assumption that organisms, including us humans, act exclusively on the basis of our momentary hedonic calculus was not then, and is not now, an empirical matter. It was, and is, a metaphysical claim. The other old chestnuts follow from this one.

If a person does the right thing out of fear of pain—whether it be produced by real parents or imagined parents (which it was, of course, was a central issue to these traditions)—it seems that the person isn't acting in a fully moral way. Such a creature isn't acting because of its perception of the morally right, but just out of its perception of what is convenient for it—and, in the perspective of a different metaphysic, say Kant's, that just isn't moral action. It was, however, enough for these theorists, because it was at least *so-called* moral action, and that was what was seen as in need of explanation.

The second chestnut is this: Such a view of morality precludes questioning the moral basis of parental prescriptions and proscriptions. If morality is nothing but the standards once enforced by one's parents, but now internalized, then the question of whether those standards are themselves moral is, quite literally, senseless. Put another way, internalizing parental prohibitions isn't a route to the development of moral thinking. If one is to become able to raise a moral question about parental rules, one must have the conceptual equipment to do so, and swallowing one's parent's rules—or for that matter becoming conditioned in certain ways—isn't a way to develop that conceptual equipment. (None of this is meant to deny the speculation that a certain sort of socialization may be a necessary condition of one's becoming the sort of person who not only makes moral judgments, but also acts on them—perhaps this is so.) But all of this is old hat. Not many academic social psychologists are either animal learning theorists or psychoanalysts. How is all of this relevant to *current* thinking in social psychology?

Well, for the last couple of decades the most prominent figure at the interface of morality and psychology has been Lawrence Kohlberg (Kohlberg, 1969). Kohlberg, as we all know, posed moral questions to subjects of different ages and documented the age-related changes in the kinds of answers the subjects gave. His theory consisted in arguing that the changes in answers constituted the development of moral reasoning. His observation was that at early ages, children tended to answer the dilemmas in hedonic terms, later they answered in terms of convention, and finally they offered principles. There is, by now, a vast empirical literature that debates the accuracy of his observations; we are not concerned with that issue, or this literature. What we are concerned with are these questions: If you pose someone a moral dilemma, and she answers that she would do this or that because it avoids pain, why would you characterize her reasoning as moral? True, it is reasoning in response to a moral question, but if you ask someone a question in physics about how hard a horse has to pull an ice-cream truck up an inclined plane, and she answers that she would like a vanilla cone, if you please, any physics professor we have met would reply not that she got the physics wrong, but that she hadn't addressed the physics of the question at all. No partial credit for *that* answer. Why not say the same of the responses to Kohlberg's questions? Many of them don't address the morality of the issue at all. But all right, suppose we allow non-moral answers to moral questions as an early stage of moral reasoning. Still a developmental theory has to explain how one stage leads to another. *How* are these a-moral responses transmogrified into moral ones? This problem persists.

Carol Gilligan, the most prominent neo-Kohlbergian, has suggested that Kohlberg has too narrow (!) a view of morality. She proposes that women have a fundamentally different moral system from men's. To support this, she argues that when posed moral questions, women answer in different ways from the ways men answer. In particular, she argues that men answer in terms of rules, but women answer in terms of caring about another (Gilligan, 1982). But even if this is so, one must ask again: But why call these answers moral? Either Gilligan has decided that any answer to a moral question is a moral answer, or she has independent reason for deciding that answers of the sort she provokes are moral. If the latter, then she has reason quite independent of the answers her subjects give for castigating Kohlberg for his narrow conception of morality—and perhaps those are good reasons. We just don't know what they are.

Our aim in recounting all of this is not to chide Kohlberg or Gilligan; rather it is to highlight the roots of this problem. If you have the view that we are fundamentally hedonic calculators, then the question you ask yourself about morality is: How do people come to do other regarding things, or in some moods: How do people come to do seemingly other regarding things? The answers Kohlberg and Gilligan adduce from their subjects *are* on that topic, therefore they are about morality.

Kohlberg and Gilligan are figures central to modern psychology as it abuts ethics, but they are not central figures to social psychology. Let us turn to how morality is placed within that tradition.

Broadly speaking, there are three core domains of social psychology. The first is the territory surrounding the notion of attitudes; the second surrounds what used to be called "person perception"; and the third has to do with emotion. Let us see how moral matters enter those concerns.

The catechism answer to the question of what is an attitude is: omnis apptitudinis divisa est in tres partes: cognition, action, and affect. Let us take capital punishment as an example of something toward which people are said to have attitudes. A person's attitude toward capital punishment is composed of, on the canonical view: his beliefs about capital punishment, his disposition to vote for or against candidates who support it, and his feelings about it. O.K., but where does a person's believing that capital punishment is morally wrong (or right, for that matter) fit? Well, that's how he feels about it. A person's moral judgments enter the model as part of the affect.

The notion is that people can have real, legitimate, cognitive thoughts about capital punishment, for example, whether it deters crime. But they also have feelings about it, and those feelings are to some degree, at least, independent of their thoughts. And among the feelings a person might have are moral feelings. Now few theorists are willing to be as blunt about the matter as I have been; most have complex ways of talking about how attitudes are complexly structured. But one hero of the field has the courage to put the matter clearly—Bob Zajonc (Zajonc, 1980). Zajonc, close enough to his animal learning roots to understand them, argues that affect, feelings, evaluations are "processed" independently of cognition. They are personal preferences to be explained by the learning history of the individual organism. Affect, evaluation, moral concerns—all of these are, from the point of view of psychology, the same; they are elements of the personal subjectivities of individuals—like a preference for Camembert over Brie.

The other core area of social psychology is "person perception." There are two branches of this field. The first is concerned with exactly the same question that ordinary language philosophers of mind worry about: How do ordinary people in their serious, that is, pretheoretical, lives talk (and presumably think) about other people's minds—and, perhaps, their own. The second branch is concerned with understanding the cognitive processes that give rise to this talk and thought. Getting the second of these questions right is, of course, dependent on getting the first right, so we will focus on that part. Now how does the moral dimension figure in that enterprise?

Well, first there is a small literature that asks about how people make explicitly moral judgments. We have nothing very interesting to say about that literature; nor is it obvious that it has anything very interesting to say about moral judgment. But the vast bulk of that literature is about something else: How we attribute traits to people. Now how are traits thought about in that literature?

Traits are treated as dispositions, as internal causes. (Although Heider, the founder of this field, surely cited Ryle, and indeed may well have picked up the notion of disposition from Ryle, there isn't the slightest evidence that he understood, or passed on, the point of Ryle's argument—that dispositions aren't internal causes. See Heider, 1958.) In any event, as this tradition sees the issue, the lay perceiver faces a fundamental problem in understanding how a particular bit of behavior is related to the actor's character. The problem is this: Was this patch of behavior internally caused or externally caused? That is: Was it consistent with the person's dispositions or not? (See Kelley, 1967; Kelley and Mischela, 1980.)

Now something not often commented on in this literature is that virtually all of the trait words we are inclined to use have a strongly evaluative force, for example, generous, greedy, and so on. Whether this evaluative force is moral or not is a matter I hold off for a moment; suffice it to say that it is evaluative. Whence this evaluative force in the social psychological view of trait ascription?

The received view has it this way: In ascribing generosity to a person's giving money to someone in need, we are asserting that the person's behavior in giving the money was internally caused—presumably by the trait of generosity, a particular internal cause (Jones and Davis, 1965; Jones and Nisbett, 1972; Nisbett et al., 1973). And, as it happens, most of us like generous people. It is because of this that "generous" has evaluative force. So in calling a person generous we are, as it were, communicating two things. The first is our discovery of a certain cause of the person's behavior, and then, in addition, we are communicating— inadvertently, one supposes—our feelings about the person. Thus, what looks like an evaluative content to "generous" isn't; the "truth condition" if you will for the description is simply the presence of a certain cause; the evaluation just adds a connotation.

The third area of social psychology that we want to touch on is its treatment of emotion, in particular, the most written about emotion—anger. How does anger come out?

Famously, Neal Miller and John Dollard brought psychoanalysis and animal learning theory together to create an account of anger: the frustration–aggression hypothesis (Dollard et al., 1939). (Interestingly it did not claim to be about anger, but about the morally laden term aggression; still the literature, if not the advertising, is about anger.) In brief, the frustration–aggression hypothesis claimed that the cause of anger is frustration—by which was meant something very precise: the blocking of a goal-directed action. What frustration was alleged to produce was an utterly blind lashing out at anything near. So according to the frustration–aggression hypothesis—and by the way, this idea is so entrenched in current thinking that we have found dictionaries that define aggression as a response to frustration—it is a fact about the way the nervous systems of organisms are wired that when an organism is frustrated it blindly lashes out. And this blind lashing out is the phenomenon we know as anger.

It is against this background that we wrote *Moralities of Everyday Life*. Our aim was to recast this general view of morality. We had the view that the moral dimension in social psychology was submerged: not in the way that a sunken treasure chest is submerged—for all intents and purposes nonexistent—but in the way that the supports for the Golden Gate Bridge are submerged—out of sight, but supporting the superstructure that everyone admires. Our attempt to raise the moral dimension used the social constructivist position of Berger and Luckmann as leverage.

THE MORAL DIMENSION IN SOCIAL CONSTRUCTIVISM

The Social Construction of Reality is a complex work, but it makes several key points that we adopted as our own. One point we embraced was the contra-relativist stance of the social constructivist position. That is to say, Berger and Luckmann took over from Schutz the claim that within the "naive attitude," people of every culture take whatever the morality of their culture might be to be *the* transparently correct set of issues, claims, and facts. It isn't that people consider and reject other possible moral worlds; rather the morality of one's culture simply is taken for granted as something real. Thus, as it happens, moral rules are seen by those seriously involved with them—those who follow or break them, rather than those who theorize about them—as objective, in the world.

Second, people participate in the creation of those rules *as things in the world* by taking part in the conversations of the communities in which specific moral rules have force. For Berger and Luckmann, moral facts are both objective *and* socially constructed. (They are socially constructed, not deconstructed.)

Third, nothing guarantees the coherence of a culture's moral code. For Berger and Luckmann, the explicit moral codes that some members of *some* cultures can produce are second-order theories about first-order moral facts. The first-order moral facts are to be found in the implicit rules surrounding the way people are typified (read traits are ascribed) in a culture. For Berger and Luckmann, then, individuals and their characters are the primary foci of social assessment. Hence theories that take cultural members' explicit moralizing as that which is to be explained are theories about theories and subject to the law of diminishing fleas.

Let us make some comments regarding this social constructivist view of Berger and Luckmann's. First, we have characterized it as anti-relativist. But we meant that as a description of the posture it takes about how ordinary people view morality. The social constructivist position is entirely neutral about the wisdom of relativist anthropologists. Perhaps you find the fact that different cultures have different moral codes reason to believe that no particular moral code is the correct one. Or maybe you don't find that any more compelling than the fact that different cultures have different beliefs about what causes diseases reason to believe that there is no right answer to the question: What causes schizophrenia? Or maybe what you find arresting is the fact that everybody in every culture believes that there is a moral right or wrong. Maybe you find it telling that about this one thing everyone agrees? In any event, we find nothing in the social constructivist position to support or refute cultural relativism as a position within ethics; we do find it incompatible with the view that ordinary people treat morality relativistically or, worse yet, as social psychology tells it subjectively.

Second, Berger and Luckmann offer a perspective on the lay ontology of morals, that of people in the natural attitude, but they do not attempt to distinguish moral matters from others which may share that lay ontology. It was not part of their (or our) social constructivist project to distinguish the moral from the not moral; our aim was, rather, to see what the implications were for the moral dimension—as well, perhaps, as others, of this lay ontology. We will return to this point later; for now we merely want to explicate how this lay ontological position worked its way through our book.

Part of our goal was to interpret a certain tradition of experimentation in social psychology in social constructivist terms. Our position was this: Precisely because people take it for granted that others perceive the same moral world they do, the failure of other people to respond to clear moral demands as we might expect them to leads to confusion, inhibition, and the possibility of embarrassment. In this sense, just because moral matters are, in lay ontology, objective, they have a certain fragility. (They also, of course, have force for that reason.) On our constructivist position, seeing that other people do not treat torturing someone as wrong—as in the Milgram experiments—leads to confusion about just what is the right thing to do (Milgram, 1974). Seeing other people not treat an obvious emergency as such leads to confusion about whether it really is—as in the Latané and Darley experiments (Latané and Darley, 1970). Seeing other people act in a brutal way to fellow subjects leads to confusion about just what is and is not brutality—as in the Zimbardo prison experiment (Zimbardo, 1970).

If morality were, as social psychologists imagine, taken by the ordinary person to be a matter of taste, then it would be difficult to explain why people in all of these studies don't follow their taste, uninfluenced by others' taste—de gustibus. . . . It is precisely because moral demands are *not* seen by actors as matters of taste that other people's views of right and wrong become determinants of one's own response—in something like the way that other people's views of the length of a line become relevant to one's own response in the Asch experiments on conformity (Asch, 1952, Chap. 16).

Our paper on gossip in that collection was simply aimed at calling attention to the other side of the social constructivist coin. Our argument there was that regardless of why people engage in gossip, in so doing they create and specify a shared sense of right and wrong in particular, concrete circumstances. More specifically, our argument was that every culture's moral code must be fairly abstract to span the variety of cases it must control. Since it is abstract, that code is in need of specification as to what is *objectively correct* in specific circumstances. Gossip seemed to us to be a social form that does just that.

A second part of our diving expedition considered traits—assessment of character. Our primary aim in that chapter was to argue that the received view of trait ascription—that it is a matter of finding causes to make predictions—is inadequate to account for the logic of trait ascription as done by ordinary people. We will not rehearse that rather tedious argument here. Suffice it to say that we argued that in characterizing an action (and a person) as "greedy," people are calling attention, among other things, to the way that action—and the person who performed it—was defective against some shared set of standards. In our view, what distinguishes greedy acts from other cases in which a person takes something for herself is *not* that greedy acts have a different cause, but rather that greedy acts have a different relation to standards of fairness. We further argued that people's tendency to describe a person as greedy on the basis of, perhaps, a single, unambiguous act of greed need *not* be an error—as social psychologists have it. It may simply be the logic of these terms that one earns, as it were, the ascription if one has done a deed warranting it. On this view, the primary point of trait ascription is to praise or blame people by calling attention to the standards that their behavior meets or falls short of. It is not to locate causes or make predictions—though both of these may follow from such ascription.

From this view of ours, the commensense actor is not seen as wasting her time on conundra, wondering whether someone took more than his due (a) because the external, temptation in the world—the overly spacious office—caused the taking or (b) because something internal—his desire for a large office—caused it. In our view, in a causal sense there is typically some internal cause matched to some external cause in this history of each act. Thus, the question of whether the behavior is internally or externally caused is usually either (a) inane or (b) a garrulous way of asking a different question: Was the person at fault in his action (internal) or not (external)—a moral question.

Finally, in this book of ours, we considered two emotions—anger and envy. With regard to anger, our aim was to argue that contra the frustration–aggression hypothesis, the typical provocation for anger isn't simple frustration, but rather the perception of some transgression (Aristotle's account had it that anger was the perception of an insult accompanied by an impulse for revenge). On this view, anger was seen not as an irrational, blind response to frustration, but rather as a fundamentally moral emotion, one grounded in moral (or perhaps other) standards. We went on to argue that even outbursts provoked by inanimate object—the car that won't start—can be incorporated in this view if: one understands such examples of anger as parasitic on more reasonable cases, and also if one accepts that even in such cases one, irrationally to be sure, treats the offending car as if it were an intransigent moral actor. Recently, Gibbard (1990) has taken us to task for tautology in this claim, but, be that as it may, our thrust in this chapter was, we still believe, sound in analyzing anger as a fundamental part not of some irrational vestige, but rather as a piece of our moral lives (cf. Gibbard, 1990, for a similar approach).

In our chapter on envy, we again attempted to recover the fundamentally moral—and social constructivist—roots of an emotion. In that analysis, we began by confronting a traditional view of envy: that it is a matter of wanting what another person has, just because he has it. We argued that people could be seen as—and be—envious even when they antecedently wanted what another has gotten—antecedent, that is, to the other's having gotten it.

Our positive conception of envy held that envy is often manifest as anger. Typically, we propose, it seems like justified anger to the envious person. What distinguishes envy from anger, we argued, is to be found in its cause. Envy, in our account, is an attempt to diminish someone (or his accomplishments) just in cases where the cause of that attempt to diminish is the other person's accomplishment, an accomplishment that makes the envious person look bad (in some sense) by comparison. We argued, then, that envy isn't the name of some raw feel, but rather is an emotion distinguished by a particular causal history, one that involves a socially constituted, objective, invidious comparison. Envy is a morally flawed emotion because (a) it involves, intrinsically, an unfair attempt to denigrate someone, and (b) it involves an illicit attempt to restore one's own status in the face of another's accomplishment. Thus, in a very complicated sense, envy too is a moral emotion.

WHY MORALITIES OF EVERYDAY LIFE?

Now we want to return to an issue we raised earlier: our studied indifference to morality per se in a book with morality in its title. Why were we so indifferent to distinguishing moral judgments from others?

The answer lies in the nature of our project. We were interested in capturing the "moral" world as it presents itself to the commonsense actor. We were accepting Berger and Luckmann's notion that the commensense actor's first-order judgments do not divide themselves neatly into moral judgments and not moral judgments. Rather, it seems, the commonsense actor's grounding judgments of good or bad, desirable or undesirable are broader than our notion of moral good or bad. (See Goffman, 1963, for a similar impulse). These "typifications," these assessments too, we believe ground the commensense actor's spontaneous emotional judgments toward other people and themselves—or so our project assumes.

To see what we mean, focus on the notion of generosity. We take it as obvious that people are pleased to be seen as generous, and would be ashamed to be seen as lacking even a trace of generosity. But let us review a familiar Kantian problem about generosity. A reasonable gloss of a generous act is one in which a person gives something to another beyond what it is her duty to give. A generous impulse is a desire to give someone something beyond what is owed him. But, at least in a Kantian view, if an act is not required by duty, if it is not done out of duty, then it is morally worthless—not evil, just worthless. Impulses are, after all, not under the control of the will; one can choose whether to *act* on an impulse, but not (in any simple sense) whether to *have* the impulse.

If a generous person is one with generous impulses, and if judging a person as generous is a moral judgment, then it is a strikingly unfair moral judgment. It is unfair because it judges a person for something beyond the control of the person's will—the having (or not) of generous impulses. We are left, then, with generous as one of those first-order "typifications" that emerge on a social constructivist account as the grounding of moral judgment, but also with the view that it is not itself a moral judgment precisely because it is wrongly located in relation to a person's will to be an authentic moral judgment. Generosity, then, is a trait of character—an assessment of a self—that is intrinsically valued and that attracts spontaneous reactions, but it is not a moral trait.

Our program assumes, then, that people's judgments of, and reactions toward, others cut across the central distinction marked by moral assessment—the will. The moral dimension, then, is not *the* dimension, or at least not the *only* dimension along which selves may be arrayed in commonsense assessments of a person's value. But this is not to say that whether an action is willed or not is irrelevant to the commonsense actor's reactions to an act or its actor. Rather it is to say that the will, and hence the moral dimension, affects assessments of selves in complex ways. One important way that the will enters into our reactions to others, we have argued, is in terms of sympathy.

There are, we suggest, three (at least) important kinds of experiences that a person might have that provoke our sympathy. These experiences are: pain, emotion, and the thwarting of a person's values. Each of these experiences stand in the same relation to a person's will; in particular, they are beyond the will. We take it as fundamental to the experience of pain, and our reaction to it, that it is beyond the control of the person in pain. People care about the fact that they are in pain, and they cannot but care about it. To the degree that pain is controllable, or to the degree that a person can control her caring about her pain, that pain is mere inconvenience and not something that engages our sympathy. So too with emotion. To the degree that a person feels, and cannot but feel, the loss of another person, say, we sympathize; to the degree that we believe that a person's experience of the loss of another *is* under the person's control, we see the reaction as merely histrionic and, thus, not worthy of our sympathy. And so too with values. We sympathize with the plight of another who must face the destruction of that which he values, *but* to the degree that we believe that this caring about what the person values is itself controlled—that is the degree to which we see the valuing as fake, and not worthy of sympathy. So, we argue, our reaction of sympathy to a person's position tracks the location of the person's will. Sympathy is rooted in the will—the moral dimension (Sabini and Silver, 1985).

Let us say a word or two to place all of this in a somewhat different perspective. In the Kantian tradition, the moral dimension is grounded in the will. But recently there seems to be a philosophical movement flourishing that is directed toward broadening the Kantian perspective, liberating morality from the will. Our position is not in sympathy with this movement. The will does seem to be the right place to anchor moral judgment. On the other hand, we do seem to make judgments about people, about whether they are good or bad, desirable or not, and some of these judgments do *not* seem to take account of the participation of the person's will. The solution to that problem, we suggest, is to recognize that our assessments of people are broader than the moral dimension. It may be that the commonsense actor's judgments of character do not honor the moral dimension; it may be that lacking generous impulses is as severe a criticism of a person as is being dishonest. Thus, the moral dimension may not easily be recovered in people's first-order typifications. But this is not to say that the moral dimension plays no role in our spontaneous reactions. Rather, we suggest, our reactions to people and their actions may involve the moral dimension in more indirect ways. We may, for example, think equally little of a person lacking generosity and a person lacking honesty, but we are moved to anger by dishonesty but pity or disgust to a lack of generosity. Our project now is to find the various ways that the moral dimension—including, at least, the will—is represented in commonsense assessment.

REFERENCES

Asch, S. E. (1952). *Social psychology*. New York: Prentice–Hall.

Berger, P., and Luckmann, T. (1966). *The social construction of reality*. New York: Anchor.

Dollard, J., Doob, L. W., Miller, N. G., Mowrer, O. H., and Sears, R. R. (1939). *Frustration and aggression*. New Haven, CT: Yale University Press.

Gibbard, A. (1990). *Wise choices, apt feelings: A theory of normative judgment*. Cambridge, MA: Harvard University Press.

Gilligan, C. (1982). *In a different voice*. Cambridge, MA: Harvard University Press.

Goffman, E. (1963). *Stigma*. Englewood Cliffs, NJ: Prentice–Hall.

Heider, F. (1958). *The psychology of interpersonal relations*. New York: Wiley.

Jones, E. E., and Davis, K. E. (1965). From acts to dispositions: The attribution process in person perception. In L. Berkowitz (Ed.), *Advances in experimental social psychology*, Vol. 2. New York: Academic Press.

Jones, E. E., and Nisbett, R. (1972). *The actor and observer: Divergent perceptions of the causes of behavior*. New York: General Learning Press.

Kelley, H. H. (1967). Attribution theory in social psychology. In D. Levine (Ed.), *The Nebraska symposium on motivation*. Lincoln: University of Nebraska Press.

Kelley, H. H., and Mischela, J. L. (1980). Attribution theory and research. In M. Rosenzweig and L. Porter (Eds.), *Annual Review of Psychology*, Vol. 31. Palo Alto, CA: Annual Reviews Inc.

Kohlberg, L. (1969). Stage and sequence: The cognitive-developmental approach to socialization. In D. A. Goslin (Ed.), *Handbook of socialization theory and research*. Chicago: Rand-McNally.

Latané, B., and Darley, J. M. (1970). *The unresponsive bystander*. New York: Appleton–Century–Croft.

Milgram, S. (1974). *Obedience to authority*. New York: Harper.

Nisbett, R. E., Caputo, C., Legant, P., and Marecek, J. (1973). Behavior as seen by the actor and as seen by the observer. *Journal of Personality and Social Psychology, 27*, 154–164.

Sabini, J., and Silver, M. (1982). *Moralities of everyday life*. New York: Oxford University Press.

Sabini, J., and Silver, M. (1985). On the captivity of the will: Sympathy, caring, and a moral sense of the human. *Journal for the Theory of Social Behaviour, 15*, 23–37.

Zajonc, R. (1980). Feeling and thinking: Preferences need no inferences. *American Psychologist, 35*, 151–175.

Zimbardo, P. (1970). *The Stanford prison experiment*. Script of the slide show.

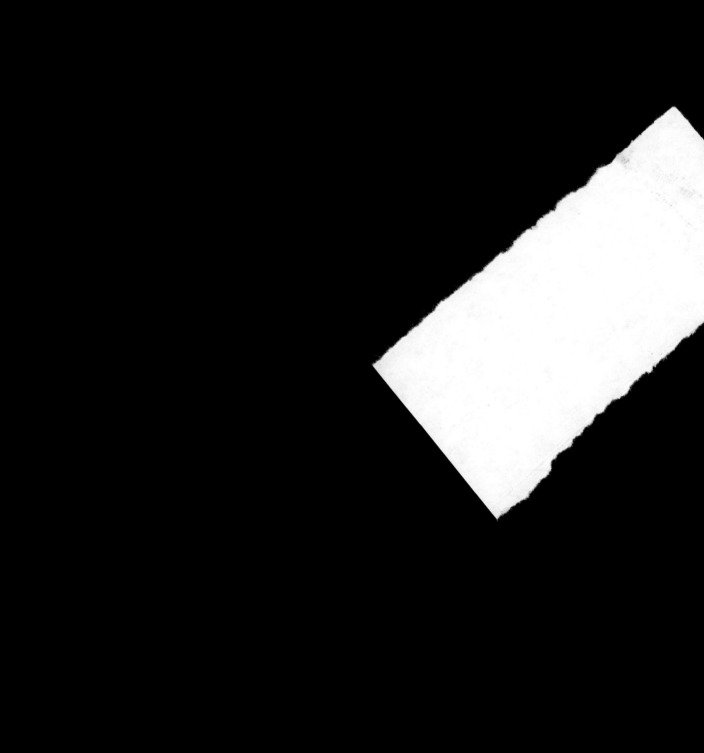

7 SOCIAL SCIENCE AND MORAL SCIENCE

Daniel N. Robinson

John Sabini provides a thoughtful and instructive review of the perspective he espouses and some of its supportive findings. As is unavoidable in redactions of works addressed to highly complex matters, "The Moral Dimension in Social Psychology" leaves a number of fundamental assumptions unaddressed, a number of core terms undefined. Part of my reply will be devoted to identifying these assumptions and terms and attempting to fill in the gaps. Just *how* this is done makes all the difference as one sets out to locate important sources of controversy. In this same chapter Sabini records the differences between traditional social science approaches to moral matters (e.g., behavioristic, psychoanalytic) and quasi-formal ones (e.g., Kohlberg and Gilligan), and then the differences between all of these and the commonsense–constructivist approach developed by Berger and Luckmann (1966) and adopted by Sabini and Silver (1982). I shall have a few words to say about these differences and the extent to which they bear on any issue reasonably regarded as *moral*. Finally, and with less hesitation than was apparent in the earlier pages, Sabini regards the will as the *sine qua non* of those moral attributions capable of engaging sympathetic responses. However, the judgments formed are not grounded solely in these attributions, but "are broader than the moral dimension" and include assessments of what Sabini refers to as *character*. On this point it will repay efforts to consider the nature of *character* and the possibility that it is not only within the ambit of moral judgment but at the very center of it.

Before beginning, though, I should say that my critical comments are broader in range than what is called for by John Sabini's useful and enlightening contribution to this symposium. Much needs to be said in support of and in reply to the constructionist literature devoted to moral and quasi-moral issues. Sabini would not claim responsibility for all of the assets of this literature and is not to be held accountable for its liabilities. Still, beyond the specific propositions he supports in his essay, there is a more general framework that he endorses and that, by virtue of its generative power, summons close and critical attention. Some of what follows avails itself of passages in Sabini's essay in an attempt to answer the more general summons. I hope not to seem, in the process, to go too wide of the mark.

As John Sabini clearly recognizes, from a Kantian perspective behavioristic approaches to morality are thwarted at the very outset by their appeals to hedonistic causes; and psychoanalytic ones by appeals to factors that are finally beyond the consciousness, if not the ken, of moral agents. But in this recognition and in the brief discussion of the Kohlberg–Gilligan controversy he does not leave room for the possibility that something more substantial than a "view" might be available to us as we begin to choose from competing alternatives. Hasty summaries of Kant's philosophy run the risk of that fatal combination— libel and parody—but the most basic tenets are clear.

Kant begins with a discussion traceable to Plato and made explicit in all of Aristotle's ethical works; viz., that if all events were solely material then only the causal laws of the physical sciences would be needed to account for everything. From the indubitable fact, however, that rational beings have the capacity for deliberated choice (*prohairesis* in Aristotle) it follows that some events must be explicated in terms that go beyond the physical. In Kant's well-known argot, the relevant distinction is between the realms he identifies as *natural* and *intelligible*. The latter is that *kingdom of ends* in which choices are governed by fidelity to principle.

Why do we not hold victims of brain-altering drugs to the terms of an agreement otherwise voluntarily joined? Why are confessions extracted by torture disregarded? Why is pain or suffering or disease a morally mitigating condition? In a word, if the actions in question are reasonably taken to be *reactions* and governed by the (nearly) unopposable laws of physical or biological nature, then they are lacking in moral content. Kant then extends this across the board and strips of moral content any and every act that has no more than physical impulses behind it and material goals before it. To those who are starving, there is this imperative: We must eat *if we would not starve*. The imperative here is what Kant called *hypothetical*. It is contingent on an existing state of affairs that is local in time and place. Further, it arises from what is biologically contingent. In these respects the resulting behavior is not essentially different from limb-flexion when a hand accidentally comes to rest on a hot object.

Moral actions are governed not by *hypothetical* but by a *categorical* imperative. Such actions express at once one's recognition of and one's exceptionless duty to a universal principle. What is morally "right" or "wrong" is just what honors or violates the principle. The celebrated *good will* in Kant is just the will that would have right prevail; the will that would, if it could, install moral principles as universal laws of nature. However, the principles themselves not only transcend the plane of what might be called the "biosocial," but are detached entirely from the even broader plane of the empirical. As Kant puts it in the *Groundwork of the Metaphysic of Morals,*

> Hence everything that is empirical is, as a contribution to the principle of morality, not only wholly unsuitable for the purpose, but is even highly injurious to the purity of morals; for in morals the proper worth of an absolutely good will, a worth elevated above all price, lies precisely in this—that the principle of action is free from all influence by contingent grounds, the only kind that experience can supply. (Paton, 1964, p. 93)

If this much of Kantian moral philosophy is understood, then it becomes clear just how much of a "social construction" of morality is possible within a Kantian context. The appeal that social practices can make to anyone must, of course, be *empirical* in the enlarged sense of the term. That is, the appeal must be representable within the arena of actual experience and must therefore be constituted of *facts*. But, from a moral point of view, this raises the animating conundrum in Plato's *Meno* and *Protagoras*. It is what so vexes Socrates in the ostensibly straightforward question, "Can virtue be taught?" If virtue is taken to be the attachment of conduct to a universal principle, and if universals are entirely outside the empirical domain, then by what means might a teacher illustrate or point to or even talk about it? The answer reached by Socrates is not unlike Kant's, both of them finally relying on intuitive or "a priori" conceptions of the sort endemic to creatures that are rational *as such*.

Many attempts have been made to "naturalize" the process by which a moral point of view comes about—even in the face of Kant's sternest warning to those who

> in a dream of sweet illusions . . . foist into the place of morality some misbegotten mongrel patched up from limbs of very varied ancestry and looking like anything you please. . . . (Ibid., p. 94)

The place of the categorical imperative in Kant's moral philosophy is the same as that occupied by the "pure intuitions" of time and space in his analysis of experience, and by the "pure categories of the understanding" in his epistemology. The pure intuitions constitute the *necessary* conditions of each and every experience; the pure categories, the necessary framework of all knowledge; the categorical imperative, the necessary precondition of all morality. Morality entails autonomy in that a moral action must be attentive to nothing beyond the principle itself in which it finds its sole sanction. Empathy, sentiment, pleasure, and the like might be coincidental with or be psychological sequellae of a moral action but are not essential aspects of it.

Again, if recent debates that owe their terms and tribulations to Kant are to be judged correctly, we will have to go beyond the politely rhetorical questions that John Sabini directs to the works of Kohlberg and Gilligan. Gilligan's distinction between "rules" and empathic feelings must be recognized as a non sequitur within a Kantian context, but to an extent not usually appreciated even by her critics. Note that a *rule* has no ontological standing outside a given social or cultural context. As Wittgenstein made clear, rules are contextual, their meaning exhausted by the conventional agreements they summarize and express. Thus, *rules are contingent* and cannot possibly qualify as *Kantian* moral imperatives. If it really is the case that Gilligan's data establish that men are rule-governed in their moral judgments, and that women are sentiment-governed, then from a Kantian point of view *neither* group has made bona fide moral judgments. The men have failed owing to their attachment to what is finally conventional, the women to what is finally psychological. And, of course, if it really were the case that in matters of this sort *gender* is dispository, then it would follow of necessity that nothing of moral consequence was involved in the slightest.

Sabini's unnamed debt to some vagrant forms of Kantian moral science has him wondering just what it is that makes Kohlbergian lower-level responses moral at all, not to mention Gilligan's appeals to "caring." He settles (comfortably?) for the criterion of other-regarding interests. He takes actions that meet this criterion as in some way challenging to those who regard persons as "hedonic calculators," though it is not clear that hedonistic considerations cannot generate the full panoply of saintly and heroic behaviors. He also seems to treat this criterion as one—if honestly adopted—that would in some way honor deontological moral theories, though Kant would regard concern for the well-being of others as *nonmoral,* even *immoral.* What a Kantian agent does or does not do for the benefit of others has to do with their *worthiness,* and not with sympathy for their plight. All this may only reflect the uncertainty recorded in his opening paragraph as to whether or not "there is a moral dimension of things. . . ." But then what is it about other-regarding conduct that would interest him or allow him to find common cause with and between Kohlberg and Gilligan? I hesitate to suggest that in these respects he well knows *that* there is a moral dimension of things but is not quite sure *what* it is, at least until he reaches the concluding sections of his essay.

It may be argued that one difference between the philosophical and the psychological mission is that the latter might be properly (safely?) confined to descriptive inquiries into practices and tendencies. The task of counting complete, the psychologist is then free to patch together some theoretical utterances that might serve either as a (veiled) restatement of the findings themselves or (more ambitiously) as a general law grounded in something more fundamental—inevitably a "process," as they say—than the observed data.

A problem with this proposal—to mention one among the legion—is that it assumes there is some way of partitioning practices and tendencies for the purpose of the desired descriptions. When Sabini recounts the work of Sabini and Silver, the approach defended by Berger and Luckmann is commended. This approach makes a distinction between the moral beliefs on which the ordinary person grounds actions and judgments, and the "explicit moralizing" of theorists attempting to assess or explain "first-order moral facts." Here Berger and Luckmann offer psychologists a nice way to avoid entry into the Long Debate but while reserving some useful function for them. The justification for the observer-role (and for the happy confidence that the observers will know what they are looking at!) is that "people of every culture take whatever the morality of their culture might be to be *the* transparently correct set of issues, claims, and facts. . . . [M]oral rules are seen by those seriously involved with them—those who follow or break them, rather than those who theorize about them—as objective, in the world" (Sabini, Chapter 6, this volume).

Needless to say, people of every culture seem to take little else as "transparently correct." So, if the anthropological claim is valid, we must be confronting in this peculiar domain a nearly unprecedented uniformity of doxastic surrender. Might it be that what is taken to be "transparently correct" by what might now be referred to as the known human race is just what is transparently correct through any essentially syllogistic mode of rational comprehension? Might it be, that is, that for creatures who are rational *as such* the awareness of their own autonomous will constitutes a recognition of the need for a principle to render its expression at once intelligible and defensible? In a word, might it be that members of the human race recognize the requirement to give reasons for those actions that impinge in consequential ways on others and, as a result of this recognized requirement, can be socialized to follow rule of law?

If all of this is at least plausible a number of otherwise imponderable questions become nearly trivial. First, the relevant comparability of observers and actors makes it possible for the former to identify and to make sense of those statements and activities on the part of the actors that may be taken as judgmental, attributional, value-laden, consistent, and, alas, authentic. They might otherwise be indistinguishable from the ordered movements of army ants and the lively sonorities of songbirds. Next, it becomes possible to rely on something more promising than "stimulus-generalization" as a tribe or society begins to dub the actions of its young as "right" or "wrong." But even more importantly, these warranted and necessary assumptions about the human race can save us from having to refer to anything as a "moral fact"—a near-oxymoron.

Moral rules, to use Sabini's preferred term, are not then "objective, in the world" as are, for example, traffic signals or statutory restrictions. Rather, certain objective facts of the world are identifiable as standing in either a contradictory or a subservient relation to a principle. The principle is irreducibly *moral* in just the sense that it is more than and different from a conventional rule, a cultural or tribal habit or any other *empirical* fact that actually is "objective, in the world."

What is *transparent* in all of this is the structure of the practical syllogism itself. The ultimate standing of the moral premises inserted into it must be the preoccupation of "those who theorize," at least until kings become philosophers and philosophers kings. The room for collisions between candidate major premises is all too ample. Consider only two Kantian injunctions: *Never lie!* and *Never punish the innocent!* And now consider only the SS-Gestapo at the door asking where the Jews are hiding. The categorical imperative provides the (transparently correct?) form of moral discourse but does not seek to give this discourse specific content. Rather, it attempts to remove moral science from those duchies of shifting belief, odd practices, and selfish or superstitious attachments that so routinely occupy the energies of the social scientist.

Having adopted the perspective of Berger and Luckmann, Sabini is not concerned to discover an algorithm or taxonomy with which to distinguish the moral from the nonmoral. Instead, he would inquire into the confusions resulting from the sorts of results reported by Milgram, Zimbardo, Latane and Darley, and others. After all, to see persons behaving brutally confuses one as to the standards of brutality. *Mutatis mutandis,* conduct discrepant with one's own standards must raise doubts as to the validity of those standards in much the way Asch's classical studies illustrate. None of this would be so were the moral domain actually a domain of mere tastes and subjective preferences.

On these points, one is tempted to remind Sabini of his entirely apt comment on Gilligan's work. If, indeed, the reasoned conclusions of moral arguments— conclusions grounded in moral theories of weight and consequence—are overcome by witnessed violations of them, one must wonder whether the audience was ever in possession of the *moral* principles in the first instance. After all, if Smith's "solution" to an arithmetic problem is entirely hostage to the false reports of a group, we have every reason to doubt whether Smith knows how to add. We might go so far as to say that he has not turned in an incorrect "solution," for he has not added anything at all. Moving the rook diagonally is not a bad *chess* move, for it is not a *chess* move at all. Similarly, waiting to see the violence others visit upon an innocent, nonthreatening other—in order to "recalibrate" one's own moral standards—is to leave the moral realm entirely and to join the mob.

But are the well-known findings best understood as sources of confusion regarding the *standards* of morality, or confusion as to what is actually going on in the minds and the general affairs of the experimental collaborators? There is always room for interpretive error when viewing the actions of others. Absent clear signs of the context and the avowed purposes of the actors, one may not know that the bloody spectacle now taking place is actually a surgical procedure intended to restore the patient to health. Gossip, then, functions not to establish what is morally correct, but whether or not a given activity instantiates or violates the (Kantian?) moral law. "Is he doing to that poor man what I think he's doing?" "No, no. He's actually a surgeon." To paraphrase Locke, who argued that madmen reason rightly from wrong premises, we might say that lay-moralists reason confusedly when (a) the factual contents of the minor premise are ambiguous and/or (b) when two equally valid and compelling major premises appear to be in conflict.

This is not to say that persons do not test their moral reasonings by engaging others in friendly debate; or test the implicit logic standing behind their moral judgments by comparing notes with others. The thickets of the real world are too dense and various to be tamed by the logic-chopper, and in the world of moral consequence few facts are mere facts. Indeed, part of what it means to order one's affairs in a principled way is to give attention to the judgments and percep-tions of others. One may give this the pejorative title of "gossip" or one may recognize it as one of the tools of self-criticism. In either case, reasonable persons invoke the principle of fallibilism when faced with difficult choices, and it is a requirement of this principle to consult what may be wiser heads. I should think this is how actual persons would explain just why they do consult friends and neighbors before reaching settled positions on moral matters. When they do not do this, they act rashly. There is, however, all the difference between such prudential measures and opinion-polling. When the latter is invoked in the moral domain, we have a version of lynch-law and most assuredly not a means by which to render moral rules—in Sabini's words—*objectively correct.*

Of the social scientists who have approached moral science, I would regard Lawrence Kohlberg as the one most familiar with and respectful of its special ontological and logical demands. If he got things wrong, these do not seem to be the things identified by his better-known critics. The story-telling method, in-debted as it was to Piaget, yielded something of an ontogenetic stage-theory of a Piagetian sort and this led Kohlberg in directions many deontologists would consider aimless. To the extent that one's judgments are a function of a stage of development, the "moral" dimension is drawn less by logic than by chro-nology—brain-maturation, learning, socialization, whatever—and to just this extent the judgments are contingent and thus morally jejune. Without putting even more words into Kant's already thick treatises, one can offer an educated guess as to his response to this sort of theory. Kohlberg, he might insist, had simply found an elaborate and all too circuitous path to the unsurprising conclu-sion that morality awaits developed rationality. *Ergo,* children need not apply. One might say, then, that what Kohlberg concluded was already established conclusively by the very logic of morals, but at least he was engaged in an identifiable form of moral inquiry.

Most of what I have said to this point is loyal to the Kantian framework and may well trigger the polite—or not so polite—query, "But just suppose Kant is wrong?" Scholarship in moral philosophy and kindred subjects (Ethics, Philosophy of Law, Political Philosophy) has never been pursued with greater vigor. The concluding decade of the twentieth century is scarcely the time to declare this part of the Long Debate complete. There have been deep problems recognized in Kant's moral philosophy from the first, and these have been discussed and examined carefully for more than a century. It has been charged with being an empty formalism. John Stuart Mill thought the categorical imperative itself could serve as a licence for unspeakable villainy and vice. The retributivistic elements have appeared to many to be vengeful and heartless. Its absolutistic requirements defy the open-texture of morally rich environments. Or, put in plainer terms—as one of my colleagues insisted a year or so ago—we all know what the categorical imperative *is,* it's just that no one can live by it!

I write now, therefore, neither to praise nor to bury Kantian moral theory or any deontological variant. Instead, I would hope to clarify the structure of such theories and their unique imperviousness to empirical modes of assessment or explanation. If Kant's theory or even approach is taken to be sound, then the social sciences simply have *nothing* to say for it, against it or about it, and there is, therefore, no point in trying. Moreover, if the approach is unsound or defective, it cannot be for *empirical* reasons (as should now be obvious, if it was not before), so the social sciences cannot even aspire to some falsificationist duty.

Where Kant's approach seems least promising, of course, is in attempts to connect *human nature* to that kingdom of ends to which we are somehow and nevertheless heirs. It does not seem sufficient to develop a logically coherent moral framework, note that only rational creatures can operate within it, and then essentially condemn as perverse or irrelevant every other attribute such creatures have apart from rationality. What might seem more promising, then, is a moral philosophy that takes morality seriously (which is to say *not* sociologically), but takes the facts of human nature where these are found. More promising, therefore, is a moral science capable of addressing the actual beings who will live according to its findings, rather than a moral science that must somehow reinvent human nature.

It is clear to me that John Sabini is striving for this sort of compromise or reconciliation, and I suggest that, at least to a first approximation, he will find a fairly well articulated version in Aristotle. Having written recently and at some length on just this possibility (Robinson, 1989), I will be quite brief here.

Aristotle's approach to everything in the animate world is *ethological.* He is at pains to observe the defining properties of creatures, the conditions under which their attributes are most fully realized, and thus the form of life such creatures are intended to live. By "intended" I refer, of course, to that *telos* identified as most sustaining and natural. Tendencies and characteristics of a persisting nature and wide distribution were evidence of important functions and purposes being served, nature not being profligate or irrational in such respects.

In his studies of human emotions, attitudes, and dispositions, Aristotle again adopts the ethological stance, but now in relation to a creature whose most signal attribute is rationality itself and thus the one creature fit for a rule of law within a political community. Unlike today's social psychologists, however, Aristotle was, to say the least, a quite sophisticated analytical philosopher wary of using dictionary definitions as substitutes for naturalistic observation; wary, too, of theories based on selective and limited observations. (Those whose estimations of Aristotle's methods differ from this characterization might return to the works themselves and not comments on them by his variously motivated critics.) So how might Aristotle approach John Sabini's brief discussion of anger, envy, and generosity, and the methods of inquiry on which the discussion is based?

As is well known, Aristotle wrote lengthily on just these attributes, especially in his *Rhetoric* and his two large ethical treatises, primarily in connection with the virtues and vices. Unlike latter-day hedonistic theories, Aristotle's theory of the virtues distinguishes among the varieties of pleasure or happiness that might serve as goals of and goads to conduct. The ultimate goal—expressed by the Greek *eudaimonia*—cannot be a sensual form of pleasure. This would at once render human motivations indistinguishable from those operating throughout the nonrational reaches of the animal economy and, at the same time, would leave no room for the participation of rationality itself. *Eudaimonia,* which Aristotle specifically reserves to human beings—proof enough that something other than sensual pleasure is involved—refers to a *flourishing form of life,* and not a specific feeling or sensation or impulse. It is not some specific state reached, but a veritable *way of life* in which ever greater harmony is reached among the defining human faculties and powers; a harmony that records what can only be called the person's essential *character* (excellence, *arete*). This is a lifelong affair, worked on like a work of art creating itself or the doctor healing himself.

The requirement of reason is proportionality. Recall that *harmonia* in the ancient Greek is not tied to music and sound (for which the relevant term is *melodia*) but more generally to *fitness,* akin to hand-in-glove. Thus, the emotions are to be deployed, as it were, in the right amounts and under the right circumstances, all this requiring rational direction or, as we are now inclined to say, "cognitive processes." The question never becomes, for example, whether anger or love or resentment is morally good or morally bad; any more than whether eating or drinking or sleeping is such. The emotions in question are entirely natural and displayed throughout most of the animal kingdom. From a moral point of view the question has to do with the conditions under which these emotions reliably surface, and the intensity with which they are expressed.

We might take as an illustration the one used by Sabini in his comments on Kant's theory and his attempt to go beyond moral boundaries and toward a kind of characterology. "A generous impulse," he says, "is a desire to give someone something beyond what is owed him." Kant, insists Sabini, would have to take this impulse as morally worthless, for it involves benefactions beyond the call of duty. Then, too, one should be praised for this sort of thing for, after all, it is an *impulse* and thus "beyond the control of the person's will."

What is odd in all this, from an Aristotelian perspective, is the notion that persons are somehow not responsible for their impulses; further—and *contra* Kant—that a disposition toward generosity cannot be morally informing unless the worthiness of the recipient is measured first. Now generosity is an especially apt choice here for, taken as evidence of that "great soul" (*megalopsychaia*) discussed in *Eudemian Ethics,* it is less a virtue than the attitude that must stand behind *all* of the virtues. It is contrasted with a mean-spirited or grudging disposition. (Imagine a solid Kantian citizen who gives each person his due, not a farthing more or less, but resents it every step of the way. His morality-index might be quite high, but on Aristotle's account we now know as much about this fellow as we care to.) But then, if it is an *impulse* rather than the expression of deliberated choice, it is simply a form of incontinence. It is a disposition the actor has not tamed and so, even if it produces just compensation for the recipient, the actor himself is blameworthy. In any case, as put forward by Sabini, one is in no position to complete the characterological or "personality" profile, for we do not know whether the generosity in question exemplifies a mere compulsion (*'orme*) grounded in appetite (*orexis*), a settled disposition (*hexis*), a choice governed by rational deliberation (*prohairesis*), or even a kind of defect of perception by which the actions of others are simply exaggerated. My point is that Aristotle would be uncomfortable with both Kant's and Sabini's assessments based on instances of generosity.

Turning now to the will, Sabini is prepared to regard it as "the right place to anchor moral judgment." Again we would find Aristotle hesitating, for again we find Aristotle sensitive to the constant interplay between the human faculties and the conditions under which they must operate. Take the captain of a ship in a turbulent sea who can save the ship only if the cargo is jettisoned. Does he *will* the act? Yes. Is it a *choice* on his part? Yes. But if we would assess the moral worth or standing of actor (or his action), it is not simply the *volitional* aspect we would anchor the judgment to, but the *principle* governing the will itself. Permitting the ship to sink is, after all, an option that could be freely but imprudently taken.

I mean not to carp here but it is important to appreciate the difference. If the will is the anchor, our moral assessments move in that noncognitive direction in which morality itself is the first casualty. Aristotle, here very much like Kant, recognized that the moral dimension is engaged not by the fact that we are emotional or motivated or willful—attributes richly distributed in phylogeny—but by the fact that we are capable of a disinterested rational assessment of maxims competing for our loyalties. A moral psychology, I submit, begins with this and probably ends with it as well. If society "constructs" anything here it is a system of supports for or obstacles to either the assessment itself or the penalties for acting on the results. Aristotle knew that children cannot be appealed to through abstract propositions. They must first be habituated to reasonable behavior, rewarded like other little animals for good behavior, and punished for misbehavior. Later, when reason is ripe, the *principle* can be understood and now tied to concrete instances.

Polis andra didaska: Man is taught by the polis. Appreciating human potentialities and the conditions needed for their flourishing, Aristotle put forth a species of social constructionism, but one limited by realistic ethological considerations and the unique problems created by a self-conscious creature able to give and expect reasons for actions.

REFERENCES

Berger, P., and Luckmann, T. (1966). *The social construction of reality.* New York: Anchor Books.

Paton, H. J. (translator). (1964). *Immanuel Kant's Groundwork of the metaphysic of morals.* New York: Harper Torchbooks.

Robinson, Daniel N. (1969). *Aristotle's psychology.* New York: Columbia University Press.

Sabini, John, and Silver, Mark. (1982). *Moralities of everyday life.* New York: Oxford University Press.

8 PSYCHOLOGY, MORALITY, AND THE LAW[1]

Jerome Bruner

When I was asked far, far in advance to participate in a conference on "Social Science and the Moral Dimension of Life," I accepted in full innocence of the duties I would be undertaking subsequently. In fact, I was asked shortly after to serve as the Meyer Visiting Professor of Law at the New York University School of Law. Almost from the beginning of taking up my new duties—which were to explore the frontier between law's empire and the sprawling commonwealth of the social sciences—I was haunted by my unpreparedness for such an exploration. It was not that I didn't know "the law": I didn't, but my colleagues in Vanderbilt Hall were swift, splendid, and generous guides on that score. It was something else.

For what struck me from the moment I set foot in the place was how different my training and my habits of thought were from those of lawyers. I was among colleagues who were quite accustomed to, quite proficient in, and very well versed in making normative judgments about the human condition—judgments that sometimes had enormous consequences not only for those being judged but for the society at large. I had none of these: no professional habits, no skills, and few procedures. Nor were the forms of judgment being made familiar to me— decisions about responsibility, about intent, about the willfulness of negligence, and the like—matters that were rarely studied in my psychological corner of the

[1] A paper presented at the conference on "Social Science and the Moral Dimension of Life" at Georgetown University, March 15–17, 1991.

social sciences. This was the realm of ethics, the "moral dimension" to which this symposium is dedicated.

Most psychological discussions of ethics are premised on an unspoken assumption that a person's ethical judgments are an expression of personal beliefs, beliefs that reflected individual needs or some vaguely depicted cultural patterns. The law and the processes of jurisprudence were rarely mentioned, and when legal matters were touched on at all, it was principally in connection with such matters as how juries come to their decisions or how eyewitnesses testify. So I was rather at sea.

During the long months following, I avidly (sometimes desperately) read not only the "standard" works on law and the legal process—from Holmes and the so-called "legal" realists, through H. L. A. Hart and the legal positivists or John Rawls and the "hidden hand" theorists, to such contemporary critics as Roberto Unger and his colleagues in the Critical Legal Studies Movement—but I also read others who, like Robert Cover, James Boyd White, and Robert Gordon, were more concerned with the constitutive or "reality making" function of law. And they had a powerful effect on my thinking, as you will see. It was a very heady time.

To my great surprise, most legal scholars, like virtually all lawyers and judges, held the view that there was a profound difference between law on the one side and morality or ethics on the other. They held this view with various justifications, all of which were interesting, and all of which seemed to converge on one crucial point, it seemed to me. The common reasoning on this point had to do with a *procedural* matter—that the procedures for coming to a legal decision were almost totally unlike what transpires when we make an ethical or moral judgment. And of course they are plainly correct in this, or *almost* right.

So I greatly welcomed the opportunity to participate in a Faculty Seminar concerned with the nature and practice of lawyer*ing*—not the nature of *law* as such, whether in the statutes or in the opinions of judges, but in the acts that constituted the legal *process*, ranging from the lawyer interviewing the client who comes to him with an ordinary trouble that needs to be translated into a legal problem, to the making of a legal opinion, say, Mr. Justice Stewart rendering opinions in two admiralty cases on the seemingly exotic issue of the conditions under which a shipowner has what is called the "duty to maintain a seaworthy vessel." It was one of my first exposures to "case law," and it was highly instructive. In one case, *Skovgaard,* Justice Stewart found that such a duty governed; in the other, *Halecki,* he found it did not.[2] Repairing the engine of an unmanned ship at dock did not entail the duty, but repairing a pump needed then and there to unload a cargo of coconut oil from a manned ship at dockside did,

---

[2] *The Vessel M/V Tungus* v. *Olga Skovgaard,* 358 U.S. 588, 1959; *United N.Y. and N.J. Sandy Hook Pilots Association* v. *Anna Helecki,* 358 U.S. 613, 1959.

even though both jobs were carried out by non-crew-members on contract. It was not exotic at all, once one knew the points of law involved.

But the opinions rendered, even in so technical a pair of admiralty cases, also seemed to go beyond pure "points of law." They seemed at certain points to touch on ethical issues as well. Indeed, Mr. Justice Brennan wrote an eloquent dissent in *Halecki* raising the issue whether the fruits of technology should always favor shipowners, relieving them of "seaworthiness" responsibility for the highly technical work that in earlier times was carried out by crew members on a manned ship. Was there not a basis for holding that *all* workers on board a ship, at sea or at a dock, crew members or workers on contract, be treated alike with respect to negligence standards? Was the equal protection clause properly served when technological advances (mostly embodied in what could be done at dry dock or on an unmanned ship) always freed the shipowner of responsibilities? All of this was neatly interdigitated in decidedly legal discussion of how "wrongful death" should be determined, but Brennan was plainly concerned with an ethical issue as well.

Cases of this sort certainly rubbed my nose in the procedural side of *legal* process, but at the same time they also made me aware of the subtle links that exist between legal process and ethical standards that are rarely made explicit in the law. Critical theorists were more ready to grant that "ideological" issues were often indirectly involved, but it seemed to me that these entailed implicit ethical standards. The sorts of ethical standards involved, moreover, were not just "raw feels" about what was right or wrong, but also had to do with how we represent social reality through our beliefs and world views. Surely any system of laws, however conventionalized its procedures, could not be alien to such beliefs. What is the relationship between them—not just historically, as when one traces the transformation of a previously ethical stance into its formulation in a statute or constitution, but psychologically as well?

The search for a resolution of this issue has been a puzzling and a consciousness-sharpening experience for me. I have found it increasingly difficult to believe that such legal doctrines as *stare decisis* or *mens rea,* for example, providing as they do the axiomatic basis of our system of laws, have, as it were, no corresponding cognitive representation in the minds of men. I have repeatedly asked myself, "Could any society operate within a rule of law that is psychologically alien or cognitively opaque to its members?" And more particularly, how in fact is law explained or justified or rationalized to the community it serves? How does one "explain" to the man in the street what is the "point," say, of filing for Chapter 11 protection under the bankruptcy law or, for that matter, of exercising the basic right of *habeas corpus?*

Asking such questions led me to some puzzling conclusions. Why were such questions so often answered in the form of little narratives about exemplifying human plights? And why were legal scholars (particularly those operating within the Anglo-Saxon legal tradition) so keen on *case* law, a system of law in which past judgments are retained in the form of a collection of relevant stories?

What I propose to do in the remainder of this chapter is to tell you what happened when I continued to push my inquiries. I have reached a few conclusions about how our system of case law manages to stay in working touch with our traditionalized way of dealing with ethical issues. We deal with such issues by the use of narrative. And we have evolved a system of case law that formalizes, proceduralizes, and enforces our modes of narrative interpretation in a manner to deal with certain crucial problems to which I will come presently. Mostly, these are problems that have to do with the creation and maintenance of meaning in a culture. But some of them have to do with managing the uncertainties surrounding the telling and the interpreting of stories that have to do with the violation of selected ethical norms. Those uncertainties, moreover, are related not only to the difficult task of reaching common agreement, but in maintaining a system that seems at least nonarbitrary even if not fully predictable.

A SYSTEM OF LAWS

Let me begin by spelling out briefly what I find to be irresistibly special about our system of laws.[3]

To begin with, it rests upon an assumed ability to decide which among a set of narrative versions of "what happened" is the "correct" version. This presumed ability is buttressed, as it were, by strict evidentiary criteria that can be made as constraining as necessary. Different systems of law require different evidentiary procedures, and case law has its own requirements.[4] The epistemological basis of our system of law is both constitutive of and constituted by its procedures. This first point may seem to lead us away from the ethical issue, but this will be seen later not to be the case.

A second feature of our legal system (and perhaps of all legal systems) is that it specifies what kinds of stories fall under the sway of law. Law is restricted with

---

[3] I do not believe that "our" system of laws and jurisprudence is *the* basic system, or indeed that there is anything that is such. Clifford Geertz's masterful account of *haqq, adat,* and *dharmma* systems in Arab, Indonesian, and Indian cultures should make it abundantly clear that legal systems are inherently local and dependent upon "thick" interpretation of local knowledge. See Geertz (1983).

[4] See Geertz (1983) on these procedural rules in the three systems of law with which he was concerned in his Storrs Lectures. In *haqq* law, for example, the court appoints a respected member of the community to gather the evidence from those who were involved, who then reports on his findings to the judge. Witnesses are neither under oath, nor does the accused have the right of confronting the accuser. But as Geertz points out, that is only a symptom of much deeper cultural beliefs.

respect to the acts that it covers: it is not about human action in general, but about certain actions. Roughly, it specifies what actions cause "trouble" and in this respect provides the crucial ingredient that makes cases translatable into narrative form (Bruner, 1991, Chap. 2). A version of this point is contained in the statement: "The law of a community is a set of special rules used by the community directly or indirectly for the purpose of determining which behavior will be punished or coerced by the public power" (Dworkin, 1977, p. 17).[5]

If someone's case is not clearly covered by such a rule (either because there is none or because the ones presumed to apply are too vague), then the case cannot be decided by applying the rule. There are various prerogatives by which a judge can "reach beyond" a rule or exercise discretion in its application, but such judicial action is controversial and generally exercised with care.[6]

This brings us to a third aspect of the legal process. The "special rules" that constitute the law of a community are not criterial subsumption rules of the kind that govern "natural kind" categories, for example, what criteria govern whether certain objects fit into such categories as "apples" or "chairs." They involve quite different principles: "These special rules [that constitute "the law"] can be distinguished by specific criteria, by tests having to do not with their content but with their *pedigree* or with the manner in which they were adopted or developed" (Dworkin, 1977, p. 17).[7]

This is perhaps a slight caricature, but it catches the spirit of the procedure. For precedents are used to illustrate acceptable applications of a rule of law. Ideally, a set of precedents are supposed to *articulate* a principle that links them. But such a principle, as we shall see, is not fully definitive of what exemplars should be included, as would be the case with an abstract subsumption rule.

If the law were governed by ordinary subsumption rules, we could get a computer to do it for us.[8] But on the other hand, the rule of precedent is not based on mere "edge matching" either—where Precedent A is like Precedent B in regard to d_i; B is like C if regard to d_j; C is like D in regard to d_k, etc. Judicial tradition, as noted, compels that precedents be conceived of as articulations of a broader principle. The principle usually takes the form of defining what we call a "functional category" (see Smith and Medin, 1981; Bruner et al., 1956, for a fuller description of category "rules").

A functional category is one that groups objects or events or cases in terms of some functional end—these things can serve as cooking utensils, these events

---

[5] The quotation is not Dworkin's own view of the matter, but his succinct summary of what is generally taken to be the positivist position.

[6] The reader is referred to the excellent summary of this issue in the chapter entitled "Design II: When the Rules Run Out" in Gardner (1987).

[7] Again, he is stating not his own position, but the traditional positivist one.

[8] For an excellent discussion of some good reasons why it is dauntingly difficult to bring judicial decisions under the umbrella of Artificial Intelligence, see Gardner (1987).

illustrate instances of repaying a debt, these cases represent violations of the right to privacy, and so on. Functional categories comprise sets of means or instruments or acts for achieving some common end. And they are typically exemplified by "prototypes" or prototypical instances. Ordinary instances of a category usually get selected, ordered, and evaluated by their "similarity" to such prototype instances. In the law, such prototypes are often illustrated by "landmark" cases. Such cases tend to become conventionalized and idealized much like prototypes in general—so to match the "prototypical" apple or the "great" base-stealer, was to have *Brown* v. *Board* or *Marbury* v. *Madison*.

There is another feature of law that needs to be noted. It is rarely univocal where its landmark cases are concerned. They are open to many interpretations and subject to years of retrospective hermeneutic ruminating. Take as just one example the famous Supreme Court ruling *Powell* v. *Alabama*, the decision in the famous "Scottsboro case" having to do with "right to counsel." It is still debated technically, for example, in terms of whether the Fourteenth Amendment incorporates the first eight Amendments to the Constitution (including the Sixth, which guarantees right to counsel), etc., etc. Does a right, for example, have to be *enumerated*, or can it be extrapolated from a general principle?

There is something very familiar about all this. We do the same thing with great literary narrative, particularly when a work is taken as prototypical of a genre. Consider the endless interpretations of Conrad's novels (Guerard, 1958). Why then is it so workaday and final to decide about legal cases, while so difficult to achieve the last interpretive word about novels? The distinguished legal scholar H. L. A. Hart provides some hints on this crucial question. All legal theorists, he tells us, cheerfully admit that it is impossible to decide whether a particular case uniquely fits a precedent or a particular rule of law. Let me quote him.

> Any honest description of the use of precedent in English law must allow a place for the following pairs of contrasting facts. *First, there is no single method of determining the rule* for which a given authoritative precedent is an authority. Notwithstanding this, in the vast majority of decided cases there is very little doubt. The head-note is usually correct enough. *Second, there is no authoritative or uniquely correct formulation of any rule* to be extracted from cases. On the other hand, there is often very general agreement, when the bearing of a precedent on a later case is in issue, that a given formulation is adequate. (Hart, 1961, p. 131)

This means, in effect, that given the absence of *subsumption* rules by which we decide whether a given case is univocally covered by a point of law, and given the absence of *similarity* rules by which we may decide whether it matches a precedent traditionally taken to have been covered by a point of law, there must be something so obvious in play that it escapes the notice of those lawyers and judges and law professors who reach the "very general agreement" that Hart celebrates so ironically in the passage just cited. What better candidate than the kinship of case law to judging the moral of a story? Let me explain.

If it were the case that in narrative there were a sharp and insurmountable separation between the "what happened" of a story (its *fabula* in the classical Formalist sense of the term) and its "moral" or interpretation (the set of precepts, legal or otherwise, that it illustrates), we would be in a terrible fix. When we decide that a Conrad story, say, "Secret Sharer," is not an adventure story but a tale illuminating the ambiguity of the line between, say, reason and impulse, we know that the "content" of the story changes with the changed interpretation. The young Captain, for example, does not bring his ship close in on the land to let Leggatt escape because he is a "daredevil," but for deeper reasons of commitment to his impulsive *doppelganger*. The modern interpretation of "Secret Sharer" simply destroys the "space" and the events of the adventure-tale alternative.

Now the passionate adherence of Anglo-Saxon law to the sharp separation of matters of fact and points of law suggests to me that it cannot abide its heritage in narrative interpretation. And this leads me to look for ways in which the legal system protects itself from this heritage. The hypothesis I now want to work out in more detail is that case law and the legal process are indeed an extension of narrative judgment. But what makes law practicable is (as mentioned at the start) its techniques for formalizing and proceduralizing its way of using the narrative method so as to achieve a workable semblance of being principled and predictable. I want to offer the hypothesis (rather Clausewitzian) that law is a way of carrying out our ordinary means of judging "trouble" stories by "other means." These means include not only codification of precepts and "morals" but also the panoply of procedures for establishing evidence, citing precedent, converting moral principles into procedural ones, etc. But for all that, the legal tradition of case law operates not just because it is buttressed at strategic points by explicit procedures and statutes, but because it rests upon our deep and abiding capacity for telling, understanding, interpreting, judging, and negotiating *stories*. It is not so outrageous to suppose that the criteria by which we judge the merit of stories and trace their pedigrees as genres are much the same as those by which we judge the convincingness of "legal" stories or by which we judge the kinship between a case now before us and a putative precedent in the past. After all, our life as members of a culture depends upon our capacity to grasp not only the specific meaning of particular stories but their generic relation to the foundational narratives that give shape to our moral convictions. For stories, as I shall try to convince you presently, are the imperfect but sole medium for structuring the implicit moral rules upon which both the law and personal morality rest.

What I want to do now is to review briefly some of the properties of that form of accounting for which we reserve the word "narrative."

LEGAL NARRATIVE

The minimal and austere definition of a narrative is that it is an account involving a sequence of events in which human (or humanlike) actors are engaged over time. The sequence of events begins with a steady or legitimate state of affairs that is then disrupted or interfered with by some precipitating event that creates a crisis that is then either redressed or allowed to perdure as a new or revolutionized legitimate state.

In legal narratives, of course, the initial or legitimate state with which the story starts is one of those domains whose violation is proscribed by a formulated rule of law—like the breaking of a contract, the violation of another's enumerated right, the causing of a harm regarded as tortious, the failure to abide by a statutory obligation, and so on. In entering litigation, a plaintiff's attorney or a public prosecutor has the responsibility to state precisely what the violation has been—that is, what is the claimed "matter of fact" and what is the "point of law" of which it is an alleged violation. This initial plea is, as it were, once for all: the point of law cannot be changed once the case is filed, and all that remains is to determine whether the "matter of fact" is, as claimed, a violation of it. And even if the case should eventually go to appeal, the appellate proceeding is limited to the point of law indicated in the initiating plea. In this respect, the narrative procedure embodied in the law differs strikingly from the freer interpretation of stories that prevails in "ordinary life." And, of course, it simplifies the interpretive task of the court in a major way.

A narrative account enacts events on several landscapes at once: human events are depicted in a "real" world, as it were, on a landscape of action; but they are depicted as well in the minds of the protagonists of the narrative, on a landscape of consciousness. The events are also taken to "exist," under some circumstances, in the mind of the narrator, whose telling of the story is taken by hearers to be only one "version." Here we must distinguish between what are taken to be "true" stories and those taken to be "fictions." In the former case, when versions vary from one narrator to another, they are ordinarily taken as "versions" that on closer scrutiny can be settled on the basis of some evidentiary criterion.[9] In the case of legal stories, the criteria to be used in decisions about the "truth" of stories are contained in the *Uniform Rules of Evidence*. What the historian Louis Munk notes about historical narrative is probably equally true about legal narratives: in both domains, there is some underlying conviction that the "true story" is in nature, to be dug out by lawyers through the adversary process and adherence to the *Uniform Rules,* and by the historian through the use of "documentation" and an adherence to strict chronology (Munk, 1978). I shall not concern myself here with narratives seen to be fictional, save that they are far

---

[9] But see Geertz (1983) for the wide variations in such criteria from culture to culture.

more open to imaginative interpretation since the only truth condition imposed upon them is that they "resemble truth" in the sense of verisimilitude. There is, of course, a fuzzy border between truth and verisimilitude. Narrative ingenuity and literary tradition provide many clever ways of achieving verisimilitude with our purportedly true accounts (Rifaterre, 1990). If truth "speaks for itself," it very often does so *sotto voce*. But for all that, we all believe at some level that it does—young children and old judges alike. But both are troubled by it nonetheless, as we shall see shortly.

"Narrative organization," the tendency to see temporally extended human events in the form of story, seems to be quite irresistible. We seem to convert all manner of scattered events, however temporally out of order they may be, into stories. If this were not so we would not have such narrative devices as flashbacks and flashforwards, and the stream-of-consciousness novel would have died unborn. The acceptability of such story-telling devices bears witness to the deeper truth that narrative is in the minds of both the teller and the told. Narratives, as it were, are made, not found, though this will be hotly denied by diehard legal scholars and historians both (see especially Schama, 1991).

Narratives consist of a story proper and an evaluative component, the latter usually cannily concealed. That is to say, a story tells what *happened* and *justifies* its telling. The justification, the latter component, inheres in the disruption of violation of legitimacy that is at the heart of any story: we tell of events *because* something went awry. We often disguise or highlight the distinction between the happening and the justification for its telling with a rhetorical objective in mind, sometimes innocently, as when we wish merely to enchant, but sometimes less so as when we tell stories as excuses or for self-aggrandizement or self-mockery. The law, of course, exaggerates the distinction by imposing its ideological and procedural divide between "matters of fact" and "points of law."

Return again to the question of why it is so difficult to tell whether stories are true or false, or in the more extended sense, why it is so difficult to know whether an interpretation handles the "facts" correctly? Neither traditional rationalism nor empiricism avails much. Rules of right reasoning that work so well for logic and mathematics do not necessarily lead to interpretive "truths." And logical empiricism rests on the presumption that the truth of the constituent atomic propositions of an account yields the account as a whole—which does not touch the case of narrative. The best we seem to be able to do in establishing whether our interpretations are "right" is to go the route of hermeneutic analysis. At the risk of gross oversimplification let me characterize such an analysis as offering an interpretation of the parts in the light of their "fit" to the story as a whole. If the parts and the whole can be made to live reasonably with each other—or in the words of the great folklorist Vladimir Propp, if the parts can be made "functions" of the whole —then we accept the "reading" as right on, though there is in principle no way of excluding alternative readings. There is always a residual discomfort among both rationalists and empiricists concerning the hermeneutic method, for it seems to chase its own tale: parts take meanings from the whole, which in turn partly (but only partly) determines what parts shall be included. This, of course, is one feature of the infamous hermeneutic circle into which all forms of historical, clinical, judicial, and moral reasoning are inexorably locked. For all that, jurists, clinicians, moralists, and historians seem to live with it—chiefly, as noted before, by formalizing and conventionalizing the process.

There may be still another reason why it is difficult to know whether a legal interpretation is "right." It relates uniquely to case law, and has to do with judgments about precedents. In law we must ask explicitly (instrumental to the pursuit of "truth") what other precedent cases a particular case is "like." And we already know H. L. A. Hart's view on the logical impossibility of making an infallible judgment of such "similarity." On what criterion does one judge similarity? Again, I believe this decision too is greatly simplified by legal procedure itself: the nature of the original plea, as noted, greatly narrows (but does not eliminate) the range of alternative precedents to be taken into account.

Let me return now to the moral or normative aspect of narrative, to the implicit "legitimacy" that is disrupted by the precipitating events in a story. In the case of legal stories, these legitimacies are not to be taken as mere public "preferences" but, rather, as collective beliefs about and commitments to a certain version of the world. They are collective not by virtue of mass psychic contagion but because they are inscribed in a code of law, in a body of relevant precedents and procedures, and in the practices of a state-authorized profession. I do not wish to make it seem that law makes narrative cold, cut, and dried, for in spite of lawyers and the courts we still take cases personally (Dunn, 1988).[10] But something becomes deeply transformed when a "moral" issue becomes transformed into the law of the land. I remarked earlier that the law carries on the narrative tradition "by other means" (much as Clausewitz intended when he remarked that war is a continuation of foreign policy "by other means"). I want now to look at what these "other means" might be and how they might have been invented or developed.

LAWS AND MORALS

Which brings me to my final topic: the relation between law as an institution of society and moral commitment in the individual. Let me review some of the standard conjectures about how this relation developed. The tough-minded view is that law is a substitute for revenge. That is to say, access to law keeps

---

[10] Dunn's work emphasizes the early origin in childhood of the rhetorical use of stories in self-justification and excuse.

contending parties from going at each other directly with the usual disruptive consequences. Oliver Wendell Holmes's classic, *The Common Law* (1881), is perhaps the great American work espousing this view. Legal doctrines, he remarks, still bear traces of their origins in revenge. Many early literary classics are similarly preoccupied with themes of revenge: the Homeric epics, the dramas of Sophocles, *Beowulf, Hamlet,* not to mention the Old Testament (Posner, 1988). For Richard Posner, indeed, the management of revenge is both the legal prototype and the *ur*-genre of literature.

But the cost of naked vengeance is too high: It breeds too intense a loyalty among aggrieved kin, and in the end escalates out of control. For what is lacking in the vengeance theory is some account of why vengeful human beings ever desist from vengeance. And, of course, they do—even in Sicily. This is what leads some legal scholars, like Robert Cover, to take a quite different view of the matter. The management of vengeance may be a by-product of a legal system, but it does not "cause" a law's coming into being. What brings on the rule of law is a much more complex and symbolic matter involving the need to create what Cover (1983) calls the culture's *nomos*. Let me quote him at some length.

> We inhabit a *nomos*—a normative universe. We constantly create and maintain a world of right and wrong, of lawful and unlawful, of valid and void. The student of law may come to identify the normative world with the professional paraphernalia of social control. The rules and principles of justice, the formal institutions of law, and the conventions of social order are, indeed, important to that world; they are, however, but a small part of the normative universe that ought to claim our attention. No set of legal institutions exists apart from the narratives that locate it and give it meaning. For every constitution there is an epic, for each decalogue a scripture. Once understood in the context of narratives that give it meaning, law becomes not merely a system of rules to be observed, but a world in which we live. (Cover, 1983, pp. 4–5)

He then goes on to characterize "great legal civilizations":

> [They] have been marked by more than technical virtuosity in their treatment of practical affairs, by more than elegance or rhetorical power in the composition of their texts, by more, even, than genius in the invention of new forms for old problems. A great legal civilization is marked by the richness of the *nomos* in which it is located and which it helps to constitute. The varied and complex materials of that *nomos* establish paradigms for dedication, acquiescence, contradiction, and resistance. These materials present not only bodies of rules to be understood, but also worlds to be inhabited. To inhabit a *nomos* is to know how to *live* in it. (Cover, 1983, p. 6)

"The normative universe," he says, "is held together by the force of interpretive commitments" (ibid., p. 6). These commitments determine what law means and what law should be. These are commitments to the system of law, and it mattes whether that system as a system—whatever its rules—is venerated or taken to be unjust, written off as the "tool of the owners" or as a just friend to all. That state of commitment also becomes part of the law. If many citizens believe that *Roe* v. *Wade* provides a licence for the murder of innocents, or that *Furman* v. *Georgia* sanctions state murder, the meaning of law changes in the society, and with it the nature of the interpretive commitment to it. The corpus juris of law exists upon a background of language, narrative, and myth.

> But the capacity of the law to imbue action with significance is not limited to resistance or disobedience. Law is a resource in signification that enables us to submit, rejoice, struggle, pervert, mock, disgrace, humiliate, or dignify. (Cover, 1983, p. 8)

Law, finally, "is a bridge linking a concept of reality to an imagined alternative" (ibid., p. 9) and the bridge cannot be crossed without narrative. Narrative is what provides the means of considering how and in what measure acts of will can transform present reality into an alternative possible world. The formal conduct of the law is judged against that background of narrative possibility: it may be seen as constricting, as enabling, as prudently delaying, and how it is seen determines the form of interpretive commitment we adopt toward it. In this respect, law can never be regarded as a fixed set of rules (as legal positivists had urged), but as a way of acting within the *nomos*.

Alas, I cannot detail fully Cover's interesting speculations about how we pass from what he calls "jurisgenesis" to a later stage of "world maintaining"—how law moves from its spontaneous origins to its later codified form. It is principally a conjectural theory about how individual moral sentiments become transformed into a collective form of commitment to a system of laws. Jurisgenesis is the process whereby legal *meaning* is established, wherein acts are imbued with narrative significance and related to personal and interpersonal commitment. World-maintaining is a subsequent process that ends by replacing the more primitive jurisgenic form of legal meaning in the interest of broader social control in a more extended community. The classic model of jurisgenesis is the small, faith-sharing, primary community—the Hebrew world, say, described by Simeon the Just two centuries before Christ:

> Simeon the Just said: Upon these things the world stands: upon Torah; upon the Temple worship service; and upon deeds of kindness. (Cover, 1983, p. 11)

That was the *nomos* of the "founding" of Jewish law and piety. Three hundred years later, after the destruction of the Temple whose service was one of the three pillars of the "world" of Simeon the Just and after exile had scattered the Jews, another great rabbi, Simeon ben Gamaliel, said:

> Upon three things the world [continues to] exist: upon justice, upon truth, and upon peace. (Cover, 1983, p. 12)

Simeon's ideal-typical world is made up of strong, "world making" forces: Torah, worship, and kindness create the normative worlds in which law is predominantly a system of meaning rather than an imposition of force. It is "paedeic" in the ancient sense of that term: pedagogy through interpretation. In Gamaliel's successor world, civil community begins: "norms are universal and *enforced* by institutions," discourse becomes objective, and the level of interpersonal commitment declines to a "minimalist" point where it is enough to assure that "objectivity" and "fairness" will not be disrupted by coercion and violence.

I am ordinarily resistant to recapitulation theories, and I shall not propose that Professor Cover's version of history recapitulates itself in each human childhood. But there is a deep sense in which modern human childhood also begins with a secularized version of the "three pillars"—the Word, the Praxis, and Affection plus the endless paidea of "drawing lessons" in the interpretive narratives of daily life.[11] It is this initial "jurisgenic" involvement in the culture-in-the-small that lays the basis for later entry into the broader, secondary community of civil life, a projection that is made possible by the creation of normative possible world in narrative.

Let me make one last point to make clearer now what must have seemed a dark comment earlier—my remark about the Clausewitzian manner in which law provides a means of conducting one's interpersonal moral commitments by "other means." Recall the characterization of the law as a set of special rules for defining those forms of conduct that require the application of coercion. I would want to urge that it is this conception of the law as a set of "limits" that also defines the range of permissible action in which "objectivity" and "fairness" are necessary for world-maintaining in Robert Cover's sense. But recall the Clausewitzian metaphor: war is a continuation of foreign policy, and to foreign policy it must return afterward. When the conduct of war negates the possibility of such a return afterward, its purpose is negated. And so with the relation of law to individual moral commitment. If the exercise of law—its decisions and its practices—undermines public faith in Gamaliel's "justice, truth, and peace," then that special form of commitment described as "interpretive commitment" is undermined. It is only then (and not in the Holmesian or Hobbesian original condition of man) that vengeance comes to loom large as a social problem. Those great novels and myths of vengeance (not to mention the child's fantasies of revenge) are not instruments of primary socialization, but expressions of the fact that neither the informal interplay of personal moral commitments nor the processes of legal decision can ever produce perfect justice.

I have taken us very far afield from the usual ways of looking at the relation of psychology and morality. Elsewhere I have tried to explain why I do not think there can ever be a full psychology that ignores or neglects man's situatedness in culture and the meanings that man creates by virtue of that situatedness (Bruner, 1991). It is this conviction that attracts me to Cover's account. Law, as I have

---

[11] On this point, the reader is referred to the rich studies of Peggy Miller and her colleagues on the uses of story in the socialization of the child. See, for example, Miller (1988).

tried to argue, is an essential aspect of culture and a crucial formative influence in the shaping of moral action. The distinguished legal scholar Alexander Bickel once characterized the judiciary as "the least dangerous branch" of government (Bickel, 1962). He chose as his epigraph Alexander Hamilton's remark in the 78th Federalist that the highest court has "neither FORCE nor WILL, but merely judgment." But the power of that judgment rests ultimately, I think, not upon the power of the executive or the Monarch to enforce it, but upon the moral commitments of those over whom it would hold sway. Public law and private morality, in this sense, become the yin and yang that define the shape of civility.

REFERENCES

Bickel, Alexander. (1962). *The least dangerous branch: The Supreme Court at the bar of politics.* New Haven, CT: Yale University Press.

Bruner, Jerome. (1991). *Acts of meaning.* Cambridge, MA: Harvard University Press.

Bruner, J. S., Goodnow, J. J., and Austin, G. A. (1956). *A study of thinking.* New York: Wiley.

Cover, Robert. (1983). Nomos and narrative: The Supreme Court 1982 term. *Harvard Law Review, 97,* 4-68

Dunn, Judy. (1988). *The beginnings of social understanding.* Cambridge, MA: Harvard University Press.

Dworkin, Ronald. (1977). *Taking rights seriously.* Cambridge, MA: Harvard University Press.

Gardner, A. V. (1987). *An artificial intelligence approach to legal reasoning.* Cambridge, MA: MIT Press.

Geertz, Clifford. (1983). *Local knowledge.* New York: Basic Books.

Guerard, Albert. (1958). *Conrad the novelist.* Cambridge, MA: Harvard University Press.

Hart. H. L. A. (1961). *The concept of law.* Oxford, England: Clarendon Press.

Holmes, Oliver Wendell. (1881). *The common law.* Boston: Little, Brown. [Reprinted, c. 1923.]

Miller, P. (1988). Personal stories as resources for the culture acquiring child. Presented at the Society for Cultural Anthropology, Phoenix, AZ.

Munk, Louis. (1978). Narrative form as a cognitive instrument. In R. H. Canary and H. Kozicki (Eds.), *The writing of history: Literary form and historical understanding.* Madison: University of Wisconsin Press.

Posner, Richard A. (1988). *Law and Literature: A misunderstood relation.* Cambridge, MA: Harvard University Press.

Rifaterre, Michael. (1990). *Fictional truth.* Baltimore: Johns Hopkins University Press.

Schama, Simon. (1991). *Dead certainties.* New York: Knopf.

Smith, E. E., and Medin, D. L. (1981). *Categories and concepts.* Cambridge, MA: Harvard University Press.

9 THE ROOTS OF MORE THAN CIVILITY

Daniel C. O'Connell

Deep within them I will plant my Law, writing it on their hearts.
Jer. 31:33 (Cf. Heb. 8:10)

The conclusion of Bruner's essay on "Psychology, Morality, and the Law" (Chapter 8, this volume) is quite succinctly the proposition that together public law and private morality define the shape of civility. The notion of "civility" is one that our popular language pundits (e.g., William Safire) might have great fun with. It is something of a soft concept. To be sure, the strength and loyalty of the Roman *civis* can still be associated with it. But what fails in it is the notion of strong obligation. At most, the notion is one of appropriateness, urbanity, politesse. Or, with *Webster* (1983), courtesy, politeness. *Ought* is smothered under all this nice stuff. The present chapter might be looked upon as an effort to disinter the foundations of obligation in the contexts of both public law and private morality, and specifically from a psychologist's point of view.

At the same time, everything Bruner wants is at least implicitly included under civility: basically a constructivism in which language plays a constitutive role in creating social reality. "Meaning is what we can agree upon," and "social realities are not bricks that we trip over or bruise ourselves on when we kick at them, but the meanings that we achieve by the sharing of human cognitions" (Bruner, 1986, p. 122). Hence, the civility of agreement and sharing is to be seen as the proper formulation of his rationale for public law and private morality.

Our beginning text from the Book of Jeremiah, however, seems to present a far different notion of the foundations of morality and law about which Bruner theorizes. Implicit here is the notion that there is indeed something substantial, something in the nature of man, that calls out for an *ought*—quite antecedent to and independent of the linguistic negotiation of reality.

Translated into some sort of psycholinguistic/moral developmental paradigm, the question might be posed: Is there something innate in the moral order? Or what sort of heart-text does God script? The rephrasing is not at all intended as either irreverent or facetious. When and how does it all begin? How does it proceed? Where do *ought, obligation, duty* really come from?

Bruner asserts that preoccupation with matters of law and morality is a rarity among psychologists, and so it does indeed appear to be. Certainly, title notwithstanding, the recent summary in the *Annual Review of Psychology*, "Moral Rules: Their Content and Acquisition" (Darley and Schultz, 1990), does little to dispel that impression. But the very rarity also piques one's curiosity: Why is it that most psychologists do not engage these issues? Are we unable or unwilling or perhaps even unaware?

My own view of the matter is that we have neither the tools nor the inclination nor the sophistication. The methods of investigation we are accustomed to make use of are suitable for discovering regularities in human activities while neglecting quite thoroughly the value systems (indeed, even the more proximate goals) that dictate these same actions. Neither the neobehaviorists nor the children of the cognitive revolution have made much room for the concepts of finality and freedom within their deliberations. Moore's (1939) original idea of cognitive psychology was complementary to his *Dynamic Psychology* (1924), but modern cognitivism has pretty well taken over the whole show by subsuming the dynamic within the cognitive. In short, instead of being concerned only with discoverable regularities in human activities we should be concerned with the genuine orderliness (and disorderliness) of human lives in the Thomistic sense: *Sapientiae est omnia ordinari.* For it is indeed the role of wisdom to order all things. A little of it would not hurt the discipline of psychology at all.

The point is by no means irrelevant to Bruner's intent, for his approach is decidedly socio-cognitive. It could hardly be accurately aligned with Moore's (1948) *The Driving Forces of Human Nature.* Bruner's emphasis is instead on learning and communicating in the moral order, and the learning is obviously to be found *only in* the communicating, and one must add—very importantly—in the *linguistic* communicating. Still, the ancient problem of the origin of *ought* cannot be so easily cognitivized. How does learning yield a *bonum faciendum, malum vitandum?* Whence the imperative, or in the present case, the gerundive? More specifically with respect to Bruner's position, how can story-telling yield a sense of obligation, be foundational to a morality? Does morality really necessarily first emerge only *after* the onset of language use and *through* the linguistic component of communication?

A STORY

In Bruner's cover letter with his manuscript, he expressed to me his interest in what I would make of it "because, as a priest, you have been dealing with moral issues in the most direct way possible" (personal communication, 1991). I deeply appreciate that sentiment from an old friend and colleague, and it is, of course, true. Nonetheless, I wish to appeal to a sort of "negotiating about the meaning" (Bruner, 1986, p. 122) that is, I think, even more direct. It concerns not my priesthood as such, but my humanity. It relies not on my pastoral experience of moralities, but on my own very personal experience of my own morality.

Accordingly, and even at the risk of seeming to wander far afield and perhaps also of becoming far too personal, allow me to insert a story of my own.

One day when I was about seven years of age and my brother 10, we joined a group of boys, mostly his age, to play a primitive form of sandlot baseball. Our contribution to the occasion consisted of an old catcher's mitt and an even older catcher's mask made of wrought iron padded over with leather—a hand-me-down bit of equipment. As things turned out, the older boys became surly and decided to subject my brother John to an ignominious "depanting," the forcible removal of his trousers. I clutched the mask by the canvas strap and held it at arm's length as I screamed, "You guys get away from my *brother* or I'll kill ya'." Instantly they freed him and disappeared. Any one of them could easily have wrung me to the ground, but I suppose I looked exceedingly murderous. *Brother,* by the way, was definitely the emphatic word, and, as I will argue, certainly carried a very concrete moral imperative for me—and, fairly obviously, also for the older boys—in this setting.

Now, I have orally related this story many times in the course of my life, but this is the first time I have ever written it down. Its pedigree or "goodness as a story" (Bruner, 1986, p. 12) I am afraid I must leave to the reader. More important, however, is the related question: Can such a story conceivably serve as one of Bruner's "foundational narratives that give shape to our moral convictions" (Chapter 8, this volume)?

By way of parenthesis, I wish to mention here that, whatever might be the foundational merit of such a story in the Brunerian sense, there is a great difference between it and parables such as those Christ narrated. The parable is a *fabula,* a fictional, possible happening, part of Bruner's "possible worlds" (1986). On the lips of the Lord, the pastoral value of parables was immeasurable; however, it is not at all accidental that He also had to go back over them to explain their moral relevance. The moral value of the anecdote taken from personal or pastoral experience is profoundly different. As a celebration of shared humanity, it has a special cogency and clarity all its own, a warmth and camaraderie about it that accomplishes wonders. There is nothing purely possible about it; it is actual and in "actual minds" (Bruner, 1986) as something that really happened.

Nonetheless, I wish now to argue that we would be confusing product and process were we to grant to such narratives the moral power Bruner wishes to grant to them.

To return to my own story, it is not by any means as simple a moral situation as one might imagine. The motive of brotherly love obviously cast out all fear and actualized both my menacing gesture and my threatening words. On the other side of the coin, however, is an apparent lack of moderation. No proportionalist, I am sure, would be willing to argue that "I'll kill ya'" was a justifiable, moderate intention (if it *was* in fact the intention to kill). But the important question with regard to the story is, for our purposes, what function it has been serving lo these many years in its *oral* version. Assuming that the story was intended to communicate and succeeded in communicating to my interlocutors the moral desirability of coming to the aid of someone we love when he or she is in trouble and one is able to do something to help the situation, are we to consider it truly a foundational narrative?

I think not. It is, in fact, both subordinate and derivative with respect to the original event itself. One might look at it this way: Were the listener instead a spectator, would not the cogency and moral import of the action be immeasurably more impressive than the story? The point I wish to make is that there is nothing particularly necessary about this second-hand morality play. Life is a better teacher in any event. Or, as my mother used to say, "Actions speak louder than words."

But such arguments beg the question anyway. For the question must be pursued back to my own morality. The single word *brother* incorporates my moral indignation totally. This brotherly defense was a moral act. Where had I learned it? Had my parents told me stories about brotherly love that carried with them such a cogency as to elicit such an extraordinarily loyal behavior from me? I find it very difficult to imagine that such an overwhelming *faciendum* could come from such story lines. I was already a young moral agent at the ripe old age of seven, and my *agendum* sprang not from foundational narratives but from my own experience of life. I knew that I had to defend my brother; that is precisely what love of one's brother *demands* and means.

What, then, *can* a narrative accomplish? Both the parable and the anecdote *celebrate* and *archivize* our moral agreements, and the factual anecdote immortalizes moral actuality rather than moral possibility. Through both genres, we exhort one another to moral *agenda,* rejoice in good deeds well done.

BRUNER'S FOUNDATIONAL SYSTEM

The theses of Bruner's foundational system are set forth quite clearly by him in his essay:

1. Stories are the imperfect but sole medium for structuring the implicit moral rules upon which both the law and personal morality rest.
2. The personal *exercise* of a moral commitment is governed not by induction or deduction or by general propositional derivation, but by *narrative pedigree.*

The first of these two principles must be taken to refer to stories or narratives in a very specific sense. Bruner defines narrative as an

> account involving a sequence of events in which human (or humanlike) actors are engaged over time. The sequence of events begins with a steady or legitimate state of affairs that is then disrupted or interfered with by some precipitating event that creates a crisis that is then either redressed or allowed to perdure as a new or revolutionized legitimate state. (Chapter 8, this volume)

This is not yet the question of narrative pedigree. If any element of this definition is lacking, there is no story at all, let alone a good one. Such an "austere" definition, as Bruner refers to it, is, I think, overdrawn. It is certainly the case that the prototypical morality play somehow recapitulates the primeval catastrophe or Original Sin that man has fallen prey to, but not every good story requires disruption. Some sort of *Ablenkung* or what Chafe (1980, p. 176) refers to as

(a) Introduction of a new character or set of characters
(b) Change of location
(c) Change of time period
(d) Change of event schema
(e) Change of world

would easily suffice instead of disruption or interference to initiate a story. I do not think it reasonable to categorize the introduction of every opportunity or adventurous challenge as necessarily disruptive or interfering, but only as exciting or interesting.

Given a story (and bypassing its pedigree for the moment), we must examine its capacity to serve as "sole medium for structuring the implicit moral rules." The distinctions I have given in the preceding regarding the moral cogency of factual stories and parables already hint at the rationale I find to be the ultimate criterion of such cogency. It is *contact with moral agency* that must somehow be verified in any instance that is foundational to either public law or personal morality. Such contact is by no means intrinsic to stories as such.

Every story must occur in either written or oral or some sign-language (e.g., ASL) form. In all these cases, though in different ways, the moral cogency of the story relies on or resides in the moral authority of the *storyteller,* not simply on the story line itself. He or she provides the nexus to the moral dimensionalities of human life. Further, the role of moral communicator is *not* in any sense limited to the role of storyteller. It is vastly broader than that.

My thesis, then, is that the foundation of both public law and personal morality is to be found in contact with moral agency. This contact is to be found in the personal experience of one's own moral agency and in the vicarious experience of the moral agency of others. In this latter case, the story is not even the most direct or adequate medium for the communication of such experience. Actions *do* speak louder than words. The observer is closer to human agency, if you will, than the listener. The story is not at all transparent in putting the listener (much less the reader) in contact with the moral agency of the storyteller.

There are hints of such an emphasis in Bruner's presentation: "Some people can make a story of anything" and "narratives are made, not found." But for Bruner, "why it *justifies* telling" resides in the story itself. "We tell of events because something went wrong," and herein is to be found the rationale for "evaluation." But the fact that something went wrong and the need to evaluate why it went wrong still do not provide an adequate rationale for *why it was wrong*. As a matter of fact, many things can *go wrong* that have no moral implications at all. Little dogs can get lost and be found again, and therein we can find a lovely story. But unless the storyteller comes through to the listener (reader) as a caring person who somehow embodies responsibility for God's little half acre and the residents thereof, there simply is no moral implication to whatever went wrong.

In any event, we must inquire further into what it might mean for a foundational narrative to "give shape to our moral convictions" or to structure "implicit moral rules" (Bruner, Chapter 8, this volume). If the rules are indeed already implicitly realized, then it would be far more accurate to say that the story simply makes explicit what is already there. The sole function of this shaping or structuring is then to serve as formulation or articulation of the antecedently given moral import that a moral agent—again, a story*teller*—wishes to communicate to another moral agent. Quite redundantly then, moral agents are in charge of moral agency.

The assumption that the moral rules are implicitly realized also requires further inquiry. On the one hand, Bruner finds it questionable that a democratic society could survive, were the principles of law "personally alien or cognitively opaque to its members." On the other hand, he finds that "the 'truth' of stories, the 'rightness' of their interpretation" remains in the last analysis somehow moot. The latter position hardly seems to correspond to a situation in which the moral rules are implicitly realized antecedent to the stories. As to the former, principles of law that are personally alien and/or cognitively opaque to the majority of our citizenry seem to be the order of the day. Thank God that our moral and juridical survival does *not* depend on such a sense of affinity and/or lucidity. The conversations of well-educated people about basic ethical questions and the front (or editorial) page of the *New York Times* should suffice to convince us that it is not only in the domain of secondary and tertiary ethical principles that alienation and opacity are prevalent in our society.

This brings us finally to Bruner's second thesis of his foundational system—the governance of personal exercise of moral commitment. The question is whether narrative pedigree is adequate for such governance.

Bruner does not really define what he means by narrative pedigree. He exemplifies it. The argument proceeds as follows: "If you ask me, . . . I will tell you stories." I find it difficult to see this as "the personal *exercise* of a moral commitment." It seems quite clearly to reflect instead an antecedent commitment, based on a prudent assessment of convergent facts. The stories consolidate and formulate one's experience, but they do not serve as an exercise of moral commitment in any foundational way.

One might argue similarly that the casuistry described by Bruner for "reconciling conflicting moral principles" is a collation of relevant considerations rather than the use of " 'interpretive' narrative." For example, "He's my *brother*" is indeed the interpretation of a case, but it is *not* a story line. The subsequent oral and written versions of the story about my brother are, moreover, precisely derivative from a previous personal moral commitment. Even "the demonstrable existence of a pedigree of like judgments in the past" is still not narrative in its nature.

Beyond his two basic theses, Bruner engages the relationship of public law and personal morality even more directly in his espousal of both the legal realists (e.g., Oliver Wendell Holmes) and the legal narrativists (e.g., Robert Cover). But although it is certainly the case that interpretive "commitments determine what law means" to a given populace, it is not the case that such commitment determines "what law should be" (Chapter 8, this volume). Neither in public law nor in personal morality, ought *ought* be defined by a counting of noses. Cover and Bruner to the contrary notwithstanding, law is not a bridge linking *a* concept of reality to *an* imagined alternative. It is not just any old concept of reality, and it is not an imagined alternative at all. Bruner's "possible worlds" (1986) are simply not an adequate basis for morality; a real world understood and cherished by "actual minds" (Bruner, 1986) is.

REALITY

It is noteworthy that Bruner's chapter has a chronic problem with the "concept of reality" in connection with the moral order. The following sequential citations from Chapter 8 are given with the emphatic punctuation or capitalization used by him in the text:

> *really*
> "reality"
> "reality"
> "correct" version of reality
> a story *interprets* the "facts" correctly
> Reality
> "really"
> "right" version of reality
> a world

The moral order is real. Moral meaning is not just "what we can agree upon" or what "we achieve by the sharing of human cognitions" (Bruner, 1986, p. 122). It is indeed spiritual and therefore capable of being distorted, disregarded, spurned entirely by the very moral agents who are responsible for its preservation. Its rationale is not discoverable merely from alternative possibilities, though these do indeed reflect man's freedom of spirit and his ability to discern and decide. Nor is our appreciation of the moral order consequent upon either the mastery of our native language or the formulation of our moral principles.

To return once again to a psycholinguistic/moral developmental framework, I would like to espouse the principle enunciated by Hörmann (1986): "Understanding is older than understanding language" (p. 87). Or, as MacNamara (1972) has put it: "Small children learn their language by first determining what the adult means independent of language" (p. 1). Granted that both Hörmann's and MacNamara's statements are primarily concerned only with very young children, the priority of understanding with respect to language is universal. We cannot use the tool of language to represent reality unless we first comprehend the reality to be communicated to one another. There is no reason whatsoever to make an exception for the moral order in this regard. We understand the moral order by engaging life and our various relationships to the world about us, especially our relationships to other moral agents. My position should not be taken to mean, however, that language in use cannot become productive rather than simply reproductive of thought (see Hörmann, 1986, p. 83).

Whence does this understanding of the moral order arise? I think it not an exaggeration to say that the combined traditions of the *philosophia perennis,* of the natural law, and of the Judaeo-Christian world agree on placing this source in the very nature of man: "Deep within them I will plant my Law, writing it on their hearts" (Jer. 31:33).

It is certainly the case that the moral virtues are exercised socially, that they need to be formulated as mandates, and that such formulation is necessarily in language. It is even true that they are often expressed by us in parables and factual anecdotes for the edification of one another. But let me express my position as bluntly as possible: They are neither logically consequent upon nor dependent upon stories or linguistic formulation.

And what about the theological virtues? Both the psalmist ("My soul thirsts for God, for the living God" [Ps. 42 (41)]) and St. Augustine ("Thou hast made us for Thyself, oh Lord, and our hearts are restless until they rest in Thee" [*Confessions,* Book 1, Chapter 1]) tell us that there is something intrinsic to man that causes him to yearn for union with God. William James (1983) sounded a similar note with respect to our "impulse to pray" as an expression of our search for the "only adequate *Socius*" (p. 301).

Ascetical theology delineates an interesting recapitulation of the prelinguistic moral understanding of the child in the postlinguistic transcendence of the linguistic in advanced stages of the prayer life. The prayer of faith, as it is commonly called, proceeds without any awareness of linguistic formulation whatsoever; for God transcends our human stammering. Sadly perhaps for some, He does *not* limit Himself to communication in English.

As a social constructivist and narrativist, Bruner comes close to defining man as *homo linguisticus*. Surely the emphasis is there, and I find it a disconcerting emphasis. The object of our psychological study is, as Herrmann (1985) has so well said, not *"the human being as language processor,"* but *"the human being who also understands language and also speaks"* (p. 41; my translation). In particular, man's moral life is far more than speaking and listening, reading and writing. These are exercised only *"occasionally, from time to time"* (O'Connell, 1988, p. 54).

William James (1983) recognized as the very first source of error in psychology "the Misleading Influence of Speech" (p. 193), because the "absence of a special vocabulary for subjective facts hinders the study of all but the very coarsest of them" (p. 194). If anything, the problem of vocabulary has become even more pronounced in modern psychology.

I think it not amiss to end with another passage from James wherein, after stating that our ethical propositions "say nothing about the time- and space-order of things," he goes on to say in all modesty that ethical propositions (along with many others) have

> grown up in ways of which at present we can give no account. Even in the clearest parts of Psychology our insight is insignificant enough. And the more sincerely one seeks to trace the actual course of *psychogenesis,* the steps by which as a race we may have come by the peculiar mental attributes which we possess, the more clearly one perceives "the slowly gathering twilight close in utter night." (James, 1983, p. 1280)

Perhaps James's very last words in *The Principles of Psychology* can be echoed with the same modesty by ourselves at the end of our own discussions of psychology, morality, and the law.

Stories are not morally foundational; they are on the upper stories.

REFERENCES

Bruner, J. (1986). *Actual minds, possible worlds.* Cambridge, MA: Harvard University Press.

Chafe, W. L. (1980). Some reasons for hesitating. In H. W. Dechert and M. Raupach (Eds.), *Temporal variables in speech: Studies in honour of Frieda Goldman-Eisler,* pp. 169–180. The Hague, Netherlands: Mouton.

Darley, J. M., and Shultz, T. R. (1990). Moral rules: Their content and acquisition. *Annual Review of Psychology, 41,* 525–556.

Herrmann, T. (1985). *Allgemeine Sprachpsychologie: Grundlagen und Probleme.* Munich: Urban & Schwarzenberg.

Hörmann, H. (1986). *Meaning and context: An introduction to the psychology of language.* (R. E. Innis, Ed.). New York: Plenum.

James, W. (1983). *The principles of psychology.* Cambridge, MA: Harvard University Press. [Original work published in 1890.]

MacNamara, J. (1972). Cognitive basis of language learning in infants. *Psychological Review, 79,* 1–13.

Moore, T. V. (1924). *Dynamic psychology: An introduction to modern psychological theory and practice.* Philadelphia: Lippincott.

Moore, T. V. (1939). *Cognitive psychology.* Philadelphia: Lippincott.

Moore, T. V. (1948). *The driving forces of human nature and their adjustment.* New York: Grune & Stratton.

O'Connell, D. C. (1988). *Critical essays on language use and psychology.* New York: Springer-Verlag.

Webster's Ninth New Collegiate Dictionary. (1983). Springfield, MA: G. & C. Merriam.

10 FREE CHOICE, PRACTICAL REASON, AND FITNESS FOR THE RULE OF LAW

Robert P. George

ON THE RULE OF LAW

Occasionally one encounters overblown claims on behalf of the rule of law. For example, thirty years ago, Lon L. Fuller, the theorist who has in our own time best explicated the content of the rule of law,[1] seemed to assert that tyrannical rulers cannot pursue their pernicious ends while at the same time scrupulously observing the requirements of the rule of law. Fuller argued, or, in any event, his critics took him to be arguing, that the rule of law operates as a procedural guarantee against serious substantive injustice.[2]

Fuller's critics responded by pointing out that wicked rulers sometimes have purely self-interested motives for eschewing official lawlessness and binding

---

[1] Fuller explicated the content of the rule of law in terms of eight constitutive elements or "desiderata" of legality: (1) the prospectivity (i.e., non-retroactivity) of legal rules; (2) the absence of impediments to compliance with the rules by those subject to them; (3) the promulgation of the rules; (4) their clarity; (5) their coherence with one another; (6) their constancy through time (enabling people to be guided by the rules); (7) their generality; and (8) the congruence between official action and declared rule. He observed that these desiderata are matters of degree; thus, legal systems exemplify the rule of law *to the extent that* the legal rules are prospective, susceptible of being complied with, promulgated, clear, etc. What was, perhaps, most controversial about Fuller's account of the rule of law was his claim that these "demands of legality" constitute an "internal morality of law." See Fuller (1969, Chap. 2).

[2] Ibid., Chap. 4.

themselves to act in accordance with legal procedures. They contended that the strict observance of legal forms by such rules cannot guarantee that the laws they enact and enforce will not be substantively unjust.

In a celebrated exchange with Fuller, Herbert Hart maintained that nothing prevents wicked regimes from pursuing manifestly evil ends through procedures that exemplify the qualities of process that Fuller correctly identified as constitutive of the rule of law (Hart, 1965). Fuller responded by claiming that grossly wicked regimes, such as the Nazi regime, do not observe even formal principles of legality. In practice, regimes of this sort depart freely from the rule of law whenever it suits their purposes. He defied Hart to provide "significant examples of regimes that have combined a faithful adherence to the [rule of law] with a brutal indifference to justice and human welfare" (Fuller, 1969, p. 154).

Fuller's critics, however, remained skeptical. Indeed, Joseph Raz went a step beyond Hart in attempting to deflate Fuller's claims for the rule of law. Raz suggested that the rule of law is simply an efficient instrument, not unlike a sharp knife, that may be useful and even necessary for governments to pursue morally decent purposes but is equally serviceable in the causes of tyranny and injustice (Raz, 1977, p. 208).

At one point, Neil MacCormick shared Raz's understanding of the desiderata of the rule of law as morally neutral (and largely technical) requirements of legal efficiency. "After all," MacCormick has remarked, these requirements "can in principle be as well observed by those whose laws wreak great substantive injustice as by those whose laws are in substance as just as can possibly be" (MacCormick, 1992). Recently, however, MacCormick has modified his view. While he continues to insist that strict observance of the rule of law is compatible with grave substantive injustice, he is now inclined to give some credit to Fuller's claim that the elements of the rule of law constitute a kind of "internal morality" of law.

> There is always something to be said for treating people with formal fairness, that is, in a rational and predictable way, setting public standards for citizens' conduct and official's responses thereto, standards with which one can judge compliance or non-compliance, rather than leaving everything to discretionary and potentially arbitrary decision. That indeed is what we mean by the "Rule of Law." Where it is observed, people are confronted by a state which treats them as rational agents due some respect as such. It applies fairly whatever standards of conduct and of judgment it applies. This has real value, and independent value, even where the substance of what is done falls short of any relevant ideal of substantive justice. (MacCormick, 1992)

MacCormick's analysis of the intrinsic, albeit limited, value of the rule of law is, I think, quite sound. I would merely add that an unjust regime's adherence to preannounced and stable general rules, so long as it lasts, will have the additional virtue of limiting the rulers' freedom of maneuver and is therefore likely to reduce, to some extent, the efficiency of their evil-doing. Even those subjected to unjust rule will be made somewhat better off to the extent that their rulers, regardless of their motives, operate according to law. To be sure, the substance of the laws may be spectacularly unjust; nevertheless, a wicked government's decision to act within the procedural constraints of the rule of law affords the general population at least some measure of security.

Plato warned that wherever the rule of law enjoys ideological prestige evil men will find it convenient to adhere to constitutional procedures and other legal forms as means of maintaining or enhancing their power (Plato, 291a–303d). He had no illusions that a ruler's willingness to operate according to law would guarantee that the particular laws he enacted and enforced would, even in general, be just. Nevertheless, he noticed that, quite apart from the self-interested motives that evil rulers sometimes have for acting according to law, men of goodwill always and everywhere have reason to respect the rule of law: for such respect manifests a degree of procedural fairness that in itself is desirable in human relations and, in particular, in the relations between ruler and ruled. While this reciprocity is often useful in securing other desirable ends—such as enabling people to understand the legal consequences of the actions they contemplate and, thus, to plan and order their lives—it is not *merely* a means to other ends (nor, I would suggest, may it lightly be sacrificed for the sake of other goods).

I think it fair to conclude, then, that if Fuller claimed too much for the rule of law, his more extreme critics have acknowledged too little. Fuller was wrong to suppose (if he did, in fact, suppose) that the strict observance of the procedural forms of legality would guarantee substantive justice; nevertheless, *pace* Raz, a ruler's willingness to observe these forms is likely to constitute a benefit to the ruled even when it is motivated by something other than a sincere regard for the morally compelling reasons that those in possession of political authority have for respecting the rule of law.

Sober accounts of the rule of law acknowledge both the contribution of formal legality to the morally upright ordering of human affairs and the limits to that contribution. Even the most illuminating of these accounts, however, typically say little about a certain very important philosophical question: What is it about (most) people that makes them fit for the rule of law?

The correct answer, I think, is suggested by MacCormick's claim that rulers ought to govern by law because people are "due some respect as rational agents." There is, however, more to be said; for today when one speaks of human rationality (in virtually any context) one will be understood to be referring to what Aristotle labeled "theoretical" rationality. *Merely* theoretically rational agents, however, could not be ruled by law and would, in any event, no more deserve to be ruled by law than computers deserve such rule. Even theoretically rational agents who (i) experienced felt desires and (ii) were capable of bringing intellectual operations to bear in order to satisfy their desires—if this were all to be said of their capacities for "practical" reasoning—would hardly be due the respect implied by the rule of law. Such agents would certainly not be capable of exercising moral judgment and making moral choices.

The rationality for which people are "due some respect" in the form of the rule of law is not primarily the rationality that enables people to solve mathematical problems, or understand the human neural system, or develop cures for diseases, or inquire into the origins of the universe or even the existence and attributes of God. It is, rather, the rationality that enables them to judge that mathematical problems are to be solved, that the neural system is to be understood, that diseases are to be cured, and that God (if He exists) is to be known and loved.[3] It is, moreover, the capacity to distinguish fully reasonable possibilities for choice and action from possibilities that, while rationally grounded, fall short of all that reason demands. In sum, fitness for the rule of law depends on our capacities as *practically* intelligent beings, that is, our capacities to grasp and act on reasons and to distinguish defeated from undefeated, and conclusive from nonconclusive, reasons for action. These capacities are, in turn, connected with our capacity for free choice, that is, our capacity to deliberate and choose (often, but not always, for conclusive reasons) between and among possibilities that provide reasons for action.

In what follows I shall explicate the phenomenon of free choice and discuss, in general terms, the relationship between free choice, practical reasoning, and morality. I shall also say why I think that beings who can make free choices and be practically reasonable are not only fit for the rule of law but, in most circumstances, deserve to be governed in accordance with it.

FREE CHOICE AND PRACTICAL REASON

People make choices; and some of the choices people make are quite unlike the "choices" made by nonrational animals. A mule may hesitate when faced with the possibilities of drinking from a pail of water or eating from a bale of hay. In the end, it will do one or the other first. Now, let us suppose that on this occasion the mule drinks the water before eating the hay. In a loose sense, the animal can be said to have "chosen" to drink before eating. Nothing *external* to the mule determined that it would drink first; what settled the matter in the end was something *internal* to the mule, namely, the mule's own desires or preferences. The animal hesitated between the pail and the bale because it was experiencing a conflict of felt desires: it felt a desire for the water and, at the same time, a desire for the hay. Eventually, the desire for the water prevailed and the mule drank.

---

[3] On the distinction between "theoretical" and "practical" rationality as herein understood, see Finnis (1983, Chap. 1). Also see generally Grisez et al. (1987).

Like mules, people can be motivated by hunger, thirst, and other felt desires. They can experience conflicts of felt desires and make "choices" in the loose sense in which mules and other animals can be said to make choices. Unlike mules and other animals, however, people can "choose" in a stricter and philosophically more interesting sense. The choices that people can make that are quite unlike the "choices" made by other animals are what philosophers mean by "free choices."

A free choice is a choice between two or more open practical possibilities in which no factor but the choosing itself settles which possibility is chosen.[4] Inasmuch as the mule's choice to drink before eating was *determined* (albeit by its own desires) it was not a *free* choice. Insofar as similar choices made by human beings are similarly determined they are not free choices. Free choices are choices that are not determined by desire. Free choices are not determined by anything. They are, in short, not determined.

Choice in any sense is possible only where someone has motives for incompatible actions. *Free* choice is only possible where these motives are reasons for action or, at least, where reasons for action are among these motives. There can be no free choice where the *only* possible motives for action are *subrational*, for example, feelings, desires, preferences, habits, emotional inertia.

Because mules can be motivated by possibilities that appeal to feelings, desires, preferences, habits, inertia, etc., they sometimes *hesitate* between incompatible possibilities and "choose" in the looser sense of the term. Because mules cannot, we must suppose, appreciate the *rational* appeal of some possibilities for choice, they cannot *deliberate* between incompatible possibilities that provide reasons for action and make free choices between or among them. People and other rational beings, precisely insofar as they can understand certain possibilities as providing reasons for action, *can* deliberate between incompatible possibilities and make free choices.

It is important to notice that reasons for action, though they are conditions of free choice, are not causes (in any modern sense of "cause") of the actions they are capable of motivating.[5] One can choose not to perform a certain act that one has a reason (and, thus, a rational motive) to perform and one can choose to perform a certain act that one has a reason (and, thus, a rational motive) not to perform. In the simplest case, one may have a reason to perform an act yet have a strong aversion to performing it (and, thus, an emotional motive for not performing it). One's failure to perform it may be due to weakness of the will (see Wiggins, 1980).

In a more interesting case, one may have a reason to perform a certain act and, at the same time, a reason not to perform it. One may freely choose to act on the latter reason. In a case of this sort where one has a conflict of reasons and no

---

[4] For a full defense of the possibility of free choice as here defined see Boyle et al. (1976).

[5] On the distinction between reasons and causes see Robinson (1985), especially pp. 50–57.

conclusive reason to act on one reason rather than the other, the choice between the two is rationally underdetermined. Nevertheless, a choice either way remains rationally grounded.[6] If one performs the act, one does so for a reason; if one refrains from performing the act, one also does so for a reason.

Let us consider an example. Suppose that Ferdinand is a bright young college senior who is trying to decide on a career. He has talent and interest in psychology and could, no doubt, contribute to the advancement of knowledge in that field. Thus, he has a reason to enroll in a doctoral program in psychology at, say, Georgetown. At the same time, however, he has talent and interest in medicine. Thus, he has a reason to forgo graduate work in psychology and go to medical school. A choice either way would be "for a reason" and, thus, rationally based; yet Ferdinand has no conclusive reason for making it one way rather than the other. A choice in favor of either possibility would be consistent with those principles of reasonableness in practical affairs that we usually refer to as moral norms. Hence, no such norm provides a reason for action that defeats one or the other of the conflicting reasons and dictates a choice one way rather than the other.

There are cases of conflicting reasons, however, in which moral norms do provide conclusive reasons to do something that one has a reason not to do or not to do something that one has a reason to do. Nevertheless, one may freely choose to defy a conclusive reason. In such cases, one's action, while not utterly irrational, is not fully reasonable. An act in defiance of a conclusive reason remains rationally grounded insofar as one performs it for a reason. Yet inasmuch as one's reason for performing it has been defeated, one's nevertheless choosing to act in this way is practically unreasonable.

Let us suppose that Ferdinand has opted for medical school. In the course of his medical studies, it becomes clear to him that it would be possible to learn a great deal about the etiology of a certain deadly cancer by performing damaging and ultimately fatal experiments on a living human subject. Naturally, Ferdinand desires to acquire this knowledge—both for its own sake and in the hope of finding a cure for the cancer. Now, it occurs to him that he could probably get away with secretly performing the necessary experiments on an advanced Alzheimer's patient who has no family and resides in a hospice that Ferdinand regularly visits as part of his practical training. So, Ferdinand faces a choice between performing the experiments and declining to do so. Like his earlier choice between going to graduate school in psychology or going to medical school, this choice is between rationally grounded possibilities. That is to say, Ferdinand has reasons for a choice either way. Here however, he has a conclusive reason for making the choice one way rather than the other, namely, the moral norm that forbids the taking of innocent human life.

---

[6] For a useful explanation of how choices between rationally grounded possibilities can be rationally underdetermined, see Raz (1986).

Moral norms are norms for free choice; they are principles of practical reasonableness that guide choices between incompatible possibilities in which one has a
reason, or reasons, for action. As action-guiding principles, moral norms are,
moreover, themselves reasons for action. They are not the most basic reasons for
action, however; for the most basic reasons are principles that guide action by
directing choice toward rational possibilities and away from what is utterly
irrational. And certain possibilities, while holding some rational appeal (and
therefore available for choice in the strong sense of the term), are, nevertheless,
not fully reasonable (i.e., the reasons for choosing them are defeated). Moral
norms guide action by directing choice toward *fully reasonable* possibilities and
away from possibilities that, while not utterly irrational, are practically unreasonable.

Moral norms (such as the norm that forbids the direct killing of innocent
human beings) are conclusive reasons for action that exclude certain possibilities
despite the fact that one has (nonmoral) reasons to choose these possibilities.
Where a moral norm excludes a possibility, one's reason for choosing that possibility (assuming that one had a reason and not merely an emotional motive for
it) has been defeated. Defeated reasons are reasons on which it is unreasonable to
act. Nevertheless, such reasons retain some rational appeal. In declining to act on
them, one forgoes some real benefit. By declining to act on a defeated reason,
Ferdinand, for example, forgoes genuine goods, namely, knowledge of the etiology of the cancer in question together with the possibility of developing a
cure.

Let us suppose, however, that Ferdinand chooses, reluctantly, to perform the
experiments on the unsuspecting Alzheimer's victim. Perhaps he has been reading the works of Jeremy Bentham or one of his contemporary followers and has
decided that the evil of performing the experiments would be outweighed by all
the good that the knowledge they would yield would make possible. In accounting for his choice, we might take note of the irrationality of supposing that the
good and evils at stake here can be commensurated in a way that would enable
someone to identify a choice one way or the other as promising the net best
proportion of good to evil.[7] We would not conclude, however, that his choice
was utterly irrational. His reasons for making it, namely, the knowledge to be
gained and the possibility of a cure, while defeated here by the absolute norm
against directly killing the innocent, remain reasons. In view of the conclusive

---

[7] For powerful arguments against consequentialism based (in part) on problems of incommensurability, see Grisez (1978), Finnis (1983, Chaps. 4–5), Raz (1986, Chap. 13), and Foot (1985). For
additional arguments that complement the argument based on incommensurability, see Donagan
(1977, especially pp. 149–157 and 172–209), Kiely (1958), and Hodgson (1967). For an ingenious,
albeit ultimately self-defeating, attempt to rescue consequentialism from its critics, see Parfit (1984),
wherein the author proposes the category of "self-effacing theory," that is, a consequentialist theory
that requires, for the sake of optimizing consequences, its own abandonment "by some process of
[deliberate] self-deception that, to succeed, must also be forgotten" (p. 42).

reason for action provided by the norm, however, his choice would fall short of what reason requires: it would thus be unreasonable, irresponsible, immoral.

ON THE INTRANSITIVE SIGNIFICANCE OF FREE CHOICE

There are two additional points about the significance of free choice that are, I think, relevant to the question of how people, as moral beings, are fit for the rule of law. Free choices are events or states of affairs in the world; they are not *merely* events or states of affairs, however, like the events and states of affairs that they bring about. In addition to their transitive significance as events that shape the world external to the chooser they have a profound intransitive significance.

First, free choices reflexively shape the personality and character of the chooser. In freely choosing we integrate ourselves around the principles of our choices. Thus, we constitute (or reconstitute) ourselves as particular sorts of persons. We construct (or reconstruct) our moral selves. Typically, this self-constitution or moral self-construction is not the precise reason for our choosing; nevertheless, it is an unavoidable side effect of that choosing. And it is the capacity for moral self-construction (and destruction) that makes us moral beings.

The second point I wish to make about the intransitive significance of free choice is that precisely insofar as our choices are self-constituting they persist beyond the behavior that executes them. Indeed, they persist in the personality and character of the chooser until, for better or worse, he repents of his prior choice and either makes a new choice that is incompatible with that prior choice or genuinely resolves not to repeat the choice he has now repudiated.[8]

The possibility of repentance of an immoral choice manifests a lack of complete integration in the human personality. Someone who has by his immoral choices constituted a wicked character can, with difficulty, reconstitute himself. Fiction and even biography are replete with examples. So long as this lack of complete integration continues, the constitution of a wicked character does not preclude the possibility of repentance and reconstitution around upright principles of action. Nor, of course, does the constitution of a good character eliminate the possibility of evil choices and the reconstitution of one's character around immoral principles. Biography and even fiction provide examples here, too.

---

[8] The resolution required to effect a reconstitution of one's character based upon repentance of one's earlier choice cannot be merely the resolution to avoid the circumstances in which one would feel it necessary to make the choice one now regrets. It can be nothing short of the resolution to choose differently even in those circumstances.

FREEDOM, REASON, AND FITNESS FOR THE RULE OF LAW

The fact that people can grasp and act on reasons, thus constituting themselves by their own free choices, does not mean that they may not legitimately be governed. The human capacities for practical deliberation and judgment and morally significant choice do not somehow make people fit for anarchy. The possibility of morally upright choice entails the possibility of immoral choice; and with respect to a great many possibilities for choice the common good of everyone in society is served by legal restrictions on the freedom of individuals to do whatever they please.

Moreover, insofar as law provides concrete norms for coordinating various types of human activity in complex societies, it is plain that legal rules would have a place even in a society of perfectly virtuous individuals.[9] Laws provide beings capable of grasping and acting on reasons with (additional) reasons for action. Where the laws are just, they provide conclusive reasons for action. The reasons for action provided by just laws are conclusive even in cases of norms (e.g., coordination norms) that come into force by virtue of the sheer legislative acts of duly qualified political authorities.[10]

Most people are capable of grasping and acting on reasons, including the reasons for action provided by laws. To subject people fit for the rule of law to rule by, say, whim or terror is an affront to their dignity. People really are "due some respect as rational agents." And such respect entails, at a minimum, the observance by political authorities of the desiderata of the rule of law.

It is true, of course, that even the most scrupulous adherence to the rule of law does not exhaust the debt owed by rulers to the ruled. As Fuller's critics insisted, the formal requirements of legality may be observed even where the substance of the law is gravely unjust. So respect for the rule of law, while (generally) required as a matter of political morality, is not all that political morality requires. Beings that are fit for the rule of law deserve, moreover, to be ruled by laws that are just.

REFERENCES

Boyle, Joseph M., Jr, Grisez, Germain, and Tollefsen, Olaf. (1976). *Free choice: A self-referential argument*. Notre Dame, IN: University of Notre Dame Press.
Donagan, Alan. (1977). *The theory of morality*. Chicago: University of Chicago Press.

[9] On the role of law in providing solutions to coordination problems, see generally Ullmann-Margalit (1977).

[10] For a useful review of the contemporary debate over the question of a *prima facie* (defeasible) moral obligation to obey the law, and for a defense of the position herein adopted, see Finnis (1989). For a vigorous argument on behalf of the counterposition, see Raz (1984).

Finnis, John. (1983). *Fundamentals of ethics*. Oxford, England/Washington, D.C.: Oxford University Press/Georgetown University Press.

Finnis, John M. (1989). Law as co-ordination. *Ratio Juris, 2*, 97–104.

Foot, Philippa. (1985). Utilitarianism and the virtues. *Mind, 94*.

Fuller, Lon L. (1969). *The morality of law*. New Haven, CT: Yale University Press.

Grisez, Germain. (1978). Against consequentialism. *American Journal of Jurisprudence, 23*, 21–72.

Grisez, Germain, Boyle, Joseph, and Finnis, John. (1987). Practical principles, moral truth, and ultimate ends. *American Journal of Jurisprudence, 32*, 99–151.

Hart, H. L. A. (1965). Fuller's *The Morality of Law*. *Harvard Law Review, 78*, 1281–1296.

Hodgson, D. H. (1967). *Consequences of utilitarianism*. Oxford, England: Clarendon Press.

Kiely, Bartholomew M., S.J. (1985). The impracticality of proportionalism. *Gregorianum, 66*, 655–686.

MacCormick, Neil. (1992). Natural law and the separation of law and morals. In Robert P. George (Ed.), *Natural law theory*. Oxford, England: Clarendon Press.

Parfit, Derek. (1984). *Reasons and persons*. Oxford, England: Clarendon Press.

Plato. *Statesman*.

Raz, Joseph. (1977). The rule of law and its virtue. *Law Quarterly Review, 93*, 208.

Raz, Joseph. (1984). The obligation to obey: Revision and tradition. *Notre Dame Journal of Law, Ethics, and Public Policy, 1*, 139–155.

Raz, Joseph. (1986). *The morality of freedom*. Oxford, England: Clarendon Press.

Robinson, Daniel N. (1985). *Philosophy of psychology*. New York: Columbia University Press.

Ullmann-Margalit, Edna. (1977). *The emergence of norms*. Oxford, England: Oxford University Press.

Wiggins, David. (1980). Weakness of will, commensurability, and the objects of deliberation and desire. In Amelie Oksenberg Rorty (Ed.), *Essays on Aristotle's Ethics*. Berkeley: University of California Press.

11 THE SWORD OF MANJUSRI: A POSTMODERN MORALITY OF INTELLECT AND SKILLFUL MEANS FOR RELATIVE WORLDS

Nancy C. Much

*Thus have I heard, once the Blessed One was dwelling in
Rajagriha at Vulture Peak Mountain, together with a great
gathering of the sangha of monks and a great gathering of the
sangha of bodhisattvas. At that time the Blessed One entered the
samadhi that expresses the dharma called profound illumination
and at the same time Noble Avalokiteshvara the Bodhisattva
Mahasattva while practicing the profound Prajnaparamita, saw
in this way: he saw the five skandas to be empty of nature. . . .
Form is emptiness; emptiness also is form. Emptiness is no other
than form; form is no other than emptiness. In the same way,
feeling, perception, formation and consciousness are emptiness.
Thus Sariputra, all dharmas are emptiness. There are no
characteristics. There is no birth and no cessation. There is no
impurity and no purity. There is no decrease and no increase.
Therefore, Sariputra, in emptiness there is no form, no feeling,
no perception, no formation, no consciousness, no eye, no
ear, no nose, no tongue, no body, no mind; no appearance, no
sound, no smell, no taste, no touch, no dharmas; no eye dhatu
up to no mind dhatu, no dhatu of dharmas, no mind-
consciousness dhatu; no ignorance, no end of ignorance up to no
old age and death, no end of old age and death; no suffering,no
origin of suffering, no cessation of suffering, no path, no
wisdom, no attainment and no non-attainment. Therefore
Sariputra, since the bodhisattvas have no attainment they abide
by means of Prajnaparamita. Since there is no obscuration of
mind there is no fear.*

Prajnaparamita Sutra [Translation,
Nalanda Translation Committee, Naropa Institute, Boulder,
Colorado]

SOCIAL DISCOURSE AND MORAL JUDGMENT

This passage is an excerpt from the Prajnaparamita [Perfection of Wisdom] Sutra, also known as the Sutra of the Heart of Transcendent Knowledge. It describes the occasion of what was known as the Buddha's second turning of the wheel of the dharma. Legend has it that when the Buddha turned the wheel of the dharma the second time, tens of thousands of arhats (accomplished monks) dropped dead. The arhats had all been trained as objectivists. They viewed the metaphysical constructs of early Buddhist doctrine from the perspective of "naive realism." In this passage, the Buddha, or rather Avalokiteshvara, speaking for him, has just told Sariputra that these ideas were actually false. The teaching became known as the "doctrine of emptiness." It was associated particularly with Nagarjuna and developed most elaborately by the Madhyamika schools of the Mahayana tradition (Ramanan, 1966; Snellgrove, 1987). The doctrine of emptiness followed upon a phase of "naive realism" in which the monks were taught the abidharma—a classification of the elementary psychophysical constituents of the universe and the means through which, by avoiding certain of these constituents and accumulating others, they could ultimately attain peace or cessation of the disturbing recycling of consciousness through the common experiences of living and dying—desire, pain, impermanence, disappointment, resentment and death—and obviate the necessity of recycling again and again through the twelve nidhanas or causal stages that result in continuity of living on earth. At this juncture (i.e., at the Second Turning) they are being told that "dharmas" (i.e., the whole phenomenal world), after all, are not real, and neither are the twelve nidhanas, the cycle of samsara, the path to attainment of liberation, nor the attainment of liberation itself. The instruction was too dangerous. The Buddha had it secured with the Nagas (serpent demi-gods) in the underworld until the time was ripe for its propagation in the world. Then Nagarjuna went and retrieved it. It spread to Tibet, Mongolia, China, and Japan. It is still a central doctrine of contemporary Mahayana schools and continues to be developed today by Buddhist philosophers.

I would like to discuss the doctrine of emptiness and the morality it generates. I shall try to expand the doctrine in relation to its postmodern cognate: discursive-constructivist psychology. I shall approach this with a view toward clarifying some misconstruals of certain subtle points of the doctrine in its best representations. Then I shall go further to discuss the kind of morality that was in fact generated by the doctrine of emptiness and suggest that it is not only consistent with postmodern constructivist psychology but suggests relevant contributions to contemporary Western moral psychology. In explicating these ideas, I shall occasionally make use of images from exotic worlds. I will do this for the same reason that, in general, one might bother to make a lifetime project of studying the psychologies, philosophies, and social theories indigenous to other societies or other times: with the thought that their images may enable us to see and understand ourselves in different ways and to notice and appreciate things about ourselves that our local habits of thought may have made obscure. Exotic theories can help to illuminate our fundamental existential problems or choices. It can be helpful to appreciate the full range of possibilities for human experience and human understanding: not to romanticize the unfamiliar, but to transcend in what may be the only way possible, the limitations of the familiar and the habitual.

The occasion for this discussion is Robert George's essay, "Free Choice, Practical Reason, and Fitness for the Rule of Law." I have been asked to comment on that essay. So basic are the divergences in the author's ways and my own of speaking of psyche, the personal entity, and the social order, that I shall have to address George's argument obliquely. In the end, I will neither agree nor disagree with the conclusions George has drawn, given the terms and premises he has chosen as the foundation for his argument. From my own standpoint, it is the terms and premises that George has chosen that inspire examination and discussion. It is the choice of the language itself that is the ground upon which the debate must take place.

DISCOURSE, RATIONALITY, AND RELATIVE TRUTH

The doctrine of emptiness was notoriously difficult to understand. With the Buddhist relish of irony and paradox, it was said that anyone who claimed to understand was a heretic. In the same vein it was said that anyone who believed that phenomena were real was a fool; anyone who believed that they were not real was a greater fool. The doctrine of emptiness was also known as the Sword of Manjusri,[1] the intellect so sharp that it cuts its own ground. According to this doctrine, that is the ultimate inevitable fate of all rationality: it just does not take one all the way. Absolute truth, such as it is, is considered to be beyond the reach of rationality, or in other words, beyond the reach of discursive thought. Rationality as we ordinarily speak of it is discursive thought. As such, it operates only within the domain of "relative truth"[2] or relative reality. Absolute reality is said to be beyond the reach of discourse and can only be indexed and not described. It is and always will remain ineffable.

Let me attempt to explicate the symbolism of this highly elliptical way of speaking in a language that is possible for a twentieth-century Western social science. Mahayana Buddhist tradition has long had an exquisite appreciation of the primacy of the indexical functions of language, even with respect to the most academic of contexts. The Buddhist teachings, they say, are like one's grand-

---

[1] Manjusri is the bodhisattva or "enlightened one" of knowledge and wisdom.

[2] This is the term that is used in most current translations. The term "truth" in this context may be problematic, as Professor Harré has suggested, since "truth" as a term implies the absolute. I shall substitute the term "relative reality," which is in keeping at least with current anthropological usage.

mother's finger pointing to the moon. She does not touch it nor can she enable us to touch it; but she causes us to attend to and notice it. Theoretical constructs or representations of the world are meant to make us notice certain things about experience and especially to help us see beyond material, empirical appearances to what is behind them. The "moon" in the proverb represents the self-existing or "absolute reality" behind the words used to describe it; the elusive truth that our theoretical constructs are intended to lead us toward.

Another story further expands the point concerning the limitations of discursive rationality. Naropa was a renowned scholar in Buddhist India around the tenth century A.D. He was the equivalent of president of Nalanda University, the ancient Buddhist equivalent of, perhaps, Oxford. This much of the story, at least, is historical. One day Naropa was reading on the lawn. A hag approached Naropa. She asked him whether he understood the words he was reading. He said that he did. She was gleeful. Then she asked him whether he understood the sense of the words. Thinking that he would please her even more, Naropa said that he understood the sense. She wept. Naropa asked her why. She said that she wept to think that a man of Naropa's intellect, understanding the words that he read, should be deluded to believe he also understood the sense (i.e., the reality they pointed to) when in fact he did not. This was a turning point in Naropa's intellectual career.[3]

Sometimes constructivist psychology has been misconstrued to mean that there is no reality beyond one's discourse—that we literally make up the world in its entirety by speaking about it and acting as if it were true. Naturally, this is felt to be an untenable position. But it is also not quite to the point. The point is rather that we never have direct access to it. Our access to reality is always mediated by our discursive language. There is nothing that we can *say* about reality outside of our own chosen or inherited and very particularistic discursive representations of it. The message of the doctrine of emptiness as developed by the Madhyamaka is not that there is nothing "out there" or "up there," or wherever things that transcend language lie, but rather that there is *nothing that we can say about it* that is true in any absolute or stable sense. We give specific substance to reality through our discursions. And we do not have access to a reality except through our discursive representations of it. Our access to whatever exists independently of our representational systems is nevertheless always mediated by our discursive language or other symbolic systems. Though there be something self-existing independent of our representations of it, we can not talk about it or reason about it independently of our discursive representations of it. And those are never the same as the thing in itself, so they are never real except in a relative sense. Language and discursive thought apply *only* to relative reality and not to absolute truth. This means they function appropriately only within

[3] Guenther (1963).

relative discursive domains. Allow me to indulge in one further story, from the Zen tradition this time; it expresses the hopelessness of trying to use language to express truth.

> At a particular monastery the monks owned a cat. Eventually the cat became an object of jealousy and contention among the monks. The abbot assembled the monks and brought the cat before them. He brought a sword and he told the monks that he was about to cut the cat in two—unless anybody could say a true word. Nobody said anything. Later a traveling monk returned to the monastery. He came to the abbot's chamber and the abbot related the story to him. The monk put his sandals on his head and walked out of the room. The abbot called after him, "Ah, if only you had been there, the cat might have been saved."[4]

It follows, I believe, from the doctrine of emptiness and from a discursive-constructivist psychology that discursive rationality can never really do very much more than to index anything that is in the absolute realm of truth. The implication most emphatically is not that there exists nothing in the world, the cosmos, or the person that is independent of our discursive constructions of it. It is rather that whatever is independent of our discourse can only be indexed or relatively described by it. The contents of descriptions themselves resides *within* the relative discursive domain. They point to and illuminate aspects of the self-existing reality beyond them. But they cannot appropriate or definitively describe it. The error that we make is to reify our descriptions. As soon as this is done, what one has is not a "truth" but an artifact. That is because artifact is what discourse produces. This is not, however, to denigrate our artifactual creations nor to imply that they are without a reality and significance of their own. The artifactual, discursively constructed world of objects, ideas, and practices has its immense importance. Actually it is quite fundamental. The fact that the world of shared meaning that we inhabit is our own discursive creation does not mean that it is *unreal* in any absolute or stable sense. Once created it is in fact existent. It is worthy of the utmost respect and attention because it is the domain of relative reality in which we live our lives, experience our experiences, and participate as immanent entities called persons. Though this reality may be our own discursive construction, once constructed, it possesses a life of its own that is a reality we are compelled to respect. This is one reason why it is said that the person who believes that the phenomenal world is not real is a still greater fool than the person who believes that the phenomenal world is real. The point is that there is nothing that we can *say* about reality that is absolutely true; there is nothing that we can say that is *outside* of our own chosen or inherited and very particularistic discursive tradition with its representations of the world. We can not actually describe the really real; we can only point to it. There is no reason to believe that our discursive language achieves any greater accuracy than that. For

---

[4] Paraphrase of Zen Koan, Nansen Kills the Cat. Yamada (1990), Kubose (1973), Ogata (1959).

this reason there is a lot of leeway in the way that it is possible to describe or represent the really real: different ideas about what natural law is; different categories of nature; different premises about persons and the social order. The world does not insist upon its description. There are relatively few "hard facts" to which every rational person must bow. There are many plausible metaphysical choices concerning concepts of personhood, the social order, and natural law. This occurs, of course, even within the local domains of discursive rationality. Robert George and myself, for example, each have clearly made certain metaphysical choices about which representations of personal entities and social orders are to be preferred. Both of our positions are products of our contemporary culture and its particular history (Kurtines and Gewirtz, 1984). I will say more on our respective choices later. The metaphysical choices made by a particular conceptual system—for example, that of the Hindu Brahmin, the Sri Lankan Buddhist, or the Tibetan Ponpo—give rise to divergent rationales—or rationalities, based upon what follows from alternative metaphysical premises and discursive traditions that are the foundations for rational thought.

Assuming that there is something self-existing independently of discursive representations of it, each of the possible discursive systems can be only an approximation at best, a relative and partial description of something outside of the language itself. There is more than one plausible version of reality and therefore of rationality, a realization that was the achievement of certain Buddhist (as well as perhaps others) philosophies more than a millennium ago. Postmodernism is a very old doctrine. Perhaps the doctrine of samsara is correct: Everything is in an endless situation of recycling itself. It is possible that every thought that can be thought and every practice that can be practiced is present as latent in every culture (universal latency; Shweder, 1991): the only difference among them is what they select for emphasis or illumination and what for obscuration and concealment.

The relation of discursive rationality to ultimate and relative reality is at the heart of the doctrine of emptiness and the Sutra of the Heart of Transcendent Knowledge. Rationality, in fact "thought" in all its forms, is discursive. It is useful and in fact necessary for the analysis of relative truth. However, its domain of operation is entirely limited to *relative* truth. It was agreed that there was something beyond relative truth; but it was also agreed that there was nothing—literally—that one could SAY about reality. In other words, culturally relative description of reality is the only kind of truth that can be spoken about because it is the only thing that linguistic categories apply to. There may be natural law as something "really real," but whether there is or not we are still constrained by our own discursive imaginations in our representations of it. And our imaginations are constructed out of the stuff of our traditional discursive systems. Whatever there is that is there independent of our imaginations, we can not make direct contact with it: at least not through our conceptual systems. It is for that reason that it is not possible (nor desirable) to avoid multiplicity or particularity in anything that is conceptualized or represented.

Rationality, it seems to me, in the sense that it is ordinarily understood, involves the manipulation of concepts. In order to have rationality at all, one has to settle for a very partial and relative, particularistic or local truth. Rationality is based upon choices involving dualistic contrasts. Something either is or is not an instance of construct "A." Without at least that minimal foundation, logic as we normally understand it is not possible. Different premises about persons, society, and nature constitute, as David Wong (1984) puts it, "differing truth conditions" for moral rationality (Professor Harré cogently recommends that "assertability conditions" would be more apt). They tend to specialize in their views of the world, their epistemologies, and the kinds of representations of reality that they generate. They highlight certain aspects of experience and obscure others. Diverse discursive systems are our symbolic pool for knowing reality. Like our genetic pool, it is not desirable to narrow the domain very much. Though some philosophers prefer to assume that disagreements can eventually be resolved by engaging in rational discourse, if the entire world were to agree on one and only one reality, it would probably be a very unfortunate thing.

Reality itself is and will remain unfathomable and literally unspeakable: not because of its "nothingness" but because of its "everythingness." Nothing thinkable or knowable is excluded. Perhaps a good deal more is included. The totality is therefore inconsistent. Here is a further subtlety of what is called the doctrine of emptiness: it is not the "nothingness" of reality that makes it empty or insubstantial: it is the "everythingness." Reality itself, whatever it is that is "really there" independent of our conceptualizations about it, is not amenable to having its possibilities appropriated or exhausted by any single and coherent interpretive system. Given the possibilities for adequate representations of reality, one can never be complete and consistent at the same time. The possibilities for choices of what to highlight and what to submerge, what to illuminate and what to conceal are multiple. In part for this reason, I recommend that we speak of "adequate" rather than "valid" or "true" representations, especially in the realm of constructs concerning personal entities and social orders.

The problem of representing reality could be thought of as analogous to the problem of the most acceptable representation of God. Which is the best and the most valid God-representation: Jehovah, Allah, Siva? A unitary God, a triune one, a God Who takes polytheistic identities, has male and female halves? One that takes incarnations on earth or one that never does? Which is the really real representation of God? The undecidability (at least in my opinion) of this question does not, as some may believe, entail that there could be no rational criteria for saying that some God-representations are more illuminating and adequate than others. There is undoubtedly an adequacy, a richness, depth, and profoundness to the God-representations of the great religions—those that are highly developed symbolically, philosophically, and morally—compared to the God-representations of cargo cults or certain evangelist preachers. These representations may be more or less adequate in certain relevant ways. The purpose of having God-representations seems to be something like the creation of certain experiences and relationships for human beings: among these a sense of reverence, inspiration, the sense of a sacred world, and a relationship with a divine order greater than one's diminutive self. Some kinds of God-representations and the practices associated with them may be more adequate and more potent creators of these important experiences than others. But when it comes to deciding on rational grounds between Siva and Jehovah, between Jesus and Padmasambhava, the going gets rough, unless one frankly relies upon the guiding coherence of a particular tradition, chosen or inherited. One can say that the most valid representation of God is ultimately undecidable by our conceptual systems, without entailing that one should not have, be guided by, or relate to God-representations, or that there is no underlying reality indexed by one's representations and yet independent of them. It is only that the human cognition, by means of its concepts, cannot go beyond one's own, or someone else's culturally constituted representations.

We have access to reality only indirectly through the language that we use to speak about it. This language has a special and peculiar kind of relation to its objects. At one and the same time it indexes or points to them, and it represents them in a certain specific and highly selective way. The selectivity of object representation is tradition bound in the large part. Individuals do not recreate the world for themselves from scratch. Every cultural tradition tends to specialize in its views of the world, its particular epistemologies, and the kinds of representations of reality that it generates and makes available. Each highlights or emphasizes certain aspects of experience and obscures or suppresses others. Rationality is always selective: If it were not, it would sink into chaos. But since it is selective, at the same time, it is always incomplete, and so in some sense inaccurate. Cultural discursive traditions involve the shaping of the attentional structures or consciousness of individuals.

Our problematic tendency is to reify our language as if it were the thing itself. This has at times been selected as a quality of "primitive" thinking (Douglas, 1966). It seems, however, to be simply a quality of the use of language. Once constituted and legitimated by tradition, our representations of things tend to take on a life of their own and "become" an illusory reality (D'Andrade, 1984). That is the creative capability of shared language. George's essay, for example, uses a very powerfully creative language that sets in motion a particular vision of persons and society. Within this particular vision, George's argumentation appears very solid, objective, and rational. However, the solidity dissolves radically and the objectivity dissolves, though the rationality remains, once one focuses upon the particular assumptions about persons and the social order that are presupposed and recognizes these as but one possible vision among rather many cogent alternatives to what personal entities, social orders, and moral practices are really like or ought to be like.

Our theoretical constructs, among which I include the terms of everyday commonsense language, as well as those of moral philosophy, "describe" reality in a certain way. But that description is always essentially relative (contestable, incomplete, inconsistent with other equally accurate descriptions, etc.): it is invalid and obscuring *as soon as we try to hold it to inappropriate standards of absolute objectivity*. However, insofar as one recognizes the creativity or constructive character of one's discursive representations of the world and does not hold them to standards of absolute objectivity, they then index and illuminate aspects of reality, and in fact have the potential to cultivate a language and practice that is eminently practical and humane because it is congruent with the way that a living, organic, and intentional world of personal entities and social orders operates: one that does not, in other words, require a frozen reality.

Both self-existing (absolute) and discursively constructed (relative) realities have practical implications. If one were to act as if either need not be respected one would rather soon be "brought back to earth" by confrontations with intense experience. To act as if absolute reality need not be respected would be to think that one has infinite and unconstrained latitude to ideationally construct any kind of reality one wanted to. The fact that this is not possible is the reason that a constructivist and relativist viewpoint still admits of judging cultures or discursive systems as more or less adequate realities with respect to sustaining and cultivating human life. Certain cultural choices just are not practical. To disrespect relative reality would be to behave as if one believed that one could do as one pleased in a social order because in fact none of it is "real" and so it does not matter what one does with it. This attitude is also likely to lead to most unsatisfactory results. At the same time, it is salutary to appreciate that relative reality is of the nature of illusion (i.e., culturally based discursive construction), since not to do so might, at any given time, be to fly in the face, if not of hard facts (of which there may be few), at least of something like powerful experience. The over-reification of the relative reality of social orders also gets one into trouble because relative reality is bound on occasion to be misleading. That realization itself is one's best protection against being wholly taken in by the particular vision of reality that one's contemporaries have created or inherited. Living organisms tend to remain susceptible to their own experience when it is powerful enough (e.g., intense pain or suffering, intense desire or longing), no matter how they would like to conceptualize it. This is part of what makes certain philosophical, cultural, or moral constructions "impractical," that is, unlivable: and thereby constitutes limiting conditions for the possibilities of discursively creating society. Though we do not construct absolute reality, we construct what we know and believe of it; and I would go so far as to say that there may be better and worse ways of doing that: more and less adequate or illuminating constructions.

FREEDOM AND TRANSCENDENCE

The doctrine of emptiness includes as its corollary the doctrine of no-self. The self has the same status as the rest of the phenomenal world. Both are devoid of independent empirical contents. As there is no self or subject, so also there is no object. The self and its objects are both empty or without substantiality; that is, they are both constituted by their mutually contingent relations embedded in a network of discursive thought. When its propositions are examined carefully, it is discovered that it is impossible to demonstrate that the data have a stable existence independent of their very descriptions. A transcendent self or self-existing entity could in principle be there. However, it acquires content only through its participation and involvement in an immanent world of tradition-based discourse. The content of immanent selves is inextricably linked to their particular symbolic and discursive world. As far as transcendent entities are concerned, they do not seem to participate in the phenomenal (relative) world at all except by becoming immanent. It is not perhaps the individual entity that is socially and discursively constituted, but the phenomena of self: that is, its experiences as described, its emotions as defined or understood. The personal entity like other entities, as an object of knowledge, is normally only indirectly accessible to us through the linguistic constructs we use to talk about it and about its experiences. We do not have direct access to it; at least not through discursive thought. I have allowed for the possibility of a self-existing individual entity independent of cultural-discursive constructions of it. However, as such it eludes the descriptions of discursive language in the same way that absolute truth does. The individual entity is accessible only as a participant in a domain of social discourse.

An inference that is sometimes made is that a constructivist psychology entails a strong determinism on the development of the individual, such that the ideas of "human nature," "agency," and "moral responsibility" or "will" must no longer apply; related to this is the supposition that under these conditions there is no such thing as morality, at least of an acceptable type since moral judgment would be seen as wholly determined by cultural rule systems. This position is also thought to entail that there can be no rational criteria for making judgments about whether some aspect of some culture is better or worse in certain respects than conceivable alternatives. The possibility that human beings discursively construct the meaning and sense of their world does not preclude there being any sort of "raw material" for them to work on. More ironically, what seems to be overlooked is the crucial observation that culture and the propensity discursively to construct a world of shared meanings *is human nature*. It is what we are about.

In the philosophical and social-scientific traditions of the West, one particularly favored characterization of the human species is to find its distinctiveness in its rationality (or cognitive capacities and activities). Culture, and the activity of constructing discursively meaningful organizations of experience, is an expression, perhaps one should say is the fundamental expression of human rationality. If the expression of human rationality is not found in culture and its discursive domains, then where is it found? Transcendent intellect, as I have already argued, is amenable to discussion only as it manifests itself immanently through particular discursive systems. It is our all-too-solid subject–object dichotomy that leads to the idea that there is a sacred self that is somehow independent of culture.

I will attempt to explicate the doctrine of emptiness with particular reference to what it does and does not mean for the agency of the individual, the quality of cultural lives, and the relation of these to "naive discursive realism." The social-discursive construction of intentionality eliminates responsibility for choice if at all only to the extent that any individual is ignorant of or unable to imagine more than one possible description of any given confrontation with experience. Even within a very localized discursive domain, some choices will be provided such that the individual can choose the best course of thought and action. Cultural discursive systems are generative systems like grammar. Even in the most rule-ridden cultures (such as India and the United States) individuals have proven to be astonishingly creative and expressive in the way they pick and choose possibilities to suit their intentions. This is in part because cultures are often more inclusive than they seem. Besides the "orthodox" version of things there normally exists an "underworld" or "black market" discourse that is going on contiguously. Although it contains the very things that are excluded from the official doctrine, it is understood by almost everyone and it is just as much a part of the culture. I call it covert culture. A complete cultural analysis would include the analysis of this underside of official doctrine. This material is often available for moral choice because it provides ways to break the (official) rules when the rules themselves seem to lead to immoral situations.

A frequent objection to a constructivist psychology is its apparent (but misconstrued) implication that human intellect is constrained by cultural rules that, it is felt, human intellect ought to transcend if the psychology is to allow for personal choice in a meaningful sense. I will argue that the particular condition or feature of a discursively constructed psychic organization that constrains intellect is precisely the mistaken belief or illusion (perhaps unconscious) that what one knows as the description of the world—especially of persons and the social order—is the only valid description and bears some special relation to absolute truth. The more a person is aware of a diversity of possible descriptions of a situation or event and of the creative act of bringing these descriptions to life, the greater the moral discretion at the person's disposal, and the more the individual is confronted with responsibility. It is only to the extent that one is bound by a naive discursive realism to a single way of looking at things that one's capacity for moral discernment and creative choice is limited. That is not to deny that this does occur in some, perhaps even many individuals to varying extents. This is in fact what the Prajnaparmita morality of liberation sees as a fundamental human problem. It is not, however, necessary that this occur: its occurrence is a matter of empirical fact and is not entailed by a constructivist psychology, although its occurrence is almost certainly one of the observations upon which a constructivist theory might be based. The determinism of ideas occurs to the extent that an individual is blind to the processes of the discursive construction and delimitation or bounding of experience—to the extent that the individual's rationality is utterly subject to or unable to resist conformity to one particular description of the world. It is not necessarily the absolute potential for human understanding and human experience that is determined by one's personal history within a particular discursive culture. What is normally determined by experiences of this kind is one's habitual patterns of rationalizing about experience. To the extent that an individual clings to naive discursive realism regarding the taken-for-granted world—and the tendency to cling is often strong—one's imagination and so one's will is bound to those patterns of cognition.

Highly developed discursive traditions such as our own allow though limit choices of many kinds within the domain of their basic premises. What is determined by the discursive tradition is a range of operations, what can be thought—the realm of the thinkable not the thought that some person is going to have at some exact moment. There is always a choice but choice—typically a dualistic one (e.g., doing the morally right versus the morally wrong thing)—exists within a particular limited rationality: what is determined is what is and what is not thinkable. Cultures and individuals are co-creative intentional systems. Some notion of teleology or directive force is embedded in traditional discursive systems; unavoidably so, since it is built into language itself as well as derivative cultural practices of all kinds. Traditions provide symbolic repertoires for the organization of experience. These order experience in such a way that it occurs as meaningful within the traditional realm of meanings. Within this domain, the individual expresses and realizes his or her personal desires, strivings, judgments, choices, and so on. Moral choices are also made within this domain.

The dangerous case is the case in which the individual is convinced that the discursive system presented by his culture is "real" in the inappropriate sense of absolute rather than relative meaning. In that case, it is possible that the phenomena of the self and its experience are utterly subject—since the imagination is constrained to move within only one sense of possible reality and cannot make the leap to other possibilities. This may or again it may not be true of large proportions of persons, who, though living currently in a society where the "knowledge" of all of the cultures of the world is more freely accessible than it has ever been, prefer to cling to a temporal and national parochialism regarding the issue of what in fact is "really real." This preference may be viewed very much as an existentialist issue. I think of Sartre's admonitions that one is always responsible for one's experience, whatever it may be; and I do not find them inconsistent with the doctrine of emptiness or a constructivist psychology. This implies that at some level one always knows what one is doing, whether one realizes it or not. It happens to be another point of Buddhist irony, but I will not go into it in depth here. If one chooses to be determined by a principle of conformity to the cultural in the doctrine of one's times, it may be because that is felt, unconsciously if not consciously, to be the safest route through human experience. Consequently one avoids admitting into consciousness at a significant level the knowledge of other realities that might quake the familiar ground on which one stands. I am, of course, suggesting that cognizing the world as a discursive relativity is not an impediment to a mature morality but a necessary condition for it.

This is not to say that one is particularly "free" to choose. Freedom would mean the absence of constraints. The constraints for remaining within one's received world are heavy. And all individual entities are born and raised into such a world. The costs of serious experimentation with other worlds may be high, the effort heroic. But the presence of constraints and heavy costs can be distinguished from absolute coercive determinism. The salutary force of describing ourselves in this way is to call attention to the possibility that the highest degree of personal freedom can come only after first recognizing the extent to which one in unfree. The individual must always function within the domain of some traditional discursive system. Each such system places constraints on what can be rationally thought; more so on what is habitually thought and taken for granted. But the individual need not be determined by any given discursive tradition precisely to the extent that the individual is aware of its relative status and the more so to the extent that other possibilities are actually learned, known, and capably experienced or practiced. To the extent that one becomes aware that the world as presented is a contestable description of reality, one is actually confronted continuously by unavoidable responsibility for choosing among possible descriptions. As long as one believes that only one pattern of reasoning and experiencing is "real" and conclusive, then naturally to the extent that one is capable of making rational choices, those choices are constrained by that particular description of reality. And insofar as it will necessarily be a limited vision, it is bound to be inadequate and misleading at (sometimes crucial) times. It is the ignorance of or refusal to consider other possibilities that is the grip of traditional determinism over the human psyche. It also follows from this position that the individual need not take or leave the local tradition as found precisely to the extent that there is cognizance and capability of other possibilities that prime the imagination concerning how things might be or how they might be accomplished. Agency is enabled to the extent that it transcends any one description of relative truth, which can only be done by cognizing others. This is one sense in which there could be a transcendent "self" compatible with a constructivist psychology. Cognizance of multiplicity actually imposes choice.

To the extent that the individual intellect can appreciate the cultural-discursive collusion to construct a particular description of reality, and its own participation in that collusion, it is also to that extent liberated from naive realism (not all realism is naive); provided, that is, that the personal entity possesses the actual skills for living out this realization—that is, for acting upon it moment by moment. That may be the even greater part of the challenge. Intellect alone, I will argue, even in its most profound cultivation, is insufficient for a completely mature morality. Certain skills must also be highly cultivated or else one's "will" is apt to come to nothing. This will be given further discussion in the final section of this chapter.

I began my argument speaking in the Madhyamika idiom in order particularly to demonstrate the idea that ultimate truth, whatever it might be, can never be accurately described; it can never be captured by discursive systems, which are inevitably based upon a logic of contrasts. However, in order for personal entities to function in the world at all, it is necessary to construct a relative reality based upon a discursive system. It is this relative reality that we know as the factual world; though it is fundamentally an artifactual world. Though it is a world of illusion, it is also the world in which we live and experience and fulfill our intentions. Once we have created it, it possesses the quality of "real." "Real" means most essentially that it has significant consequential implications for the beings that inhabit it. It must therefore be respected in a pragmatic sense as real, though potentially interchangeable with other realities.

Our relative descriptions of the world may be more or less adequate in their potential to illuminate experiences and phenomena of the world rather than obscure them. I recommend the use of the term "adequate" to replace the term "valid" when referring to the appraisal of discursively created realities. This is appraised relative to how they enable the cultivation of human potentialities. Ironically and elegantly, the ultimately real can only be experienced by the personal psyche by experiencing its ineffable presence—this has been described as the quality of richness or value—through its expression in the dignity of cultural (relative) forms. Some forms enhance this potential more than others. The embeddedness of ultimate reality—or value—in relative forms is the other reason for saying that the individual who believes that phenomena are not real is a worse fool than the individual who believes that they are (in the naive sense) real. The adequacy of various relative forms for enhancing the human potential to experience reality and cognize value may turn out to be something open to actual investigation.

INTELLECT AND SKILL

The explicit morality generated by the Prajnaparamita teachings[5] was motivated by the intention of liberating sentient beings from suffering, especially extreme forms of suffering. The problem of the personal entity according to this vision was twofold obscuration compounded of (1) primitive beliefs about reality and (2) conflicting desires or conflicting emotions. Primitive beliefs about reality refer to the naive discursive realism of the ordinary person whose problem is taking too literally what was actually something of a masquerade. The Mahayanists were keenly aware of the dramaturgical qualities of social existence. The mistake also included taking for stable and solid what was actually more like a mirage or a dream. Care must be taken at this point to avoid the mistaken inference that this meant that relative reality is superficial and of no account. As already discussed, that is not the case because the individual entity is fully engaged in it and can not be otherwise as long as the individual lives in the world. The error is mistaking the principles of operation that rule phenomena in the realm of relative reality. The problem of conflicting desires is related to the problem of primitive beliefs. Taking as naively real the discursive constructions of the world, one also takes as naively real the discursive constructions of one's own intentionality. This causes illusory and unnecessary mental conflicts and inappropriate (misdirected) desires that lead to actions that fail to fulfill their aims or to aims that are impractical in themselves.

The compassionate goal was to rescue every individual being from imprisonment in repetitive cycles of self-frustrating activity caused by their not realizing what it was that actually motivated them nor what was actually required to cultivate a mind capable of cognizing value and experiencing a joyful existence. The antidote to the obscurations is to cultivate the intellect that sees through the discursive processes. One of the techniques is simply the contemplation of the doctrine of emptiness. The result is the intellectual achievement known as the perfection of wisdom, or transcendent knowledge or the sword of Manjusri. It is also known as "discriminating awareness wisdom." Only when the two obscurations have been overcome and this capacity for moral discernment has been achieved is it possible to possess full moral discretion.

The cultivation of intellect, however, is only one of a pair of interdependent moral techniques. Both are necessary to fulfill moral action. They are said to operate together like the two wings of a bird. When one possesses the realization of how the relative world operates, one must also possess the personal skills to act effectively upon that realization. This, it happens, is a very rigorous undertaking and requires quite a lot of skill indeed. The second unit of the pair is known as

---

[5] It is encoded in many sources, among them Gampopa (1981).

skillful means. In its embryonic form it begins as compassion: the simple intent to liberate others from the bonds of the obscurations and to cultivate oneself as necessary to do so. It is a moral intentionality based upon the realization of the interdependence of one's individual entity with the individual entities of others. The intention in itself, however, is no more than embryonic. It must be followed through with disciplines for the cultivation of skills that enable one to act effectively according to the (moral) requirements of all kinds of situations. These skills traditionally are known as the six paramitas or six perfections: patience, generosity, ethics (cultural competence), exertion, meditation, and wisdom. The sixth is the same as the perfection of wisdom. There is somewhat of a rank order implicit, though training for the six is also simultaneous. When these are achieved, it is said, "skillful means" arise automatically as the ability to follow through on moral discernment and not only know but also perform what is morally appropriate in any situation. The morality of Mahayana is particularist, contextual, and strongly situated in social relations. However, the distinctness of morality in the full sense of Mahayanist compassion from mere "cultural rules" is shown in the fact that "ethics" as competence in cultural rules and mores of the place and time is simply a subsidiary skill for the practice of morality. Only at the point when skillful means arise (as more or less integrated, stable, and complete skills) is one finally able to apply a fully mature moral intelligence to situations in the world. The training was rigorous and intense, even heroic.[6]

I would suggest that this is a vision of morality that makes perfect sense both in contemporary Western society and in the context of a constructivist psychology. I will outline what I see to be its primary features and in particular those features that contrast with the person-rational-agent position inherent in Professor George's essay.

1. Moral freedom is not something that individual entities natively possess, except as potential. They are rather in need of being freed from deluding processes of mind so that they can come to possess an intellect capable of incisive moral discernment.

2. The epitome of moral intellect is expressed as the intellect that is able to see through its own discursive processes and the discursive processes of others, defeat false consciousness, discern situations adequately, and use the discursive powers creatively. It is not rationality in the sense of a criterion of empirical objectivity. It includes nonempirical as well as empirical and nonlogical as well as logical processes (e.g., recall the Buddhist narratives that express liberating knowledge with nonlogical and even illogical forms of argumentation). Rational, nonrational, and irrational thought processes all have a place in the discernment of realities.

---

[6] Much but by no means all of this training occurred in monastic-yogic contexts. There were also nobles and other householders who undertook the training.

3. Moral intention is not sufficient to produce moral action, even in combination with adequate discernment. The cultivation of skills that enable one to follow through on intent is necessary.

4. The idea of liberation from false consciousness and naive discursive realism (moral rationality) is only one-half of the relevant description of freedom or freedom as a moral agent. The other half is the cultivation of the personal skills that actually empower the individual to follow through and to act effectively to intervene in the creation of situations.

5. Moral intellect and moral skill do not develop spontaneously. Training and cultivation are required.

6. Moral capacity as here described is not something that individual entities possess natively merely by virtue of being born a human being with normal capacities. It is natively present only in its embryonic form of an impetus toward compassion and a restlessness or desire to liberate oneself from pointless suffering. It so happens, however, that it takes rather extraordinary skills to accomplish these things so that a fully mature moral capacity requires extensive cultivation and training through the individual's life. Morality could be thought of as a process of cultivation rather than as a quality or possession or inherent ability (except as embryonic) of personal entities. It requires training.

7. Not intellect but emotion or desire is the root impetus or motive to moral action. Intellect and discipline are means to achieve the capacity to fulfill this intention. The impetus provided by desire is twofold. It consists of (a) the desire to rid oneself from suffering and (b) compassion for others. The former becomes discriminating awareness wisdom; the latter becomes skillful means.

Though the discursively created relative reality is a world of illusion, it is also the world in which individual entities live and experience. It contains the only possibilities for contact with self-existing reality that, though independent of our discursive processes, is experienced only as immanent in the relative worlds created by them. If one fails to respect its presence, one will create untenable situations of suffering. At the same time it is necessary to appreciate that the nature of the discursive world is illusion. I hope by now it is realized that this term is not used with a derogatory sense: this philosophy delights especially in the play of illusions, once, that is, they cease to be the sources of suffering because one does not recognize them for what they are. It is not the illusory nature of the relative world that is the problem. It is the attempt to reify or solidify it. If one reifies it too solidly, one will confront its limits as painful experiences because one has applied the wrong expectations by misconstruing the principles of how the world operates.

I hope that the reader will not have minded my importation of an exotic vocabulary into contemporary moral discourse. It is an attempt to create a few additional possibilities for that discourse. I will borrow a justification from Peter Winch (1986):

> What we may learn by studying other cultures are not merely possibilities of different ways of doing things, other techniques. More importantly, we may learn different possibilities of making sense of human life, different ideas about the possible importance that the carrying out of certain activities may take on for a man, trying to make sense of his life as a whole. . . . The concept of learning from what is involved in other cultures is closely linked with the concept of wisdom. We are confronted not just with different techniques but with new possibilities for good and evil, in relation to which men may come to terms with life.

I will close with a traditional supplication to one's lineage: Grant your blessings so that I may realize the inseparability of samsara (illusion) and nirvana (reality).[7]

REFERENCES

D'Andrade, R. G. (1984). Cultural Meaning systems. In R. A. Shweder and R. A. LeVine (Eds.) *Culture Theory: Essays on Mind, Self and Emotion.* New York: Cambridge University Press.

Douglas, M. (1966). *Purity and Danger: An Analysis of Concepts of Pollution and Taboo.* London: Routledge and Kegan-Paul.

Gampopa. (1981). *The Jewel Ornament of Liberation.* H. V. Guenther, Trans. Boulder, Colorado: Prajna Press.

Guenther H. (1963). *The Life and Teaching of Naropa.* Oxford: Oxford University Press.

Kubose, Ven. G. M. (1973). *Zen Koans.* Chicago: Henry Regnery Company.

Kurtines, W. and Gewirtz, J. (1984). Certainty and Morality: Objectivistic versus Relativistic Approaches. In W. Kurtines, and J. Gewirtz, (Eds.) *Morality, Moral Behavior and Moral Development.* New York: Wiley and Sons.

Ogata, S. (1959). *Zen for the West.* Westport Connecticut: Greenwood Press.

Ramanan, K. V. (1966). *Nagarjuna's Philosophy.* New York: Samuel Weiser Inc.

Shweder, R. A. (1991). The Astonishment of Anthropology. In R. A. Shweder, *Thinking Through Cultures: Expeditions in Cultural Psychology.* Cambridge, Massachusetts: Harvard University Press.

Snellgrove, D. (1987). *Indo-Tibetan Buddhism: Indian Buddhists and Their Tibetan Successors.* Vol. 1 and 2. Boston: Shambhala Press.

Winch, P. (1970). Understanding a Primitive Society. In B. R. Wilson (Ed.), *Rationality.* Oxford: Blackwell.

Wong, D. (1984). *Moral Relativity.* Berkeley: University of California Press.

Yamada, K. (1990). *Gateless Gate.* Tucson: University of Arizona Press. Second edition.

---

[7] From verses written by Pengar Jampal Zangpo. Trans. Nalanda Translation Committee, Naropa Institute, Boulder, Colorado.

12 CAN THERE BE A JUST AND MORAL SOCIAL CONSTRUCTIONIST PSYCHOLOGY?

George S. Howard

I take the answer to my title's question to be "yes." But rather than making a general argument designed to apply to several forms of social constructionist theory, I will first sketch one form of constructionist theory with which I have wrestled of late. Then I will delineate the sense in which this form of constructionism might be seen as being locally moral and just. In so doing, I hope to highlight the sense in which the morality and justice contained in any constructionist system is with respect to that system's internal criteria of reasonableness, and thus might not suggest any universalizable criteria for justice and morality. But issues such as morality are moot (in my opinion) unless humans possess some power of self-determination in their actions—that there exists some degree of freedom of the will.

IN WHAT SENSE ARE HUMANS FREE?

The specter against which I have struggled for the past decade is the possibility of complete mechanistic (i.e., nonagentic) determination of human action. Sources of coercion in human action can be thought of as emanating from biological (genetic or physiological), psychological, environmental, social, and cultural factors. My central concern lies with the question of whether any room remains for concepts such as self-determination, free will, and true agency, once the influence of the numerous nonagentic causal influences upon human action have been considered. That is, if a Laplacean-type omniscent calculator (possessing complete knowledge and infinite power of calculation) was able to precisely predict all human actions based upon nonagentic influences, then there would be good grounds for believing that there is no room for genuine self-determination in human action.

There have been many different construals of free will (van Inwagen, 1983) over the last two and a half millennia. Some of these construals (e.g., free will results from the absence of any physical constraint upon the agent) clearly do not square with the arguments and research to be summarized herein. However, whenever an agent makes a choice (and then acts for the sake of that choice) one might see it as a free choice (and act) if indeed the agent might have chosen to do otherwise *ceteris paribus* (i.e., all other things being equal). The notion of free will entertained herein is seen in Robert Frost's poem "The Road Not Taken":

> Two roads diverged in a wood, and I—I took the one less traveled by,
> And that has made all the difference.

If Frost's traveler had also been able to choose "the road more traveled by" but instead opted for "the road less traveled by," one might assert that he/she had made a free choice. But since the time of Heraclitus (with his point that one can never step in the same river twice), we have recognized the virtual impossibility of meeting the demands of the *ceteris paribus* condition in such cases. Fortunately, new experimental methodologies now allow us to test the causal force of free choice in human action in a manner that fully meets the requirements of the *ceteris paribus* assumption (see Howard and Myers, 1989).

One of the benefits of weathering peer scrutiny in science is that it allows one to make remarkable claims while only citing the arguments and evidence that fully justify those claims. In a series of studies (Howard, 1988; Howard, DiGangi, and Johnson, 1988; Howard and Conway, 1986, 1987; Howard, Curtin, and Johnson, 1991; Howard and Myers, 1989, 1990; Howard, Myers, and Curtin, 1991; Howard, Youngs, and Siatczynski, 1989; Lazarick, Fishbein, Loiello, and Howard, 1988), my colleagues and I were able to demonstrate the causal force of self-determination in human action in a wide array of domains. The remarkable aspect of this line of research is that one can precisely quantify the proportion of variance in human action unequivocally attributable to self-determination (or freedom of the will). The word *unequivocally* here refers to the fact that in making these quantitative estimates, the influence of all possible nonagentic (e.g., biological, environmental, intrapsychic) factors in the genesis of this action has been completely eliminated via methodological control procedures. Again, space constraints preclude a thorough explication of the logic and data that justify the claim for the importance of self-determination in the genesis of everyday human action. But to say that self-determination is an important causal element is *not* to say that humans are free to act in any manner they so desire. Rather, the studies cited demonstrate instances of the entire range of volitional control from complete (100%) to null (0%) variance attributable to self-determination.

HOW IS THE CAPACITY TO SELF-DETERMINE ACHIEVED?

Because we are human beings, all of us have extensive first-hand knowledge of how it is that we are sometimes able to control our actions, while at other times we seem to be incapable of acting in ways that we desire. One might expect that research designed to highlight the factors related to subjects' ability to demonstrate increased amounts of self-determination in their action would confirm the findings suggested in our everyday experience. This turns out to be exactly the case. Once an agent decides to demonstrate his/her ability to self-determine his/her actions in some domain (i.e., decides to take part in a particular study), then aids to his/her continued attention to the task (e.g., reminders) and incentives made contingent upon successful performance (e.g., bribes based upon successfully completing tasks) do reliably augment subjects' ability to provide evidence of self-determination. While it might lead to philosophical conundrums, factors that are often seen as material and efficient causes of human behavior actually represent conditions that enable agents to be more (or less) successful in achieving their self-determined goals. This is but another way of demonstrating that an agent's actions are not performed in a vacuum. Rather, our agency is nested within a world of nonagentic causal influences, and thus bounded by the particulars of those circumstances. In order to consider the morality of any action, one must have tempered his/her evaluation of the act by consideration of the circumstances under which the agent toiled at the time of the action.

In addition to nonagentic influences that impact our lives and actions, we are also the beneficiaries (and sometimes the victims) of our own life-narratives. There is a sense in which each of us is both the protagonist *and* the author of our own life-story. Rather than seeing the meaning of our life-stories as a given, social constructionist thought entreats us to see the meaning of agents' lives and actions as negotiated constructions—interpretations of a flow of events and action that could just as well have been seen as representing or signifying something quite different than the chosen meaning. Among the cast of negotiators in this process, the person whose life is under consideration and the dominant beliefs of his/her culture represent important voices. Long ago Harré taught me that agency was (in part) a belief that endowed the believer with certain powers that he/she might not possess under a different set of beliefs. And so I looked for experimental evidence of self-determination in human action at Notre Dame— that bastion of Catholicism, rugged individualism, and midwestern self-reliance. Happily the evidence for self-determination in South Bend was strong—for if one could not find any evidence of free will there, it might not exist anywhere! And if I had been unable to demonstrate the power of free will, the specter of complete nonagentic determination in human action might have grown even more ominous for me. Such are the risks one takes when he/she subjects his/her beliefs to the scrutiny of fair empirical tests.

Of course, we have witnessed only the beginning of research in this domain. It remains for researchers to specify exactly how it is that human self-determination achieves its effects in a world of nonagentic, coercive mechanisms. Science always strives for a deeper, richer understanding of powers (or capacities, or generative mechanisms) that underlie observed experimental relationships. Watkins (1984) notes that "our supreme demand is that our science will penetrate deeper and deeper until eventually it achieves ultimate explanations of all phenomenon" (p. 128). Recall, for example, that since the time of Gregor Mendel scientists could specify the relationships between certain characteristics (e.g., eye color, height) of parents and the likelihood that their offspring would exhibit those characteristics. But it was only in the last thirty years that the mechanisms responsible for the transmission of hereditary traits became clearly understood by scientists. Similarly, demonstrating that humans can (to some extent) self-determine their actions represents an important experimental demonstration. But these demonstrations do not (in and of themselves) shed light on the particular mechanisms that enable humans to exhibit this remarkable power to self-determine. What are the mechanisms—analogous to the sequence of purine and pyrimidine bases occupying specific locations on the DNA molecule that transmit genetic traits from parents to offspring—that are responsible for the human capacity to self-determine?

My colleagues and I believed that the meaningfulness of an action should be related to an agent's ability to self-determine actions in that domain. But it was initially unclear exactly how one could demonstrate that an agent achieved the power to self-determine actions in a domain as a result of the meaningfulness of the action.

If you would, imagine that you are a research subject in a study designed to test your ability to demonstrate fine-grained control over the number of alcoholic drinks you consume each day. The experimenter explains that you would demonstrate control by trying to hit a "target" number of alcoholic drinks each day. The sequence of targets over 24 days was 1, 2, 1, 0, 1, 1, 1, 0, 1, 0, 1, 0, 0, 1, 2, 2, 0, 1, 1, 0, 2, 0, 2, 0. What percentage of days do you believe you would be able to hit the exact target value? If you hit each of the 24 targets exactly, that might suggest excellent fine-grained control on your part. Conversely, if you tried to hit the targets but were always unable to do so, that would suggest that you lacked the ability to control your consumption of alcohol. In one study on University employees (Howard, Curtin, and Johnson, 1991), subjects hit targets about 47% of the time. Do you believe you would have had a better or worse hit rate?

But, I'm afraid I described the study only as it would appear to control group subjects. For another group of subjects the task was made *more meaningful*. These subjects were told that the random-appearing sequence of targets had really been determined in a precise manner. The sequence of daily drink targets of 0, 1, and 2 spell out a message in Morse Code. Imagine that a target of two drinks represents a "dash," a one drink target depicts a "dot," a single 0 drink target represents a space between letters, and finally two consecutive 0 drink targets signals a break between words. Thus, the message contained in the sequence of intervention phase targets reads "FREE WILL." Subjects were told that if they "hit" every target, they would have demonstrated complete power of self-determination of alcohol consumption in this study.

Thus, two groups of subjects attempted to "hit" the exact same sequence of daily drink targets. Presumably, the task was more meaningful for the Morse code group subjects. It is rather surprising that the amount of self-determination evidenced by subjects in this more meaningful condition was about twice as large as that exhibited by their control group counterparts.

An immediate replication and conceptual extension of this finding was undertaken. Sixty subjects (29 male, 31 female) were grouped in triads and one subject from each triad was randomly selected to be in the Involvement/Meaning (IM) group. These subjects were told that the sequence of targets would spell out the word or short phrase of his/her choice in Morse Code. Each IM group subject selected his/her own word or phrase, then converted it into Morse Code, and filled in their sequence of daily targets on his/her data sheet. The second member of that triad (again randomly chosen) received the sequence of targets chosen by the IM group member of the triad, and was shown that it rendered a meaningful message in Morse Code (thus, this group is referred to as a meaning-only (MO) group). The final member of each triad was simply given the sequence of targets and urged to hit as many targets as possible to establish their fine-grained control of behavior (FC group). Intervention time ranged from 14 days (required to spell out LOVE) to 26 days (required to spell out SUCCESS).

Thus, three groups of subjects who were initially equivalent in all respects (motivation, intelligence, etc.) were asked to hit the exact same sequence of target drinks (due to the matching procedure). These groups only differed in the meaning that their task possessed for group subjects. Subjects in all three groups exhibited a significant ability to pattern their consumption of liquids in response to the prescribed targets, but there were important differences among the three groups in their ability to precisely hit their sequence of targets. Control group (FC) subjects exhibited about a 61% ability to self-determine their rate of liquid consumption. (More precisely, they demonstrated a 61% decline from baseline to intervention phase variability attributable to the targets.) A much greater degree of self-determination (84%) was shown by subjects in the more meaningful MO group. Finally, subjects in the most meaningful (IM) condition were able to self-determine their drinking to an astonishing degree (95%). And so we have again experimentally linked the meaningfulness of actions to subjects' ability to self-determine in that domain. But before pursuing that story further, a brief explanation of why these findings are so astonishing needs to be given.

ON THE EMPIRICAL (IN) ADEQUACY OF PSYCHOLOGICAL THEORIES: INFERENTIAL STATISTICS AND POINT ESTIMATION

One sure sign, we are told, that psychology is still at a formative stage of development as a science is our inability to precisely predict and/or control human behavior in real-world settings. Our failures in this regard are so obvious that we have often given up this ambition in our empirical efforts. The concession of defeat in the prediction and control domain can perhaps be seen in the widespread acceptance of inferential statistics in psychological research rather than point estimation approaches or proportion of variance accounted for (PV) approaches more commonly seen in the "harder" sciences. Authors sometimes contrast the use of inferential statistics in psychology with proportion of variance accounted for approaches, model fitting, or point estimation techniques. While there are differences among these latter three groups of techniques, they are considered herein as a generic type of statistical analysis, and contrasted with the array of inferential statistics (where the goal is simply to eliminate chance as the sole cause of an observed relationship) typically reported in the psychology research literature. Obviously, some inferential statistics can easily be converted to PV indices (e.g., omega square, partial eta square, r^2), so the barrier between these generic types of analysis is somewhat permeable. Many PV and model fitting research techniques are already known to psychologists.

Using strength of relationship measures would be advantageous in psychological research. They are easily understood because, unlike inferential statistics, they correspond to how we naturally think about relationships among events, and magnitudes of association. However, use of strength of relationship measures in psychological research brings home the reality of our failure to achieve prediction in nonlaboratory settings comparable to our colleagues in other sciences.

> The only difficulty arising from the use of PV measures lies in the fact that in many, perhaps most, of the areas of behavioral science, they turn out to be so small! For example, workers in personality-social psychology, both pure and applied (i.e., clinical, education, personnel), normally encounter correlation coefficients above the .50–.60 range only when the correlations are measurement reliability coefficients. In PV terms, this *effective upper limit implies something of the order of one-quarter or one-third of variance accounted for*. The fact is that the state of development of much of behavioral science is such that not very much variance in the dependent variable is predictable. This is essentially merely another way of stating the obvious: that the behavioral sciences collectively are not as far advanced as the physical sciences. (Cohen, 1977, p. 78; emphasis added)

Nunnally (1960) suggested that our infatuation with inferential statistics represents a natural outgrowth of our inability to achieve predictive accuracy in human behavior. "It is hard to find principles of human behavior. Consequently, psychological research is often difficult and frustrating, and the frustration can lead to a 'flight into statistics' " (p. 649). Meehl (1978) makes a similar point in noting that psychologists are bogged down in tests of statistical significance, whereas their colleagues in the physical sciences are engaged in the more rigorous endeavors of model fitting and point estimation.

> Nothing is as stuffy and pretentious as the verbal "pseudorigor" of the soft branches of social sciences. In my modern physics text, I am unable to find one single test of statistical significance. What happens instead is that the physicist has a sufficiently powerful invisible hand theory that enables him to generate an expected curve for his experimental results. He plots the observed points, looks at the agreement, and comments that "the results are in reasonably good accord with theory." Moral: *It is always more valuable to show approximate agreement of observations with a theoretically predicted numerical point value, rank order, or function form, than it is to compute a "precise probability" that something merely differs from something else.* (Meehl, 1978, p. 825)

The real culprit is not inferential statistics per se, but rather the predictively weak theories that psychologists have thus far been able to produce (see Meehl, 1978, 1990).

> Naturally, theories differ in how well they achieve the desiderata of good theories regarding predictions—that is, they differ in how easily empirical predictions can be derived and in the range and specificity of these predictions. Unfortunately, psychological theories, particularly in recent years, tend to be very restricted in scope. And, unlike physics, the predictions that psychological theories do make are typically of a nonspecific form ("the groups will differ") rather than being point predictions ("the light rays will bend by x degrees as they go past the sun"). (Maxwell and Delaney, 1990, p. 16)

Thus, while Meehl (1978, 1990) suggests that our empirical efforts might be improved if we turned to point estimation, Cohen (1977) implies that to do so would highlight the current dilemma in psychology—that our current psychological theories and experimental methodologies are inadequate to predict more than a small fraction of human behavior. As long as psychologists' efforts to employ point estimation techniques serve to dramatize the predictive poverty of many current theories, these individuals are unlikely to adopt point estimation approaches in spite of their relative scientific superiority.

NEW GOALS FOR A SCIENCE OF SELF-DETERMINED ACTION

This impasse, however, may be resolved more readily than it first appears. As will be demonstrated, the problem, in part, results from an overly narrow view of both human functioning and the nature of prediction in a social science. The present section of this chapter will argue that Cohen's effective upper limit of prediction in real-world settings, which appears to be "something of the order of one-quarter or one-third of variance accounted for," is disappointingly small *only if one assumes* that a mature science of human behavior should allow for prediction (*by the scientist*) of 100% of the variance in human action. Why would anyone make such an assumption? Because that is precisely the goal that the physical sciences (almost) actually achieve in many of their empirical efforts. Then why should a psychological theoretician/researcher settle for anything less than that lofty ambition? Because there is good reason to believe that human beings are active agents with some degree of ability to self-determine their actions. To the extent that humans possess the power of self-determination, scientists will only predict a fraction (roughly, $1.0 - PV$ due to self-determination) of human behavior as an ultimate scientific ambition. Thus, Cohen's (1977) effective upper limit of prediction of 25 to 33% would not be at all disappointing if the circumstance was, for example, that self-determination accounted for say 60% of the variance in a particular domain of human action.

Unfortunately, until quite recently, all sciences assumed that the possibility of self-determined action lay outside of the realm of scientific analysis. Berger (1963) put it quite eloquently, describing the sense of freedom one would have if humans were truly self-determining active agents.

> Freedom is not empirically available. More precisely, while freedom may be experienced by us as a certainty along with other empirical certainties, it is not open to demonstration by any scientific methods. . . . Every object of scientific scrutiny is presumed to have an anterior cause. An object, or an event, that *is* its own cause lies outside the scientific universe of discourse. Yet freedom has precisely this character. . . . The individual who is conscious of his own freedom does not stand outside the world of causality, but rather perceives his own volition as a very special category of cause, different from the other causes that he must reckon with. This difference, however, is not subject to scientific demonstration. . . . There is no way of perceiving freedom, either in oneself or in another being, except through a subjective inner certainty that dissolves as soon as it is attacked with the tools of scientific analysis. (pp. 122–124)

Berger's claim, that science could not furnish empirical documentation of human freedom, was originally factually correct. However, methodological refinements in psychological research now make possible the very demonstrations Berger claimed to be impossible. That is, we are now able to provide scientific evidence of self-determination or behavioral freedom in human actions.

Do active agent theories allow for greater predictive accuracy in human action than standard nonagentic psychological theories? Consider that in a hypothetical study, 70% of the within-subject variance in a particular domain (e.g., peanut eating) might be attributable to agentic self-determination when the influence of all other nonagentic causes of the behavior are systematically, methodologically controlled (cf. Howard and Conway, 1986). If we were then able to predict another (let us say) 20% of the variance via nonagentic factors (e.g., levels of hunger, environmental factors, etc.), we would have an instance of impressive prediction of 90% of the variability in human behavior. The missing 10% of variability could be attributed to unidentified nonagentic factors, errors in measurement, and random disturbances (random error) involved in the study. In this scenario, psychologists would approach the levels of prediction in human action heretofore seen only in the more mature sciences. But doing so implies measuring and taking seriously that portion of human action due to self-determination, rather than having it simply swell the error terms of our statistical analyses, as has been the case heretofore.

STORIES, STORIES EVERYWHERE—BUT NOT A TRUTH TO THINK

If, as demonstrated earlier, an agent's ability to self-determine his/her actions in a domain is (in part) a result of the meaningfulness of that action for the agent, then one might wonder, "Where does meaningfulness come from?" An answer to this question might be found in the recent explosion of literature in the domain of narrative (or story-telling) psychology (Bruner, 1986; Howard, 1989, 1991; Mair, 1988; McAdams, 1985; Polkinghorne, 1988; Sarbin, 1986; Spence, 1982). For narrative psychologists, thinking often represents instances of meaning construction via story-telling. I am a bit more radical than most narrative psychologists in that I hold that all thinking represents instances of meaning construction via story-telling (Howard, 1991). For example, the meaning of the current war in the Persian Gulf (and all actions associated with it) are quite different if you see it as the latest round in a long struggle by the Arab world against Western domination (Saddam Hussein's story) rather than as a test-case of whether naked aggression against a weak, peace-loving state (Kuwait) will be tolerated in a post-Cold War world (George Bush's story). Bush and Hussein tell radically different stories, but both of their tales are of the same sort—historical/political analysis—and both stories "fit" the facts of the matter reasonably well. But the implications of "seeing" the issues from one perspective rather than another are enormous. This is the point at which the perspective being offered in this paper most clearly makes contact with recent constructionist thought. Whatever "truth" or "reality" or "facts" we come to hold are not simply "out there" to be discovered, but rather are constructed by the interpretive template (or story) that we choose to tell about them. While Bush and Hussein both tell (quite different) stories of the same historical/political genre, sometimes competing stories are of radically different genres—as one might argue that this has been the heart of the creationist versus evolution debate. One genre of story might see *The Bible* as "the Good Book"; whereas from a different story genre, Darwin's (1859) *The*

Origin of Species might seem like a very good book. Both stories might be true (i.e., might actually have occurred), and the relative validity of the two stories depends on the perceived plausibility of the two interpretive frames (science and religion) to each listener. Cronbach (1982) has instructed us that "validity is subjective rather than objective" (p. 102). It is an argument's (or a study's) plausibility that counts—and plausibility (as his modified cliché suggests) "lies in the ear of the beholder" (p. 102).

Narrativists claim that the dominant cognitive capacity shared by all human beings is meaning-construction via story-telling. This predisposition can be seen when children at a very early age are intrigued by stories told to them by parents, in children's books, through television cartoons, and the like. In fact, one might argue that the ideal of a liberal education is found in a person who is able to apply an array of types of stories (scientific, political, religious, economic, etc.) to a problem. One source of our freedom arises, I believe, from our ability to envision problems from different story-perspectives. Our possibilities for alternative thoughts and actions change dramatically when a problem is seen against the template of one story, and then from another completely different perspective. But whereas education urges people to entertain a plurality of perspectives in understanding and dealing with problems, developing a plurality of storied voices is not considered an appropriate strategy for all tasks. For example, McAdams (1985) sees the formation of identity as a process where "We make our existence into a whole by understanding it as an expression of a single and developing story" (p. 150). And the type identity stories favored in Western societies frequently see persons as self-contained individuals (cf. Geertz, 1979; Sampson, 1977; Shotter and Gergen, 1989). But this tendency to see ourselves in this manner does *not,* constructionists argue, tell us anything fundamental about human nature. Rather, the phenomenon of Western individualism tells us more about the stories of identity that are currently held to be "true" of human nature in Western cultures. The situation tells us more about how we have chosen to construct human nature, as we depict it in the dominant stories of our culture, than it does about the way human nature *must be.* One must be vigilant to never mistake what *is* for what *must be,* when studying *Homo fabulans* (Man the storyteller). Thus, investigations of the personalities of Westerners might be seen as revealing a good deal about the dominant stories of our culture. This view, of people being lived by stories, was made nicely by Mair (1988):

> Stories are habitations. We live in and through stories. They conjure worlds. We do not know the world other than as story world. Stories inform life. They hold us together and keep us apart. We inhabit the great stories of our culture. We live through stories. We are lived by the stories of our race and place. It is this enveloping and constituting function of stories that is especially important to sense more fully. We are, each of us, locations where the stories of our place and time become partially tellable. (p. 127)

Thus, there are stories everywhere. Stories are all about us, like the air. But no story or stories tell the "Truth" about human nature, the world, reality, the good life, human history, and so forth. Each story attempts to tell a truth from its perspective. It is problematic to claim that one perspective is "truer" than another—they are simply different, and thus noncomparable.

WHAT IS THE PLACE OF CONCEPTS LIKE JUSTICE AND MORALITY IN A WORLD OF STORIES?

One of the most important immediate benefits of social constructionist thought has been the warranting of voices and stories of previously disenfranchised minority groups such as gays, women, and ethnic or racial minority group members (e.g., K. J. Gergen, 1989; M. M. Gergen, 1991; Kitzinger, 1989). As oppressed groups tell tales of their experience as minority perspectives within a dominant culture, one often sees the ways such individuals have been victimized—one can see the manner in which they have been treated unjustly. And every genuinely caring person would want to see such unfairness cease. But the fact of prior victimization does not imply that "anything goes" for victimized individuals or groups—they are not completely free to reinterpret and remake society into the ideal image that individuals from their perspective might desire. But they do have the right (at least in so-called "free societies") to attempt to alter society to correct the more obvious instances of injustice. But the problem is that action that looks just and moral from one perspective can be seen as an abomination when viewed from a different storied perspective. (Recall the Hussein versus Bush tales of what is now occurring in the Persian Gulf.) One can always tell a story that will seem to justify any action an agent desires (here I refer to what is clearly a case of self-serving rationalization). Does this mean that narrative psychologists are doomed to a vicious relativism in evaluating the appropriateness of human actions? I hope not.

The grounds for assessing the appropriateness (or morality) of an agent's action that I would like to suggest are a refinement of the Western judicial notion of a trial by a jury of one's peers. All of us at the Georgetown conference are fairly well acquainted with mainstream notions of science, the logic and procedures of Western psychology, and contemporary constructionist views. In a certain sense we represent a jury of peers for one another. A negative decision by the overwhelming majority of this group on any part of our papers should give any one of us real reason to doubt the wisdom of the position we adopted and/or the moves we made in the story elaborated in our paper. Of course, we still have the right to maintain our beliefs in the face of negative evaluations—and, in fact, great scientific developments might be saved by that strategy—but such criticism by like-minded peers usually points toward faulty or strained reasoning and beliefs. Analogously, if George Bush couldn't have gotten strong agreement to go to war in the Persian Gulf from the leaders of the industrialized nations, he would have had good grounds for doubting the morality (to say nothing of the wisdom) of his decision to go to war. Similarly, if Sadaam Hussein was unable to get approval from the other Arab leaders of the world for his stance, he likewise would have had good grounds for self-doubt.

Of course, a positive evaluation from a like-minded peer jury is a bit more difficult to interpret. Sharing our worldview (and perhaps our interests also), their sympathetic evaluation may represent too lenient a moral hurdle to pass. Finally, a jury can be "stacked" to virtually assure a positive judgment. As examples, the morality of Hitler's actions should not be judged by a jury of Nazi party regulars: nor would we want to limit Michael Milliken's peer group to only Drexell, Burnham, Lambert investment bankers. An agent's peers should be able to easily understand the storied perspective from which the agent operates. But peers must possess sufficient perspective to be able to find fault with excesses of the per-spective itself and/or to criticize an agent's actions performed under the guidance of that storied perspective.

But, you will argue, this is not a blueprint for a constructionist ethics—it more resembles a hopeful wish that constructionist metatheory does not preclude considerations of morality and justice. You are quite right in finding the present argument incomplete and unsatisfying. My hope for constructionist morality and justice lies in the fact that while one's choice, of an interpretive frame from which to view the world, is clearly underdetermined, once the choice has been made, a determination of moral and immoral actions (or just versus unjust treatment of agents) can be made based upon the internal standards of that perspective.

For example, I understand a good deal of my life within the stories of science and Western democratic traditions. Once having committed myself to those traditions, I am inundated with a plethora of nonarbitrary (at least within those traditions) criteria against which my behavior should be measured. More than criteria, MacIntyre (1981) argues that traditions prescribe certain practices, and virtue is seen in an agent's fidelity to the spirit contained in those practices. Serious failure to act virtuously with respect to those storied traditions implies some degree of responsibility and blame. The fact that I believe that there is no ultimate justification for science and Western democracy does not in any way imply that I should not be censured for violating the canons of those traditions. I have been indoctrinated by stories that describe scientific behaviors that are unethical: and I recognize treason when I see it. I am as responsible for violations of those codes as is any other denizen of those traditions. But I have no desire to subject all humans into my belief systems, since I understand in advance that there is no "best" or "assumption free" perspective.

Having endorsed an extremely tolerant, pluralistic view, I should note that it is quite possible for stories to go completely mad. Hitler and Naziism represent obvious choices for condemnation. With rare exceptions, by the beginning of World War II, Hitler and Naziism were seen as pariahs by the world community. Condemnation was expressed, not only because Hitler represented a threat to many nations, but also because Nazi treatment of racial groups (such as Jews) and sovereign states (such as Poland and Czechoslovakia) violated quasi-universal ethical principles (such as Kant's Categorical Imperative: Roughly, to act in such a way toward others that if the positions were switched . . .). Thus, there are some grounds for hope that perspectives themselves might be subject to some form of nonarbitrary scrutiny, with principles of negotiation and arbitration by neutral third parties holding some promise. But the possibility of adjudicating disagreements between discrepant perspectives seems fraught with difficulties, as power considerations seem to always intervene.

I should emphasize that I see these arguments, that constructionist thought might not force us to lose all sense of ethics and justice in the evaluation of our actions, as rather weak arguments. Perhaps they represent no more than my hope that constructionist thought will not inevitably lead us to a state of vicious relativism. But at least in my case, I feel I have freely chosen to see the world from at least two storied perspectives—science and Western democracy (the benefits of education exposed me to several alternative worldviews that I might have chosen to see as fundamental to my life instead). Both of my favored traditions provide standards for appropriate action that seem reasonable within their separate worldviews. I feel that I should be bound by the duties and obligations inherent in those systems. Do not other responsible worldviews possess different (but reasonable nonetheless) internal standards against which agents' actions might be measured?

Even though I am not an ethicist or a legal scholar, I can foresee numerous difficulties that would need to be overcome before most constructionists would be comfortable in endorsing any set of legal or ethical principles. But to say that we cannot know Truth absolutely does not, I believe, imply that we cannot establish minimal standards for responsible conduct (and discriminations of the relative merit of various courses of action) *within* each constructed worldview or tradition. Might not these seeds of value discrimination among practices within perspectives serve as the first impulses toward constructionist worldviews about which determinations of justice and morality can be offered?

REFERENCES

Berger, P. (1963). *Invitation to sociology: A humanistic perspective*. New York: Doubleday.
Bruner, J. (1986). *Actual minds, possible worlds*. Cambridge, MA: Harvard University Press.
Cohen, J. (1977). *Statistical power analysis for the behavioral sciences*. New York: Academic Press.

Cronbach, L. J. (1982). *Designing evaluations of educational and social programs.* San Francisco: Jossey-Bass.

Darwin, C. (1975). *The origin of species.* New York: W. W. Norton. [Originally published in 1859.]

Geertz, C. (1979). From the native's point of view: On the nature of anthropological understanding. In P. Rabinow and W. M. Sullivan (Eds.), *Interpretive social science,* pp. 24–41. Berkeley: University of California Press.

Gergen, K. J. (1989). Warranting voice and the elaboration. In J. Shotter and K. J. Gergen (Eds.), *Texts of identity.* London: Sage.

Gergen, M. M. (1991). Finished at 40: Women's development within the patriarchy. *Psychology of Women Quarterly, 14,* 471–493.

Howard, G. S. (1988). Science, values, and teleological explanations of human action. *Counseling and Values, 32,* 93–103.

Howard, G. S. (1989). *A tale of two stories: Excursions into a narrative approach to psychology.* Notre Dame, IN: Academic Publications.

Howard, G. S. (1991). Culture tales: A narrative approach to thinking, cross cultural psychology, and psychotherapy. *American Psychologist, 46,* 187–197.

Howard, G. S., and Conway, C. G. (1986). Can there be an empirical science of volitional action? *American Psychologist, 41,* 1241–1251.

Howard, G. S., and Conway, C. G. (1987). The next steps toward a science of agency. *American Psychologist, 42,* 1034–1036.

Howard, G. S., Curtin, T. D., and Johnson, A. J. (1991). Studies of the role of meaning in self-determined action. Using point estimation techniques in psychological research. *Journal of Counseling Psychology, 38,* 219–226.

Howard, G. S., DiGangi, M. L., and Johnson, A. (1988). Life, science, and the role of therapy in the pursuit of happiness. *Professional Psychology: Research and Practice, 19,* 191–198.

Howard, G. S., and Myers, P. R. (1989). Some experimental investigations of volition. In W. A. Hershberger (Ed.), *Volitional action,* pp. 335–352. Amsterdam: North-Holland.

Howard, G. S., and Myers, P. R. (1990). Predicting human behavior: Comparing idiographic, nomothetic, and agentic methodologies. *Journal of Counseling Psychology, 37,* 227–233.

Howard, G. S., Myers, P. R., and Curtin, T. D. (1991). Can science furnish evidence of human freedom? Self-determination versus conformity in human action. *International Journal of Personal Construct Psychology, 4,* 371–395.

Howard, G. S., Youngs, W. H., and Siatczynski, A. M. (1989). A research strategy for studying telic human behavior. *Journal of Mind and Behavior, 10,* 393–412.

Kitzinger, C. (1989). The regulation of lesbian identities: Liberal humanism as an ideology of social control. In J. Shotter and K. J. Gergen (Eds.), *Texts of identity.* London: Sage.

Lazarick, D. L., Fishbein, S. S., Loiello, M. J., and Howard, G. S. (1988). Practical investigations of volition. *Journal of Counseling Psychology, 35,* 15–26.

MacIntyre, A. (1981). *After virtue.* Notre Dame, IN: University of Notre Dame Press.

Mair, M. (1988). Psychology as storytelling. *International Journal of Personal Construct Psychology, 1,* 125–138.

Maxwell, S. E., and Delaney, H. D. (1990). *Designing experiments and analyzing data: A model comparison approach.* Belmont, CA: Wadsworth.

McAdams, D. (1985). *Power, intimacy, and life story.* Homewood, IL: Dorsey Press.

Meehl, P. E. (1978). Theoretical risks and tabular asterisks: Sir Karl, Sir Ronald, and the slow progress of soft psychology. *Journal of Consulting and Clinical Psychology, 46,* 806–834.

Meehl, P. E. (1990). Appraising and amending theories: The strategy of Lakatosian defense and two principles that warrant using it. *Psychological Inquiry, 1,* 108–141.

Nunnally, J. (1960). The place of statistics in psychology. *Educational and Psychological Measurement, 20,* 641–650.

Polkinghorne, D. P. (1988). *Narrative psychology.* Albany, NY: SUNY Press.

Sampson, E. E. (1977). Psychology and the American ideal. *Journal of Personality and Social Psychology, 35,* 767–782.

Sarbin, T. R. (Ed.). (1986). *Narrative psychology: The storied nature of human conduct.* New York: Praeger.

Shotter, J., and Gergen, K. J. (Eds.). (1989). *Texts of identity.* London: Sage.

Spence, D. P. (1982). *Narrative truth and historical truth: Meaning and interpretation in psychoanalysis.* New York: Norton.

van Inwagen, P. (1983). *An essay on free will.* New York: Oxford University Press.

Watkins, J. (1984). *Science and skepticism.* Princeton, NJ: Princeton University Press.

13 THERE CAN BE A JUST AND MORAL SOCIAL CONSTRUCTIONIST PSYCHOLOGY, BUT ONLY IN A SOCIAL WORLD THAT IS HOMOGENEOUS AND/OR STATIC

Fathali M. Moghaddam

OVERVIEW

George Howard, in Chapter 12 of this volume, proposes that a just and moral social constructionist psychology is possible when judgments of justice and morality are made with reference to a system's internal criteria. But he neglects to convey what is a just and moral psychology. I begin by suggesting that a just and moral psychology may involve, first, establishing criteria for just and moral behavior; second, identifying what people believe to be just and moral behavior; and, third, identifying the conditions in which just and moral behavior is more likely to occur. On this basis, I argue that social constructionist psychology can be just and moral in conditions where cultural homogeneity exists and/or where the social structure is static and groups do not interact. Possibilities for the achievement of these conditions are examined and I conclude that such conditions are not at all likely to be met. Consequently, a just and moral social constructionist psychology seems not to be possible. Howard seems to implicitly accept this conclusion when he makes claims, by reference to some non-relativistic ideas of just and moral behavior, that he expects us to accept about the mistreatment of gays and other minorities. Finally, universals seem to be implicit in attempts to arrive at one common answer for all societies to the question, "Can there be a just and moral social constructionist psychology?"

Perhaps it is the fate of all challengers to be expected to succeed where the current champions have failed. Social constructionism is a notable challenger to positivistic approaches to psychology. As such, social constructionism is being asked to meet the requirements of a "just and moral" psychology—a task that has been consciously sidestepped by positivistic-oriented psychologies.

But it is not only "mainstreamers" who sidestep complex challenges in this realm. In the preceding chapter George Howard presents various intriguing arguments to explain how his

> hope for constructionist morality and justice lies in the fact that while one's choice, of an interpretive frame to view the world, is clearly underdetermined, once the choice has been made, a determination of moral and immoral actions (or just versus unjust treatment of agents) can be made based upon the internal standards of that perspective.

Nowhere in his elaborations, however, does Howard explain what exactly *constitutes* a just and moral psychology. The meaning of this pivotal idea is left for readers to construct and deconstruct as their hearts desire. This opens the door for all kinds of "audience improvisations," so that our impressions of what Howard means may come and go, rather like characters in a "neo-dada" play presenting us with different versions of an evasive plot.

But a reply to Howard's essay cannot afford the luxury of neglecting the question of what exactly constitutes a moral and just psychology. Consequently, it is with this thorny issue that we begin our discussion, before turning to the central question of the ways in which a social constructionist psychology may meet the requirements for a just and moral psychology.

In brief, my conclusion will be that social constructionism can, indeed, achieve a "just and moral" psychology, but not in a culturally diverse world of interacting and transforming social groups. It is only in a social world that is culturally homogeneous and/or has static social groups that a "just and moral" social constructionist psychology can be achieved.

WHAT CONSTITUTES A JUST AND MORAL PSYCHOLOGY?

There are at least three ways in which a psychology can be "just and moral."

Establishing the criteria   First, by establishing the criteria for "just and moral" behavior. For example, what system of reward allocation is "just and moral" when individuals are distributing resources to members of their own and other groups? Such general questions of inquiry lead to many more specific issues. For example, should reward allocation take place on the basis of individual merits only? Should the group membership of people be taken into account? Such questions are viewed by positivistic researchers as falling outside the realm of science, and being fit for ethicists and other "nonscientific" scholars.

Establishing the conditions   Second, a psychology may be just and moral when it establishes the conditions in which just and moral behavior can be achieved. For example, researchers have examined the extent to which individuals follow "just and moral" procedures under different conditions when allocating rewards to ingroup and outgroup members (Taylor and Moghaddam, 1987). The simple event of social categorization, involving the placement of individuals in group "X" rather than in group "Y," has been found to be associated with consistent bias in favor of the ingroup (Tajfel, 1978). The concern of scientific research has been simply to demonstrate that such bias exists, rather than to evaluate this bias according to criteria of justice and morality.

Appropriate consequences   A third way in which a psychology can be just and moral is when the fruits of this enterprise have "just and moral" consequences. For example, researchers have attempted to identify social psychological processes associated with intergroup discrimination (Moghaddam and Stringer, 1986; Wright, Taylor, and Moghaddam, 1990). Through highlighting processes associated with discrimination, researchers may help eliminate such "problems," and in this way influence society to become more just and moral. The value-laden nature of such studies is made explicit in most research reports. For example, the introductory remarks to a recent volume entitled *Prejudice, Discrimination and Racism* were as follows:

> The United States is a country whose fundamental values demand liberty and justice for all. It is a country founded on the proposition that all men [sic] are created equal. Nevertheless, it is also a country with racist traditions and contemporary manifestations of racial prejudice and discrimination. (Dovidio and Gaertner, 1986, p. 1)

The explicit assumption throughout this collected volume is that prejudicial and discriminatory behavior is wrong, and that psychologists should study such phenomena as a means of helping to end them.

Positivistic-oriented psychologies may claim to be just and moral on the basis of the second and third, but not the first of these criteria. That is, researchers following this tradition are concerned with remaining objective and avoiding value judgments about what is or is not just and moral behavior. As scientists, they wish to remain impartial judges, rather than to become entangled with issues of good and bad behavior. However, researchers in this tradition do attempt to identify what is understood by others to be just and moral, and the conditions in which behavior meeting the conditions of just and moral behavior can arise. Through these efforts, researchers may "present the facts" about the circumstances in which just and moral behavior can be achieved. Such findings may in turn influence society to become more just and moral. For example, when research has established that (1) racism exists and (2) there are specific conditions that promote more just and moral race relations, then society will be better armed if it chooses to turn away from racism.

Apart from a claim to objectivity in research methodology, positivistic researchers tend also to assume that certain fundamental universals exist with respect to what is just and moral. Thus, various models of moral development and justice have been proposed, incorporating assumptions about universal laws of behavior in this domain (Moghaddam and Vuksanovic, 1990). A more specific example is that prejudice against minority groups, such as Blacks and women, has been assumed, sometimes explicitly, to be unjust.

The assumption of universality of course makes decision making much more simple, and also perhaps rather simplistic and unrealistic. Decision making is simplified because we need to refer to fewer value systems for establishing just and moral behavior. At the same time, in this culturally diverse world the suspicion arises that such a simplistic system may be neglecting important complexities of social life.

The appeal of social constructionism arises in part from its apparent ability to incorporate the complexities of cultural diversity. Thus, Howard (Chapter 12, this volume) is appealing when he states that "the morality and justice contained in any constructionist system is with respect to that system's internal criteria of reasonableness, and thus might not suggest any universalizable criteria for justice and morality." But do such statements promise more than the social constructionists can deliver? The claim that social constructionists can deliver a just and moral system as long as the assessment is within the system's internal criteria may seem a modest enough goal. We shall see, however, that this goal is very difficult if not impossible to achieve through social constructionist models.

JUST AND MORAL BEHAVIOR ACCORDING TO INTERNAL STANDARDS

"Does this mean that narrative psychologists are doomed to a vicious relativism in evaluating the appropriateness of human actions? I hope not" (Howard, Chapter 12, this volume).

Having followed the social constructionist tradition of rejecting universal standards by which to judge the morality and justice of an action, Howard expresses a hope that social constructionism may avoid what he calls a "vicious" relativism. This hope is derived from the seemingly plausible idea that we should rely on notions of moral and just behavior internal to each group. But before I review the case for such internal value systems, there are a number of seemingly minor but, nevertheless, troublesome points that I would like to clarify.

First, the use of phrases such as "*vicious* relativism" and "*oppressed* groups" is problematic, as are claims such as "every genuinely caring person would want to see such *unfairness* cease" (Howard, Chapter 12, this volume; my emphasis). From which perspective and according to which set of "internal" values pertaining to moral and just behavior is Howard making these claims?

For a relativism to be judged "vicious," there must be some value judgment made. Who is establishing the criteria for deciding what is "vicious"? One person's "vicious relativism" may be another person's "absolute universalism."

Howard makes explicit his belief that gays, women, and various ethnic and racial group members have been mistreated. He also claims that these groups, as well as their sympathizers, have the right to "attempt to alter society to correct the more obvious instances of injustice." But, according to social constructionism, a group can only be "mistreated" in terms of a set of internal standards accepted by those making such a judgment. There are many people who *do not* believe that gays and other minorities have been mistreated. Indeed, it would not be difficult to identify various groups who feel that gays, to take one example of a minority group, have been treated much more positively than they deserve. Why should we not accept their internal values for assessing moral and just behavior, rather than Howard's (Chapter 12, this volume)?

For example, the treatment of gays in the Islamic Republic of Iran has been described as "barbaric" by various gay-rights groups in the West. But according to standards of just and moral behavior internal to the Islamic Republic of Iran, it is gays who are "barbaric" and inhuman in their behavior. One way to end such "barbarism" is to punish Iranian gays so that they will behave in a just and moral manner, according to the criteria internal to *their own Iranian society*. Any condemnation of such treatment of gays could only be valid if we stepped outside the "vicious relativism" arising from social constructionism.

THE SOCIAL PSYCHOLOGICAL STUDY OF FASCISM

But we need not wander to distant lands to find examples of how cultural relativism falls short when attempting to arrive at a just and moral psychology. Within Western societies there exist many subgroups who not only uphold different notions of morality and justice, but are making efforts to overthrow democracy and discard democratic notions of moral and just behavior.

Consider the case of fascist movements, which have been the focus of a number of social psychological studies. The classic study on fascism was conducted in the immediate post World War II era and the impetus for this research was a concern that potentially fascist personality types may pose a threat to democratic systems (Adorno, Frenkel-Brunswik, Levinson, and Sanford, 1951). Research on *The Authoritarian Personality* led to the development of the F-scale, which was originally designed to identify pro-fascist tendencies in individuals. The explicit value system guiding this research was that fascism must be fought, and that democracy is something of value that is worth defending against fascists and other anti-democratic forces.

More recent studies of authoritarian or "potentially fascistic" personality types have been just as explicit about the value systems they endorse. For example, Billig (1978) conducted a study of members of the National Front, a pro-fascist political group active in England. In this analysis Billig (1978) makes explicit his strategy of *rejecting* the value system of the individuals he is studying, and of getting "behind the mask" of the National Front members. Only through this process of "unveiling" could Billig (1978) expose the fascist personality and apply his own value system for assessing moral and just behavior. Similarly, Altemeyer's (1981) research over the last twenty-five years toward developing a scale for measuring Right-Wing Authoritarianism has involved explicit biases, as suggested by the main title of his recent book, *Enemies of Freedom* (1988).

(It is worth noting that Altemeyer (1988) perceives the threat to democracy arising from *Right-Wing* authoritarianism. He shares with many other social scientists a tendency to assume that *Left-Wing* authoritarianism either does not exist or does not pose the same threat to democratic values as Right-wing authoritarianism. As an educator in Iran during the postrevolution era, my sense of the situation was that there were identifiable left-wing groups who did behave in ways that were very similar if not identical to groups typically described as "Right-Wing Authoritarian.")

These examples from the literature on fascism suggest that various researchers adopting "objective" methodologies have made explicit the influence of value systems on their work. But they have made it equally clear that they consider their value system to be "better" than the one adopted by the pro- or potentially fascist individuals they have studied. For example, Adorno et al. (1951) made it clear that they consider democratic notions of moral and just behavior to be universally better than those of fascism. Furthermore, Billig (1978) has suggested that it is only through adopting an ideology that perceives the authoritarian personality as deceptive and tries to get behind the mask of the authoritarian that a researcher could uncover realities behind the mask. By implication, the mask is "faulty," the authoritarian personality is "problematic," and the researcher is in a better position to evaluate events and issues of justice.

But Howard is not ready to admit to value judgments that would suggest certain worldviews to be more just than others, or some value systems to be "better than" others. Given this reluctance, his "slide" into using value-laden language *is* problematic. If he is not ready to claim that certain systems for judging moral and just behavior are better than others, then how does he expect us to accept his claim that gays and other minorities have been mistreated? Why does he not accept the claim that gays and other minorities have been treated unfairly *favorably* rather than unfairly unfavorably?

DOES SOCIAL CONSTRUCTIONISM NECESSARILY LEAD TO A FOCUS ON MINORITY GROUPS?

Another issue that needs to be clarified is Howard's claim that "one of the most important immediate benefits of social constructionist thought has been the warranting of voices and stories of previously disenfranchised and minority groups" (Chapter 12, this volume). It is certainly true that a number of social constructionist researchers have focused on minority groups, but this should not lead us to conclude that the philosophy or the methodology of social constructionists somehow is more likely to lead to such a focus than is the philosophy or methodology of positivism.

In terms of the influence of social constructionist philosophy, implicit in Howard's essay is the claim that because each group has an internal system for justice and morality, researchers should pay attention to each different internal system. This "intervention" by researchers will lead to a highlighting of the worldview of minority groups, who have thus far supposedly been neglected. As a consequence, researchers may help change the status quo, which is in favor of majority groups.

But if each groups' views simply reflect their own internal notions of justice and morality, on what basis can social scientists intervene to change the status quo? Minority groups claim the status quo to be unjust, but why should we support this claim rather than the claim that the status quo is just?

Any intervention to change the status quo will be attacked as unjust from the perspective of some group or other. Only by standing outside internal systems of just and moral behavior and by referring to some universal system can we justify intervening on behalf of one group or another to change the status quo.

Consequently, from a relativist viewpoint we do not have valid reasons for attempting to change the status quo. It is only with reference to a system of justice and morality that extends beyond one group's boundaries that we can legitimately take actions that impact on more than one group.

As to methodology, "account gathering" of various sorts, whether it be attached to ethogenics, narrative psychology, discourse analysis, symbolic interactionism, or whatever, does not "inevitably" lead to the study of minorities anymore than it does of majority groups. The focus on minority groups arises from a *political* decision taken by researchers. This decision involves a value judgment about the unequal and unjust relations between majority and minority groups. Through a focus on minority groups, researchers have attempted to highlight the unjust conditions of such groups and identify how minority group members could escape this injustice (Taylor and Moghaddam, 1987).

It is exactly this political orientation that differentiates between the social psychology of Europe and that of the United States (Moghaddam, 1987, 1990). European social psychology has evolved in part as a reaction against the reductionism of U.S. social psychology. Such reductionism has involved a tendency to ignore societal processes, and to attempt to explain social behavior by exclusive reference to dispositional (intrapersonal) processes.

Thus, a *political* concern for the state of minority groups has led Henri Tajfel (1984), Serge Moscovici (see Moscovici, Mugny, and Van Avermaet, 1985), Willem Doise (1978), and various other European social psychologists to focus on minority group behavior, and to develop models that attempt to incorporate societal processes. However, the main body of research generated by these scholars has been in the *laboratory* tradition. The work of Moscovici (1982) on minority group influence is an important example of how one need not adopt "account gathering" methods to study minority groups. Also, one need only refer to the handbook of discourse analysis to recognize that the adoption of account gathering methods does not necessarily lead to a focus on minority groups.

CONDITIONS THAT WOULD PERMIT THE DEVELOPMENT OF A JUST AND MORAL SOCIAL CONSTRUCTIONIST PSYCHOLOGY

The critical points that I have raised vis-à-vis Howard's thesis do not lead to the conclusion that a just and moral social constructionist psychology cannot evolve. Indeed, in this part of the discussion I shall outline two conditions in which such a psychology could develop.

Condition One: Cultural Homogeneity

A just and moral social constructionist psychology becomes possible in a culturally homogeneous world. (We use the term culture in the anthropological sense, to refer to all that is human made. Thus, we are not concerned with evaluative notions of "high culture" as opposed to "popular culture.") In such a world, all individuals would share the same values and abide by the same "internal" system for judging the justice and morality of behavior. Consequently, there would be no need or possibility for referring to external value systems, since everyone would agree that the internal value system is the best, and no external value systems would be available.

In such a culturally homogeneous world, the system of justice and morality would be universal. Thus, there would be no need for a culturally relativist perspective. In conclusion, there can be a just and moral social constructionist psychology in a condition where there is a universal system of justice and morality, and there is no role for cultural relativism.

Condition Two: Static Social Groups

Second, a just and moral social constructionist psychology can evolve in a condition where social groups do not interact, but exist as independent units with fixed boundaries in a static social world. In such a world, the members of each group would interact only with other ingroup members.

One important consequence of such a situation would be that individuals would only interact with others who *share their particular system of just and moral behavior.* More specifically, individuals would only interact with others who choose to adopt the same interpretive framework.

Within such a world, judgments about the justice and morality of a particular act would be decided only by reference to internal value systems. Any attempt to make reference to external value systems would be a violation of rules, and would be treated as such by all group members.

The effective functioning of this system would require that all individuals who choose to change their interpretive frameworks would exit from the group. Whether they leave by choice or are forced out, or whether they choose to remain alone or opt to become a member of a group that upholds their (different) interpretive framework, are issues outside the domain of this discussion. The point relevant to the present discussion is that for a social constructionist psychology to be just and moral, a group should consist only of individuals who share common interpretive frameworks and who apply identical criteria for evaluating the justice or morality of an act.

MEETING THE CONDITIONS FOR A JUST AND MORAL SOCIAL CONSTRUCTIONIST PSYCHOLOGY

How likely is it that the conditions that we have outlined for the development of a just and moral social constructionist psychology could be met? We shall consider each condition in turn.

Homogeneous Culture

At a superficial level, at least, the world seems to be moving toward a homogeneous culture. Improved communications systems seem to be leading us toward the "global village," so that events such as the re-unification of Germany and the recent Gulf War can be witnessed by billions of people around the world as they occur. At the same time, increasing international trade and the expansion of multinational corporations have led to the same products being found in almost all societies. For example, McDonald's hamburgers and pizza from Pizza Hut can now be "enjoyed" by residents of almost every major city in the world, including Moscow. Increasingly similar material conditions for social life may gradually lead social behavior to also become similar in different societies.

Thus, there do seem to be ways in which culture is becoming homogeneous around the world. If this trend continues, we could, in theory, reach a situation in which the standards used for judging just and moral behavior would be similarly universal.

At the same time, the movement toward a "global village" is accompanied by what is perhaps an even more powerful movement toward separatism. (Perhaps as a result of actually eating the McDonald's hamburgers! Surely people will have more sense than to want to be a part of *that* global village.) The apparently contradictory forces of globalization and separatism are present in almost all geographic areas. For example, the European Economic Community (EEC) is at present preparing to become one economic unit in 1992, and there are also plans to bring members of this community closer together politically and culturally. But, at the same time, numerous nationalist movements, such as the Welsh, Scottish, and Irish Nationalists in the United Kingdom, the Basques in Spain, and the Flemings and Walloons in Belgium, are attempting to break away and establish smaller independent states. Separatism is not confined to Europe, but is also thriving in most other parts of the world, including Eastern Europe and the former Soviet Union (Boucher, Landis, and Clark, 1987).

Separatist movements have been influential in countering attempts to force the assimilation of ethnic minorities and achieve cultural homogeneity. In summarizing the situation, Moghaddam and Solliday (1991) have commented that "whether the attempt to force assimilation stems from a Third World government's desire to 'modernize' or from a communist government's desire to comply to the Marxist model of social class progression, ethnicity seems to be firmly rooted in the foundations of social life, making assimilation difficult" (p. 55). With respect to the possible motivational basis for a desire by ethnic minorities to resist assimilation and cultural homogeneity, Moghaddam and Solliday (1991) speculate, using the case of Iran as an example:

> no matter how quickly . . . Westernization proceeded, Iranian society could still only *approximate* a Western society. Since Iranian elites pushed traditional Iranians to become something which they could never be—"more British than the British" or "more American than the Americans"—they effectively created a scenario in which the traditional Iranian—or any minority population—could never succeed. Within the average Iranian, this constant failure seemed to reinforce a negative view of Iranian identity. . . . This phenomenon of "never measuring up" is shared in varying degrees by all populations which attempt to assimilate into an "ideal," yet unattainable, culture. . . . The Iranian revolution of 1978 was, first, a violent reaction against assimilation and, second, an attempt to re-establish the traditional minority cultures which had been discarded in the name of "Westernization." The Shah encouraged the Iranian people to imitate and emulate the Swiss, for example, effectively sending the

message that Iranians are "second rate." Ayatollah Khomeini, on the other hand, urged Iranians to emulate the ideal *Islamic* society, emphasizing that they were the "best" in the eyes of God. Each of these messages had a fundamentally different psychological effect. In exaggerated terms, these two opposing approaches reflect both the fatal flaw of assimilation and the idealistic attraction of heritage culture maintenance. (pp. 64–65)

Thus, there seem to be strong forces pushing the world toward cultural diversity rather than cultural homogeneity. This same trend is present in North America, where recent research has documented a systematic trend toward heritage culture maintenance among ethnic minorities (Lambert and Taylor, 1990; Moghaddam and Taylor, 1987; Moghaddam, Taylor, and Lalonde, 1987, 1989). Increasingly, immigrants to North America are reporting that they have come to North America to take part in the American economy, but not the American culture, to have children who contribute to and benefit from prosperity, but not to bring up children who behave like American children. Most importantly, these immigrants are learning English, but they are also insistent that they should retain their heritage languages. Despite the efforts of various pro-assimilationst groups (e.g., the English-only movement), cultural and linguistic diversity seems to be increasing rather than decreasing in North America.

In summary, although at a superficial level there does seem to be movement toward cultural homogeneity and a "global village," in practice the world situation is far more complex and reflective of a strengthened cultural diversity. An "ethnic revival" is under way, both within North America and throughout most of the world. There seems to be very little possibility that we shall arrive at cultural homogeneity, a condition necessary for the achievement of a just and moral social constructionist psychology.

Static Social Groups

The possibility of achieving the second condition for the development of a just and moral social constructionist psychology seems to be even more remote than the first. Let us remind ourselves that if a social structure is static and groups do not interact, then individuals will only need to make reference to internal systems for judging just and moral behavior. Since all interactions will be with ingroup members, and the members of each group share systems for judging justice and morality, then there need not arise any disputes about the relative merits of different systems.

For example, if all Muslims only interacted with other Muslims, and Protestants only with Protestants, and Catholics with Catholics, then the members of each group could decide the justice and morality of behavior by reference to their own internal, and in important ways different, systems. In such a context, a social constructionist psychology may function to be just and moral.

But the contemporary social world is far removed from this static situation, as exemplified by the ongoing Salman Rushdie affair. Rushdie is a Muslim who, like millions of other Muslims, lives in England (a Protestant country). He interacts with both Muslims and Christians, and is judged according to the internal value systems of both of these groups.

Even a brief survey of movements of populations in different parts of the world suggests that contacts between culturally diverse groups are increasing rather than decreasing (see the journal of *International Migration Review* for current surveys). Consequently, far from becoming static, the world is becoming increasingly interactive in terms of contact between different groups.

CONCLUDING COMMENT

Social constructionism *is* doomed to a "relativism" referred to by Howard (Chapter 12, this volume). This may be interpreted as the bad news. However, there is also some good news. This relativism is only "vicious" from some perspectives; the alternative exists of interpreting this relativism in a positive light. I believe we should seriously consider the possibility that social constructionism may arrive at a just and moral psychology *in some societies, but not others.*

Howard adopts a social constructionist perspective, but asks questions in a universalist fashion. Surely the question should not be, "Can there be a just and moral social constructionist psychology?" in the universal sense, because the implicit assumption is that there are universals that can lead to one answer. Perhaps the question should be, "In what kinds of societies can there be a just and moral social constructionist psychology, and what are the kinds of societies in which this cannot be achieved?"

REFERENCES

Adorno, T. W., Frenkel-Brunswik, E., Levinson, D. J., and Sanford, R. N. (1951). *The authoritarian personality.* New York: Harper & Row.

Altemeyer, B. (1981). *Right-wing authoritarianism.* Manitoba, Canada: University of Manitoba press.

Altemeyer, B. (1988). *Enemies of freedom: Understanding right-wing authoritarianism.* San Francisco: Jossey-Bass.

Billig, M. G. (1978). Fascists: A social psychological view of the National Front. London: Academic Press.

Boucher, J., Landis, D., and Clark, K. A. (1987). *Ethnic conflict: International perspectives.* Newbury Park, CA: Sage.

Doise, W. (1978). *Groups and individuals: Explanations in social psychology.* Cambridge, MA: Cambridge University Press.

Dovidis, J. F. and Gaerntner, S. L. (Eds.) (1986). Prejudice, discrimination and racism. New York: Academic Press.

Lambert, W. E., and Taylor, D. M. (1990). *Coping with cultural and racial diversity in urban America*. New York: Praeger.

Moghaddam, F. M. (1987). Psychology in the Three Worlds: As reflected by the crisis in social psychology and the move toward indigenous Third World psychology. *American Psychologist, 42*, 912–920.

Moghaddam, F. M. (1990). Modulative and generative orientations to psychology: Implications for psychology in the Three Worlds. *Journal of Social Issues, 46*, 21–41.

Moghaddam, F. M., and Taylor, D. M. (1987). The meaning of multiculturalism for visible minority immigrant women. *Canadian Journal of Behavioral Science, 19*, 121–136.

Moghaddam, F. M., Taylor, D. M., and Lalonde, R. N. (1987). Individualistic and collective integration strategies among Iranians in Canada. *International Journal of Psychology, 22*, 301–313.

Moghaddam, F. M., Taylor, D. M., and Lalonde, R. N. (1989). Integration strategies and attitudes toward the built environment: A study of Haitian and Indian immigrant women in Montreal. *Canadian Journal of Behavioral Science, 21*, 160–173.

Moghaddam, F. M., and Solliday, E. A. (1991). Balanced multiculturalism and the challenge of peaceful coexistence in pluralistic societies. *Psychology and Developing Societies, 3*, 51–71.

Moghaddam, F. M., and Stringer, P. (1986). Trivial and important criteria for social categorization in the minimal group experiment. *The Journal of Social Psychology, 126*, 345–354.

Moghaddam, F. M., and Vuksanovic, V. (1990). Attitudes and behavior toward human rights across different contexts: The role of right-wing authoritarianism, political ideology, and religiosity. *International Journal of Psychology, 25*, 455–474.

Moscovici, S., Mugny, G., Van Avermaet, E. (Eds.). (1985). *Perspectives in minority influence*. Cambridge, England: Cambridge University Press.

Tajfel, H. (Ed.). (1978). *Differentiation between social groups: Studies in the social psychology of intergroup relations*. London: Academic Press.

Tajfel, H. (Ed.) (1984). The social dimension. 2 vols. Cambridge, England: Cambridge University Press.

Taylor, D. M., and Moghaddam, F. M. (1987). *Theories of intergroup relations: International social psychological perspectives*. New York: Praeger.

Wright, W. C., Taylor, D. M., and Moghaddam, F. M. (1990). Responding to membership in a disadvantaged group: From acceptance to collective action. *Journal of Personality and Social Psychology, 58*, 994–1003.

14 SOCIAL CONSTRUCTIONISM: RELATIVISM, MORAL SOURCES, AND JUDGMENTS OF ADEQUACY

John Shotter*

What reflection in this direction would entail is already fairly well known. It involves, first, conceiving reason differently, as including—alongside the familiar forms of the Enlightenment— a new department, whose excellence consists in our being able to articulate the background of our lives perspicuously (Taylor, 1987, p. 481)

The real foundations of his enquiry do not strike a man at all. Unless that fact has at some time struck him (Wittgenstein, 1953, no. 129)

Our task in this symposium is to explore the moral dimension(s) of everyday social life, and what a social constructionist psychology may, or may not, have to say about it or them. The thesis that I want eventually to explore comes from Vico: social processes, he claims, are based or "rooted," not in anything pre-established in people, nor in their surroundings, but in socially shared *identities of feeling* they themselves create or "construct," in some sense, within the flow of activity between them. These identities he calls "sensory topics"—*sensory* because they are to do with shared feelings for shared circumstances; and *topics* (Gr. *topos* = place) because they give rise to "common places," to moments within an otherwise continuously changing flow of social activity, to which shared references are possible. Such *topoi* are the sources of shared feeling within a community, against which the adequacy of any linguistic formulations by its members can ultimately be judged as to the sense they make (Shotter, 1986, 1991; Vico, 1948). Also, I shall link these claims to Taylor's (1987, 1989)

* Written while Cornell Visiting Professor, Department of Psychology, Swarthmore College, Swarthmore, PA 19081, 1990–1991.

recent discussion of the inherent tensions[1] in the "moral sources" of the modern self, to show the point of a social constructionist psychology in illuminating the nature of these tensions—not with the purpose of resolving them, but of understanding what, from a practical–moral point of view, is involved in living more productively *with* them.

That we "construct"—or better, that we are still in the process of "constructing"—the moral sources by which we live is the central social constructionist thesis that I want later to put forward. But much more must be said first. For there is little point in launching straight into arguments for social constructionist approaches in psychology and hoping to have them properly understood, without first saying something about the rather different academic "background" from out of which they have arisen, and within which they play their proper part (draw their life)—hence the point of the two epigraph quotes above. Arguments will fall on deaf ears, or be misunderstood, without the formation also of a new academic "common sense." And this is the aim of both Wittgenstein and Taylor: to attempt to break the hold a particular way of thinking has upon us, that incorporated in the "epistemological standpoint," which has so dominated modern philosophical thought. And here, let me add straightaway, for them as for me, it is not so much *foundationalism* (the justification of one's claims to knowledge by their "rooting" in stated, supposedly self-evident principles)—as many now claim is Rorty's (1979) central point—that is the dominant characteristic of that project, as a commitment to a model of knowledge as *representation,* to knowledge as a "correct representation of an independent reality"—where this picture of knowledge is rooted in the same image of agency (the atomistic, "punctual self"), and the same moral and spiritual ideals (to do with taking to some extent an instrumental stance toward people) that characterize our civilization today (Taylor, 1989).

The great paradox of that image, as Taylor (1989) shows, is that although we ourselves in our everyday social institutions, in our practices, and in other forms of social activity have historically developed it, and continue within the form of many of our (official) social relations to sustain it, it is an image of us as being completely self-contained, as owing nothing of who or what we are to ourselves, to our own social activities, or to those of our predecessors. Hence, if it ever does strike us (as in Wittgenstein's example) that the real foundations of our inquires are unknown to us—that they perhaps have a socio-cultural, historically developed and developmental nature—then that fact must be continually recovered, so to speak, against the grain of our thinking. We must "deconstruct" just the very

---

[1] Such tensions as those between the project of disengaged reason to *find* the solutions to problems, and the more Romantic project to do with *making* or *creating* alternatives, will be apparent throughout this article.

detached, disengaged, instrumental forms of thought into which, as psychologists, in the face of, if not our own at least the disbelief of others, we struggled so hard to fit ourselves in becoming practitioners of modern psychology.

TRANSCENDENTAL PRACTICAL REASONING: FIRST STEPS

Now we must train ourselves in a new enterprise, an enterprise that, in one of its forms, as we shall see, holds the seeds of an escape from the supposed wholesale *relativism* to which many critics of social constructionism claim it *must* fall foul. It is a form of argumentation that finds its origins in Kant's "transcendental or conditions of possibility" arguments: We argue for the inadequacy of the concept of the self-contained self, and motivate the need for an alternative, by showing the indispensable social conditions required for such a form of selfhood to be possible in the first place; and we do so, from a "transcendental" position implicitly made available to us (but not yet articulated), within the very contexts in which we have our being. However—and here is its new twist—the form of reasoning or argumentation involved is first of all of a *practical* rather than a theoretical kind, that is, it is a reasoning not in terms of principles and procedures (which would still sustain the epistemological project), but a form of reasoning, as I said earlier, based in the "moral sources" of which Taylor (1989) speaks.

Second, in the attempt to "see" the nature of such implicit sources, it makes use of a "unit"—"joint action" (Shotter, 1984)—which, as we shall see, has the special quality of being a *particular* form of human existence (with all its tensions and uncertainties), which can be *used* as a "psychological instrument" (in Vygotsky's sense) *through* which we may "see" the nature of social life *generally*—just as the blind person's stick is a general-purpose instrument for the "seeing" of a terrain. This is an example of its second new twist. Instead of theories in the strict sense of systems of propositional statements, our "theory" will consist in a whole set of linguistic formulations, *useful* in the sense that as *prosthetic* extensions of ourselves, we can explore the nature of our social world *through* them, thus to reveal features that otherwise would remain hidden. Our "theory" then will be unsystematic, an "analytic toolbox," for use in linguistically articulating the possibilities "hidden" in our spontaneous, social activities, thus to actualize those possibilities as amenable to our own voluntary control. It is a form of reasoning, as is already clear, attuned not to abstract universals or generalities, but concerned with the irremediably "local," and particular character of truth, argument, and validity. To the extent that its aim, at least in academic life, is to "articulate" in some way the otherwise unformulated moral sources against which all our linguistic formulations may be judged as to their adequacy, it *is* concerned with an overriding good (a "hypergood"—Taylor, 1989[2]), and has thus a limited moral vision. Furthermore, to the extent that it aims at uncovering, or "deconstructing" what has gone into our current forms of thought about ourselves—for only if error is recognized can the search for alternatives be motivated—it is a form of reasoning concerned with the undoing of conceits or illusions.

In moving toward the substance of my argument, let me begin with a bit of personal history: I want to say that, as it happens—under the influence first of Vygotsky and Mead, and then of Wittgenstein and Vico (as will appear in the following)—my work has always been centrally concerned with questions of *moral* accountability. I was concerned with the questions of, not only what it is for us in our everyday affairs to account either ourselves or others as autonomous, responsible persons, but also, and primarily, what is involved in people (children) developing from a state of moral dependency to one of moral autonomy (Shotter, 1974). Indeed, in my first book (Shotter, 1975), in echoing Koch's (1964) complaint about the morally demeaning "image of man" projected by modern psychology, I attempted to reformulate psychology—or at least, to argue for a new "position" in academic psychological discourse—for psychology as a "moral science of action" rather than as a "natural science of behaviour." For, as I said in that early work, "people must not be treated like organisms that respond directly in relation to their position in the world, but rather as special organic forms which deal with nature in terms of their knowledge of their "position" in a culture; that is, in terms of a knowledge of the part their actions play in relation to the part played by other people's actions in maintaining (or progressing) the culture" (Shotter, 1975, p. 14).

Indeed, my project then was (and still is) to fashion a psychology that is of some help in us understanding precisely and accurately how we are "placed" socially, historically, morally, and thus politically, in relation to those around us, now, in our current, "local," historical circumstances. Thus: to grasp what moral resources there are available to us that we might draw upon in acting as we ourselves, rather than our circumstances require; or, if such resources are lacking, to understand why, and what kinds of changes are required in one's social conditions for them to become available. In other words, my project was concerned with how one transcends one's present, local conditions, for conditions that, in some way, can be deemed morally better—whether one has experienced such conditions before or not.

---

[2] In general, in offering a vision of the good, Taylor eschews the offering of basic reasons, the formulation of an overriding "hypergood that puts all other goods under suspicion. As he sees it, an ethical outlook organized ahead of time around any particular hypergood is inevitably conflictual and in tension with other goods.

IDENTITY AND ARTICULACY

In exploring these questions further, at least two distinct paradigms, in tension with each other, are available to us: (1) In one, we might explore (with Vygotsky) something of what is involved in a child developing into a morally autonomous person, a responsible member of a (modern?) society, able to contribute to the maintenance (if not the transformation) of its culture. (2) In another, we might explore (with Vico) what is involved in a whole people developing its culture in response to new conditions, not always of its own making. Both paradigms are important ones, for I think we can all take it for granted that, as Vico puts it, in social life "things do not settle or endure out of their natural state" (Vico, 1948, para. 134). Stable social practices have to be sustained in existence by being continually reproduced in all significant details in people's everyday social activities, and by transgressors being held responsible and sanctioned in some way—this is the whole point in people knowing how to play their part in life, and being held responsible for their failures. When routines break down, restitutions and repairs are required. In the first paradigm then, in which individuals must find a place within a society, people's potential behaviors are always in excess of what is required; there is a surplus. But in the light of the second, we find that social practices can never be completely stabilized, as a result of either internal or external influences, they must continually "develop," and as they do people become anxious as to whether their past activities are still adequate to their needs. Here they have a sense of deficiency; there is a lack; and they seek a better form of life. Thus for the child, the freedom and excess of play is a source of creativity; while for the people, their creativity is to be found in their anxiety at the inadequacy of their mode of being, and its failure as a basis for the production of the mutual understandings upon which a tolerable social life depends.

Vygotsky: The "Development" of Responsible Action

It is against this perhaps puzzling background—of the indeterminate,[3] two-sided nature of human nature—that we can turn first to an exploration of what is involved in a new member of a society, an infant, learning how to maintain (if not to transform) its society's culture, by learning how *him* or *herself* can control (in a socially responsible manner) his or her own activities. My aim here is to try to

---

[3] Macmurray (1961, p. 60) perhaps goes too far when he says: "In the human infant—and this is the heart of the matter—the impulse to communicate is his sole adaptation to the world in which he is born." But he is surely right when he says (1961, p. 67): "That man is social by nature is true, but highly ambiguous. Many animals are social; yet no species is social in the sense in which we are, for none has the form of life determined from the beginning by communication."

understand not just how a child gets to *know* what we as adults know, but becomes literally "one of us" in the sense of sharing or coming to share our "form of life" (Wittgenstein); or, as Taylor might put it, to *see* our circumstances in the same terms as our tutors do theirs—an ontological rather than an epistemological problem. We shall find three interlinked issues central: (1) the question of the child's identity or selfhood; (2) the transformation of socially distributed, lower, spontaneous activities into higher, individual, self-controlled activity; and (3) where the process of "internalization" involves not a spatial but a moral "movement."

(1) First to discuss the matter of identity, what it is to be an identifiable someone. We can discuss it from within two perspectives: either from the "outside," from the point of view of the kind of beings required for a self-reproducing, self-sustaining community to be possible; or from the "inside," in terms of what a person must know in order to be a self-responsible person, able to sustain completely the management of their own affairs within a moral community—a community that, if they fail, will sanction them.

To turn first to what is required for the sustaining of a community: Clearly, being *like* a socially responsible person is not a matter of making certain, special patterns of movements. Nothing anyone could detect and identify in a merely *observed* pattern of movements made by infants would indicate that infants *themselves* had detected and identified their own activity in the same way. Even less would such observations indicate that infants already knew the meaning or significance of their actions, what they implied in relation to them dealing *properly* with their circumstances, with whether they had made any mistakes or not. Something more is involved in people acting in the knowledge of what they are doing than merely behaving in a situation in ways that others can recognize: if they are to be accounted fully responsible members of their society, they must not only be able to recognize it in the same way themselves, they must know what part their action plays in relation to the activities of the others around them in sustaining, progressing, or degrading the culture. To become socially responsible agents, then, children must learn not just to control their own behavior and to control it intelligently, in relation to their own needs, but also intelligibly and responsibly, in ways that not only make sense to others, but that also relate in some ways to what, overall, others are trying to do in their lives. The child, then, must acquire some knowledge of *him* or *herself*, that is, more than a simple sense of his or her own functioning, children must learn *who and what they are* in relation to all those with whom they share their lives. It is this knowledge that enables them to order and structure those aspects of their lives that they share with others, and to make recompense when they go wrong. Without such knowledge, their behavior must remain of a vague and indeterminate kind, not necessarily related to other people's activities at all.

Turning now to the perspective from within the person: The question of "Who am I?" or "How can I be a responsible person?" cannot of course be answered by looking into oneself and hoping to find the answer in one's subjective make-up—just as it could not be found from the "outside" in the pattern of one's movements. To know who I am, and that my actions are indeed *my* own actions, and relate to who I am, I must know where I stand, how I am "placed" with respect to the "others" who are important to me in my life—as a result, I may find myself badly rather than well placed, of course, and feel both a sense of failure and worthless, and a lack of opportunity to ameliorate the situation. Whatever: my identity is known to me in terms of *my situation;* whether I like it or not, that is how I *find* myself to be. Thus the question "What is it like to be *me?"* is answered by me describing my "world": (i) the "things" I perceive in it; (ii) the values I attach to them, and the embodied reactions I have toward them; (iii) the opportunities for action it now "permits," or "affords" me, that "I" can take; and (iv) especially its "horizon," that is, what is not actually at present "visible" to me but what it "hints" at it being reasonable for me to expect in the future —for although I am depressed now, there are still *grounds* for hope.

(2) But how might all this be possible? How can infants become beings, not only able to sustain stable social practices by continually reproducing their significant details in their own everyday social activities, but also able to feel depression and hope? And how, also, can they learn, if they fail in their actions to sustain a practice, to make restitution, to reinstate it? In other words, how are lower, spontaneous activities, usually performed only in reaction to circumstances, transformed into higher ones, into activities for which people *themselves* can be held responsible?

A first clue can be found, I think, in what one might take to be a first law of social constructionism. Gergen (1985, p. 267) states it thus: "The terms in which the world is understood [and dealt with practically] are social artifacts, products of historically situated interchanges among people." In Vygotsky's (1966, p. 41) Marxian version, it becomes: "The relations between higher mental functions were at one time real relations between people." But perhaps we need to add yet a little more to the "workings" of such a process for an understanding of what precisely is being claimed here to become clear.

As I see it, the origin of the process involved is as described by either Mead (1934, pp. 77–78), when he claims:

> The mechanism of meaning is present in the social act before the emergence of consciousness or awareness of meaning occurs. The act or adjustive response of the second organism gives to the gesture of the first organism the meaning it has.

or by Vygotsky (1987, p. 189), in his statement that:

> It is a general law of development that conscious awareness and mastery characterize only the higher stages of a given function. It arises comparatively late and must be preceded by a stage where conscious awareness is absent . . . , For conscious

awareness of a function to be achieved, the individual must first possess what he is to become consciously aware of.

In other words, what is being claimed here is that it is in the very nature of social activity itself that individuals "stimulate," "motivate," or "call out" in each other different forms of mental activity, thus providing occasions upon which they may each call attention to the nature of what the others around them are *already doing*. In other words, whatever the inner, physiological "mechanism of learning" might be, within social activity itself are the social conditions required for the spontaneous "creation" of new forms of mental activity, and their transformation—in the process of what Vygotsky calls "instruction"—into forms under our own self-control.

(3) Thus, in the development of behavior, says Vygotsky (1966), "the child begins to practice with respect to himself the same forms of behavior that others formerly practiced with respect to him" (pp. 39–40). What at first appears on the social plane as something (lower and biological) between people, later appears as something (higher and cultural) on the psychological plane *within* the child alone. Thus—to digress for a moment—unlike Rorty, who might want to say that we are "making" all the way down, Vygotsky would say that "making" (culture) and "finding" (biology) are intertwined (in "instruction"), all the way down, and all the way back.

But let us explore what Vygotsky actually means when he talks of the process of *internalization*. Is he talking about it as a *physical* or a *psychological* movement inward? In other words, is he talking about how what is "outside" us geometrically or geographically, so to speak, gets "inside" us or is he using the word "internalize" to characterize something not essentially spatial or geographical at all, but to do with a transformation in our *responsibility* for things? Or to put it yet another way, is he talking about a merely epistemological[4] process, in which what was at first inside only the adult's head is transferred into the child's head, or is he talking about an *ontological* process in which the very *being* of the child is being changed in some way? The question is a pertinent one, for it is not so much a matter of the form of the child's behavior as the locus of its control. For things that at first a child only does spontaneously and un-self-consciously, under the control of an adult, later come under the control of their own personal agency.

Here then we meet a tension in Vygotsky's own thought. The matter remains moot, for on one interpretation, one must argue that Vygotsky's whole approach is a paean to disengaged and instrumental modes of thought, and issues of "mastery"—and the emancipatory importance of taking an instrumental attitude

---

[4] In an epistemological process, there is a merely cognitive effect upon the content of people's "minds," while an ontological process affects people in their ethical being; it determines the kind of "world" to which they are responsive and within which they must act.

toward one's own abilities. But the ontological interpretation is also possible, for although Vygotsky never explicitly made the distinction between spontaneous, lower forms of activity and higher, voluntary ones in ethical terms, this is clearly what is involved. But this is obvious in accounts of what happens when mistakes are made, and where blame is apportioned. Indeed, as Bakhtin (1986) shows the same ethical concerns that hold in the social realm are still of importance in the "inner," psychological realm of the individual. Clearly, one can say, what is involved is an ontological rather than an epistemological problem.

The unit of analysis: joint action   But if ontological, what might be the nature of the changes in the child? It is not so much that in this process children learn new forms of action, perception, thought, and feeling that would otherwise (as biological beings) have never occurred to them, but that they learn socially significant *uses* for the functions that they (biologically) already have or may make use of at any time; they learn how *to order* their activities in relation to the requirements of others. The child learns *him* or *herself* how to act, not like infants who are *reliant upon others* to complete and give meaning to their behavior, but, to repeat, to relate what they do and what they feel to their knowledge of their own momentary "position" in their social situation.

Now here is not the place to get into the specifics of what Vygotsky calls the process of "instruction"—it has many and various "local" forms. But I do think it is worthwhile, after an initial comment upon what it involves, to outline what one might call the "basic or paradigmatic unit of analysis," what Vygotsky called "the single living 'cell'," the microcosm that provides a view of the macrocosm.[5] The comment is this: Vygotsky struggled with the unit of analysis problem because he wanted a "unit" that did not separate the biological from the social, the natural from the historical, or the organic from the cultural. As he saw it, everything of importance took place within a *zone of activity,* what he called the "zone of proximal development." It is within that zone that culture is appropriated from nature, and within which nature (our living, material bodies) reappropriates culture. It is in this zone that already fashioned "psychological instruments" may be transmitted to the child, or new such instruments fashioned, which, in "mediating" mental activities, transform them from lower to higher forms. Such "instruments," like a knot in a handkerchief as an aide memoire, have their significance (as for Wittgenstein) only in terms, as I have already said,

---

[5] "The whole of *Capital* is written according to the following method: Marx analyzes a single living 'cell' of capitalist society—for example the nature of value. Within this cell he discovers the structure of the entire system and all its economic institutions. . . .Anyone who could discover what a 'psychological' cell is—the mechanism producing even a single response—would find the key to psychology as a whole" (Vygotsky, 1978, p. 8).

of what can be achieved *through* their *use* (for an extensive account of mediation, see Shotter, 1989). In one sense, it is a zone of indeterminacy, a zone of uncertainty between *actions* (What I do) and *events* (What merely happens), and as such, does not seem amenable to characterization. This, however, is not entirely the case. It is its very lack of specificity that is its central defining feature.[6]

Elsewhere (Shotter, 1984), in the spirit of Vygotsky, I have attempted to formulate just such a "unit of analysis" as a "psychological instrument" for use by us in our analyses of social activity. I have called activity in this zone of uncertainty "joint action." It has two major features:

1. As people coordinate their activity in with the activities of others, and "reply" to others in what they do, what they as individuals desire and what actually results in their exchanges are often two very different things; in short, joint action produces unpredictable and *unintended* outcomes—these generate a "situation," or an "organized setting" existing between all the participants. As its organization cannot be traced back to the intentions of any particular individuals, it is *as if* it has a "given," "natural," or "externally caused" nature; although, to those within in it, it is "our" situation.

2. Although such a setting is unintended by any of the individuals within it, it does have an *intentional* quality to it: it seems both to "contain" something and always to "indicate" or to be "related to something other than or beyond itself,"[7] that is, participants find themselves "in" a *given* situation that has a *horizon* and is "open" to their actions. Indeed, its "organization" is such that the constraints (and enablements) it makes available influence, that is, "invite" and "motivate," their next possible actions.

And as Giddens (1980, p. 8) describes it, such socially constructed but "unintended consequences may systematically feedback to be the unacknowledged conditions of further acts."

In the ordinary flow of activity between people, in fact, a changing sea of *moral* enablements and constraints, of privileges and entitlements, and obligations and sanctions is created. The changing settings created are *moral settings* because the different "positions" they make available have to do with "rights" and "duties," with the nurturance or injury to the being of a person. For instance, the rights and duties associated with being a 1st-person speaker, a 2nd-person listener, or a 3rd-person observer are quite different from each other. As a 2nd-

---

[6] Indeed, as Wittgenstein (1953, p. 227) writes, "What is most difficult here is to put all this indefiniteness, correctly and unfalsified, into words." For: "The difficulty of renouncing all theory: One has to regard what appears so obviously incomplete, as something complete" (I, 1980, no. 723).

[7] "Ahead of what I can see and perceive, there is, it is true, nothing more actually visible, but my world is carried forward by lines of intentionality which trace out in advance at least the style of what is to come" (Merleau-Ponty, 1962, p. 416).

person one has a status quite different from that of a 3rd-person: one is involved in and required to maintain the action; we do not have the right to step out of our personal involvement with the speaker and attend to aspects of their person or performance to which they do not intend us to attend. The figure below is intended to show the nature of the difference between being "inside" or "outside" "THE SITUATION."

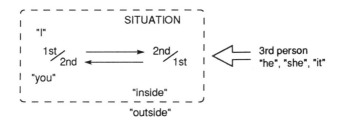

The obligations upon those "inside," however, do not extend to 3rd-persons, those "outside" it. Hence our unease when as 1st-person performers attempting a tricky interpersonal encounter, we find ourselves observed by a 3rd-person outsider: we experience ourselves as someone else's "object," fearful that we shall be judged and questioned about those aspects of our behavior over which we had no control. My point in making these distinctions is this: the conduct of social life is based upon a right we assign to 1st-persons, a right to make nonobservational self-ascriptions, to *tell* us about themselves and their experiences, by saying, for example, "I'm frightened" or "I'm puzzled" or "I love you," and to have what they say taken seriously as meaning what they intend it to mean—as long as, that is, we also feel that they *already* have the social competencies required to sustain the society within which this right makes sense.

The view of the 1st-person here, then, is of someone always "in" a given but changing, socially constructed situation; that is, in a "made" situation, but one not wholly of their own making, where the "openings" (to action) in such a situation are, in the course of a discourse, always changing. This, as I have already outlined earlier, *is* my *identity* in the situation. And it is of such a nature that I can be empowered by being embedded in such discourses, but can also be entrapped and disabled by them as well. Indeed, it is the 1st-person right to speak and act, and have what one does or says taken seriously, that is continually in contest. It is continually in contest because there is an intrinsic scarcity associated with it: a "political economy" is at work because, if I am to be someone else's listener, I cannot be the speaker, if I am to be someone else's reader, than inevitably I cannot at the same time be a writer; and I cannot simply assert my right to be a writer on my own, a writer is useless without readers. Clearly people, although essentially concerned to retain their membership in their society—for it is only in terms of their "belonging" that, as we shall see, they have their rights—act whenever they can to increase their own 1st-person rights and to reduce their obligations. Thus at every moment then, "where" one is, how one is placed in relation to the others around one, both in terms of what one has a right to do and in terms of the resources made available to one there, is important knowledge in determining one's momentary action.

Articulacy: social accountability   The concept of joint action thus allows us to articulate something of the character of the unacknowledged conditions of action constructed as an unintended consequence of previous actions, and to elucidate the importance of these conditions for our identities, our social ontology. Indeed, as I have already made clear, as an aspect of that ontology, to qualify for the special, socially autonomous (1st-person) status of adult persons, human agents must possess as a special aspect of their perceptual awareness of their surroundings an awareness of how they are (currently) "placed" or "positioned" in relation to all the other agents around them. They must be capable of perceiving themselves as being, not in an everywhere indifferently textured physical space, but as surrounded by an invisible "landscape" of morally textured "opportunities for action" made differentially available to them according to their location among the other agents around them. In other words, they must possess a *practical–moral* consciousness, a consciousness whose functioning, as we shall see, must be described in a language of *touch and feeling*[8], rather than sight and seeing. Those who do not properly *grasp* "who" they are, so to speak, the momentary state of their identity, do not know how to act in ways appropriate to their situation—where that knowledge we have of our "location," the "unacknowledged conditions" of our acting, is given us in our *feelings*.[9] It is this new language of feeling and the practical–moral reasoning it involves that are central to all that follows.

As the primary function of language in this approach is—rather than the representation of reality—*to give form to feeling* in the coordination of social action, we must now examine again our ways of talking, and the part they might play in the socio-historical processes involved in the formation of people's subjectivities and identities. Again elsewhere (Shotter, 1984), I have discussed these

[8] The point about what we know *practically* is that it cannot be surveyed (Wittgenstein). Its nature is only revealed to us in our uses of it, and our use of it depends upon our *sense* of its shape, so to speak.

[9] Where what is meant here by the term "feeling" is not anything to do with our own emotional state, but with our sense of the situation we are in: whether, for instance, it presents us with a difficulty of a certain kind to which we must respond—our sense of its nature guiding us in our response to it.

(2) This brings us directly to Vico's second *boria* and the claim he makes that, for the purposes of our study, "we must reckon as if there were no books in the world" (Vico, 1948, para. 330). What extraordinary stance is required if we are to take this claim seriously? Vygotsky (1962) puts it well when he says that "in learning to write the child must disengage himself from the *sensory effect* of speech and replace words by images of words" (p. 98, my emphasis). It is this sensory or sensuous aspect of speech that is so difficult for us now, as literate people, to recognize and to describe; it is, however, this sensuous, moving, rhetorical aspect of speech that will be our main concern in the following.

This, then, is the force of Vico's correctives: If we are to grasp the nature of the beginnings of language, and reckon as if there were no books in the world, it is the (for us) extraordinary nature of oral, preliterate, nonconceptual, nonlogical forms of communication that we must understand. We must grasp the nature of a form of communication that consists not in a sequential occurrence of events or things, not in a series of products or of component meanings, but that "subsists" in the continuous flow of sensuous, "moving" activity between people.

Vico and "Sensory Topics"

In such an unbroken flow of responsivity, in which at first, as Vico puts it, "each new sensation cancels the last one" (para. 703), how do people manage to create and establish within the flow of experience between them a "place" (*topos*), an "is," within the flux of sensation that can be "found again"? How is a recognizable distinct, but socially shared *feeling* about one's circumstances, to which all those involved can later return, formed? For without the possibility of referring to something recognizable as familiar, individuals would live, as Mead (1934, p. 351) puts it, "in an undifferentiated now," responsive like animals only to immediate and proximate influences. Without the metaphor of written texts, and of meanings as static images (representations) to help us, how might we imagine the nature of people's first mental activity?

While modern theories of knowledge begin with something present to the mind—for example, Descartes begins with self-evidently true, clear, and simple innate ideas—Vico begins by asking how it is that the mind comes to have anything present to it at all (Verene, 1981). And it is precisely to this question that Vico claims to have an answer, indeed, it is the master key of his science:

> We find that the principle of these origins both of languages and of letters lies in the fact that the early gentile people, by a demonstrated *necessity* of nature, were poets who spoke in poetic characters. This discovery, which is the master key of this Science, has cost us the persistent research of almost all our literary life, because with our civilized natures we moderns cannot at all imagine and can understand only by great toil the poetic nature of these first men. (Vico, 1948, para.34, my emphasis)

But to understand what he means here by saying that the early people were, by necessity, poets (where the word "poet" is from the Greek *poitetes* = one who makes, a maker, an artificer), we must divide the process of making into two parts: the first, to do with the forming of a *sensory topic,* and the second, with the forming of an *imaginary universal* that from a "rooting" in it, "lends" the topic a determinate form. We shall find the resources we need in characterizing both in the following paradigm example.

In paragraphs 379–391 of the *New Science,* Vico analyzes what he calls the "civil history" of the saying that it was "From Jove that the muse began." Taking it seriously, he suggests that fear of thunder indeed functioned to give rise to both the first sensory topic and imaginative universal. For, as everyone runs to shelter from the thunder, all in a state of fear, an opportunity exists for them to realize that it is the *same thing* that they all fear; and a look or a gesture will communicate this. What we might call a "moment of common reference" exists between them. What "inner mechanisms" might be making such a realization possible is not Vico's concern here; his concern is with the "outer" social conditions. And here it is the fear shared in common that provides the first fixed reference point that people can "find again" within themselves and know that others "feel the same way."

For this kind of fear, this fear of thunder, is not an ordinary fear of an immediately present dangerous event to which one can respond in an effective manner. There is no immediate practical response available to them in response to thunder. It is "not a fear awakened in men by other men, but fear awakened in men by themselves" (para. 382). Their fear is of a kind that seems to point *beyond* the thunder. When people hear it, they become confused and disoriented, they move furtively and with concern for each other—the thunder's presence is the *unspoken* explanation of their actions. And often, "when men are ignorant of the natural causes producing things, and cannot explain them by analogy," says Vico (axiom, para. 180), "they attribute their own nature to them." Thus at this point:

> The first theological poets created the first divine fable, the greatest they ever created: that of Jove, king and father of men and gods, in the act of hurling the lightning bolt; an image so popular, disturbing and instructive that its creators themselves believed in it, and feared, revered and worshipped it in frightful religions . . . . They believed that Jove commanded by signs, that such signs were real words, and that nature was the language of Jove. The science of this language the gentiles believed to be divination . . . . (para. 379)

And it was by learning to read the auspices (natural "signs") that one could learn how, ahead of time, to conform oneself to Nature's (Jove's) requirements.

But the fable of Jove, the imaginary universal, "lent" form to, and was "rooted" in, the prior establishing of a *sensory topic,* a sensuous totality linking thunder with the shared fears at the limits of one's being, and with recognizing the existence of similar feelings in others because of shared bodily activities. It is created, not out of a heterogeneous amalgam of events, but *within* a developed and developing totality of relations between people: "The first founders of humanity applied themselves to a sensory topics, by which they brought together those properties or qualities or relations of individuals and species which were so to speak concrete, and from these created their poetic genera" (para. 495).

The sensory topic from which the image of Jove originated is thus a "topos," a "place" in which it is possible to "re-feel" *everything* that is present at those times when "Jove" is active. And, as such feelings are slowly transformed into more external symbolic forms, the inarticulate *feelings* remain as the "standards" against which the more explicit forms may be judged as to whether they are adequate characterizations or not.

Sensory topics are the primordial places, the *loci,* constituting the background basis of the mentality of a people. They make up its common sense, its *sensus communis.* Without a common sense, there is no basis in which to "root" the formation of any imaginative universals. Yet, such a common sense is in no way *systematic.* It is, says Heider (1958, p. 2), "unformulated and only vaguely conceived." According to Schultz (1964, p. 72), "it embraces the most heterogeneous kinds of knowledge in a very incoherent and confused state." It is "immethodical," says Geertz (1983, p. 90), that is, "it caters both to the inconsistencies and diversity of life," it is "shamelessly and unapologetically ad hoc. It comes in epigrams, proverbs, *obiter dicta,* jokes, anecdotes, *contes morals*—a clatter of gnomic utterances—not in formalized doctrines, axiomatized theories, or architectonic dogmas." Yet strangely, as Geertz goes on to say, for all its disorder, such knowledge has "accessibleness" as another of its major qualities. Indeed, as Vico points out, it is first in *practical* activities that people must create (by ingenuity/*ingengno*) the meaningful links between (i) "what" is demanded in a situation and (ii) "what" is available (by way of resources)[10]—a meaning must be "lent" to the sensing of one's surroundings.

What Vico outlines here, then, is a poetic image in terms of which one might understand the *mute,* extraordinary, commonsense basis for an articulate language—where such a basis constitutes the unsystematized, primordial contents of the human mind, its basic paradigms or prototypes. They are a special set of feelings or intuitions, the topics or moral sources (Taylor) defining a form of life, against which the adequacy of any conceptual or linguistic formulations within that form of life may ultimately be judged as adequate.[11] If we are to understand

---

[10] Vico saw also the conceit of scholars as due to their detachment from the necessities of life. Indeed, in his history, they came last on the tree of knowledge: "First [were] the woods, then cultivated fields and huts, next little houses and villages, thence cities, finally academies and philosophers: this is the order of all progress from the first origins" (Vico, 1948, para. 22).

[11] "Giving grounds . . . , justifying the evidence, comes to an end;—but the end is not certain propositions striking us immediately as true, i.e., it is not a kind of *seeing* on our part; it is our *acting,* which lies at the bottom of the language-game" (Wittgenstein, 1969, no. 204).

their nature, it is not a logic—not a system of propositions—that is needed, but a poetics. A particular, concrete way of talking is needed that "shows" what cannot be "said," a particular way of talking *through* which we can see the general nature of extraordinary, originary events.

TRANSCENDENTAL PRACTICAL REASONING: NEXT STEPS

Where, now, do we stand? Well, although it is clear that the end is not yet in sight, we no longer stand like Beckett's characters: "In this immense confusion one thing alone is clear. We are waiting for Godot to come" (Beckett, 1956, p. 80). Waiting for the "theory of everything" that the epistemological project promised no longer makes any sense. Hence the values of both Vygotsky's psychology and Vico's science of history: they place us in the middle of something that is ongoing; and they are both concerned with how, nonetheless, within this immense confusion, with a little help from our friends, we can and do get by. Indeed, to digress upon this point for a moment, it is worth reminding ourselves that, as a matter of fact, science has not yet achieved the success for which we were meant to wait: we have not yet managed to substitute a clear order for the vagueness and mystery, uncertainty and conflict apparent in our current forms of everyday social life, as well as the occasional appearance of the extraordinary and the surprising—thus we still cannot provide ourselves ahead of time with a mechanical guide as to what we should always do for the best. We still must decide practically, on the spot, in the circumstances as they arise. In the terms of Clov (in Samuel Beckett's *Endgame*), we have as yet failed to put "everything in its last place under its last dust," to give the final reasons for it all.

Acting "Through" Tools-of-Practical-Reasoning

But if vagueness and mystery, uncertainty and conflict, and the extraordinary are really there in the actual nature of our social lives together, if we are to construct a realistic account of our actual social being, an account of who we are or might be, and of the nature of our relations to each other, then this indeterminacy cannot be ignored—indeed, in its positive aspect, it is what makes for the "openness" of our lives. And this is why, I think, we must give up the epistemological (and Enlightenment) project of formulating *principled* foundations for our lives. Indeed, as Taylor (1989, p. 77) says, "What is relevant to my argument here is that articulating a vision of the good is not offering a single, basic reason." But if we are to *articulate* it, what actually does it involve in practice? For there is no doubt at the moment, once outside the routines of everyday life, we find ourselves confronting many genuine dilemmas, or situated in many (as I have called them) zones of real uncertainty or tension—tensions whose resolutions cannot easily be decided ahead of time, on principle. What in the practice of ordinary everyday life is involved, and what especially is involved for academics—given their special position (?) in relation to all the rest of us?

These are, I think, the kinds of problems that not only worry us generally, but are also the ones with which critics always confront social constructionists. If so, they are precisely of the kind explored by Vygotsky: they are problems that arise when one is at a boundary, or in a zone of disorderly activity between two relatively orderly forms of activity.[12] And at such boundaries, or in such zones, there are inevitably uncertainties and tensions. Some of these we have already met, both with Vygotsky's own approach and in confronting Vygotsky with Vico: the tension between dispassionate modes of instrumental reason and more engaged, passionate, and poetic forms. But there are other genuine tensions we face too: between the individual and the collective; between rights and duties; between self-fulfillment and benevolence to others; justice for ourselves and mercy toward others; the "natural" and the "artificial"; the "ordinary" and the "extraordinary"; and so on. But how to practically deal with and decide between such tensions—by our embodiment of "psychological instruments"—is, for Vygotsky, precisely the nature of the process in which our *higher* forms of mental functions are developed from *lower* forms. This, as I have argued here and elsewhere (Shotter, 1989), is his central and most important notion.[13]

But what I think needs to be added to his insight about the nature of psychological instruments is this: that in one of their forms we use them as *embodied prostheses,* that is, as historically developed, socio-cultural forms of practice, ways of acting and communicating, modes of being-in-the-world, forms of talk, *through* which we make a particular kind of sense of the world, one that is a part of what we (and others) take our cultural identity to be. Hence, in talking to and about, say, *persons* in our culture, we talk to and about them *through* an embodied *sense* of their nature, a body of knowledge that leads us to value—without quite knowing why—*both* self-expression and self-fulfillment (self-making) with its "downside" of seemingly externally imposed traditions *and* the task of "finding" one's natural, authentic self, along with whatever help one can get

---

[12] No prizes for noticing the influence of Chaos Theory on my formulations here. These are further worked out in Shotter (1991).

[13] To give an example: Vygotsky (1966, pp. 24–27) discusses what people might do in finding themselves in the position of Buridan's ass—apparently unable to decide which of two equally attractive foods to eat. Unlike the ass, they solve the problem by use of an artificial device, by casting lots: the person's behavior would be determined "not by the stimuli on hand, but by a new or invariably man-made psychological situation" (ibid., p. 27). Later, of course, they may not need to resort to the actual casting of lots, or toss of a coin at all, but could use an imaginary equivalent, making use of it as a "psychological instrument." It is this that sets people apart from animals. Here, Vygotsky was influenced by Engels's *Dialectics of Nature* (quoted in Vygotsky, 1966, p. 22): "the animal merely *uses* external nature, man, by his changes, makes it serve his ends, *masters* it," and in mastering it, Vygotsky adds, learns how to master himself.

from the techniques and discoveries of science, *along with* the feeling that one *ought* to be an integrated self—a rather peculiar idea within, as Geertz (1976) remarks, the context of the world's cultures. But for us this is normal. Something "in" us "shapes" our perceptions and actions such that, among other things, we distinguish normal (those like us) from abnormal people (those unlike us). But it is in the very nature of the (socially and communicatively developed) prostheses through which we make these judgments that—just as we feel the surface of the road *through* the steering gear of our cars as wet, icy, or dry, and *not* (as long as it works "properly") the workings of its cogs, pinions, or hydraulic pumps—their "workings" remain invisible to us . . . but not entirely.

For the main function of our psychological instruments, of our forms of talk, is not as the epistemological project would have it—to "represent" things—but to "give shape" to our activities, to our lives together. Thus, the "workings" of such "instruments," what their nature "is," is revealed to us at least in their use. And so their nature can be discovered, not from a study of how we talk about them in reflecting upon the structure of our language, but from a study of how "they" necessarily "shape" those of our everyday social practices in which they are involved. Their influence is revealed in the "grammar" of such activities. Hence Wittgenstein's (1953, no. 373) claim that "grammar tells us what kind of object anything is." Except, it must be added, that ultimately our "grammatical" studies will lead us beyond the realm of the ordinary into the extraordinary, that is, into the need for the poetics of which Vico speaks.

And this, I think, is the form of the new department of (poetic) reason, "whose excellence consists in our being able to articulate the background of our lives perspicuously," of which Taylor (1987, p. 481) speaks. Its task consists in the fashioning of, as Wittgenstein (1953, no. 122) termed them, "perspicuous representations." For, as he said:

> A main source of our failure to understand [how language works] is that we do not *command a clear view* of the use of our words.—Our grammar is lacking in this sort of perspicuity. A perspicuous representation produces just that understanding which consists in "seeing connections." Hence the importance of finding and inventing *intermediate cases.*
>
> The concept of perspicuous representation is of fundamental significance for us. It earmarks the form of account we give, the way we look at things. (Is this a "Weltanschauung"?)

Intermediate cases, cases on the boundaries between otherwise well-known entities, the unclear cases that make bad law and that *do not* give rise to the mechanical rules (needed by those who lack practical mastery), are just the ones we *do* need to reveal the nature of our practical-moral skills. And in the paradigms of both "joint action" and (Vico's account) the creating of "sensory topics," I have tried to provide just such prosthetics, a couple perspicuous representations *through* which we can "see" some of the issues in question.

Indeed, put this way, we can see that Wittgenstein's claim that our project must come to an end simply in a recognition of the "hurly-burly" (Wittgenstein, 1980, II, no. 629), or practices of everyday life,[14] is a "cop out"—for the source or sources of perspicuous representations, what might motivate their fashioning, still remain hidden from us. Our doctrines must take their beginnings from that of the matter of which they treat. We must reach back to the extraordinary phenomena, the lower forms of social life from out of which we have fashioned our higher forms, in order to "see" the fact of their continuing presence—in practices of child care, schooling, family life, education, public ceremonies and rituals, and other communicative practices in general—in the background of our current everyday social lives. Amid the routines (which can be *almost* emptied out into systems of rules), there are fleeting moments in which we must, in varying degrees of depth, be able to perceive ourselves as being (as already mentioned) surrounded by an invisible "landscape" of morally textured "opportunities for action," made differentially available to us according to our "position" in relation to the others around us. Without such a sense, the others around us would see us as "out of touch with reality," as lacking a proper social competency.

Thus, Taylor (1989) is clearly right, methodologically, to stress the continuity between later, higher, more autonomous forms of being and earlier, more "primitive" forms, in which one is more immersed in a community. Communal or relational forms of being are not only ontogenetically prior, but the necessity for a practical–moral sensibility—even if for only fleeting moments—makes it impossible for us, whether as ordinary people or academics, to adopt an independent, disengaged stance toward the whole range of our (or other's) thought and language. Methodologically, our individuality remains immersed, as it were, in relations of immersion. And without a sense, at the *moment* of our acting of the "position" we occupy in relation to (at least a partial) landscape of moral sources, we would be unable to show any consistency in our own activities— we would lack an intelligible identity, we would be unable ourselves to sustain our way of being in the world. We would be a mere creature of circumstances. But Taylor is concerned with more than these technical matters. He also wants to point out how, through language—even when it creates in us the illusion of our separateness from others—we remain related to our partners of discourse, either in real, live exchanges or in indirect confrontations. The fundamental dependence of our thoughtful way of being upon or ways of speaking makes interlocution, in one or another of these forms, inescapable for us. Thus, the same *moral* and *political* uncertainties and tensions influencing our relations with those around us come to be incorporated in the sensuous makeup of our very bodily being.

---

[14] See note 11.

CONCLUSIONS

Social constructionism, rather than assuming that reality has an as yet un-discovered order, recognizes that, as a matter of present, contingent fact, none of the social or mental forms of which we currently speak has an objective nature. In reality, they are all partial, provisional, and intersubjective (and probably, although there is not space to discuss it here, imaginary). If vagueness and mystery, uncertainty and conflict are *really* there in the actual nature of our social lives together, then, if we are to construct a realistic account of our actual social being—of who we are or might be, and of the nature of our relations to each other—they cannot be ignored. Account must be taken of them too. And this is in fact what I have taken to be a central feature of the moral worlds of our social being.

In such uncertain worlds, if there is to be any reliable intelligibility in them, then it is crucial whether people can and do take responsibility for their actions. If they do, then in Arendt's (1959) words, "even if there is no truth, men can be truthful, and even if there is no reliable certainty, men can be reliable" (p. 254).

Thus vagueness and mystery at the heart of a moral world do not preclude the possibility of an intelligible and satisfying social life. In fact, their presence motivates the attempt to achieve it, and makes the living of our lives the task it is; this "is" our nature: as only partially formed beings, living with only a partial knowledge of ourselves and our circumstances, we cannot avoid our continual moral *worries*. But, as Taylor (1989) argues, to live a properly moral life is not to live with a single, particular "hypergood" in mind that you can both state as a principle to others and "prove" to them that you are incontestably justified in following, but simply to live in touch with the tensions between the marvelous, socio-cultural, historical, dynamically developing but complex range of moral sources available to one in one's culture.

But, if one is in touch with the moral sources that give one's culture its identity, then one may always act in ways others will at least understand, if not always account right—indeed, one may feel that one has acted wrongly, and regret the fact. Yet, these self-same moral sources drive at least some of us (still under the influence of the Enlightenment and the epistemological project) to search for an end to such a state of affairs. And without a doubt, disengaged and instrumental modes of thought have (as well as enabling us to be "masters and possessors of Nature"), when turned around and applied to ourselves, emanci-pated us . . . to an extent. But, when elevated to the position of a hypergood, they have occluded, not only other important goods, but the very idea of the practical-moral life, in which such goods must play a part. Thus the search by many others, for something in terms of which to restore depth, richness, and meaning to life, to recover what our current knowledge disciplines have occluded or rendered "rationally-invisible"[15] to us.

Indeed, it was the failure of a natural scientific psychology to treat people as if they existed in a social, institutional, cultural, and historical vacuum. In so doing, morality became a kind of "bolt-on" extra, something that was required *if* we were going to be social beings–hence the need for it to be explicitly justified, theoretically. Whereas, in the social constructionist approach I have outlined here, our individuality is "constructed" and sustained only within "joint action" with others (Shotter, 1984). We cannot not be moral beings in one way or another. Even our attempts to hide that fact from ourselves are done in the service of a certain moral preference (an escape from *imposed* social orders) (Taylor, 1989).

Thus, as I see it, one conclusion we come to is this: social constructionism, in some of its forms at least, not only *can* but *must* embody the moral moment in life and in the living of it, in a way that is excluded in all the stances driven by the epistemological project—for *they* all ignore the social moment in which the ethical deed in the making is at work. In acting morally or not, the question is not whether one is acting according to justifiable "principles" or "standards"— because there are none. Constructionism in that sense *is* radically antifoundationalist. But not being able to offer, like good epistemologists, external, decontextualized criteria for their claims does not mean that they have no standards at all. As I have already made clear in discussions of the nature of joint action, the very nature of the context in which one's practical reasoning takes place is such as to provide, moment by moment, its own sensory or felt standards as to what is or is not fitting to it. Only if one is still something of an unreconstructed epistemologist, who still feels [sic] that *all* one's actions should be founded or rooted within a single hypergood—and clearly, the neo-Nietzschean hypergood of breaking with all existing contexts because (as another aspect of one's unreconstruction) one feels they all constitute closed systems is an obvious one at the moment—will one's "constructionism" not yet be completely antifoundationalist. One has not accepted yet, as Wittgenstein (1981, no. 656) put it, that one's language "is variously rooted, it has roots, not a single root," that our rootings are historical, socio-cultural products, and that is it up to *us* to make them.

Indeed—to emphasize the nonrelativistic nature of social constructionism—it is worth adding here that (1) it is in the very nature of the contexts of joint action that they provide or afford one a *sense* of what is fitting in the context or not and (2) that (although there has been no space to discuss this) as one moves from the center of such activity to its boundaries, and comes more into contact with the activity of those toward the "outside" of one's own social surroundings, so one

---

[15] To invert a term of Harold Garfinkel's (1967).

comes more into contact with the "otherness" in terms of which one's own form of social life has its being. In other words, it is in the very practical-moral nature of our constructed being that we *must* continually come up against that which is other-than ourselves. Our practical–moral reasoning does not, and cannot, take place solely within a system of any kind, whether it consists in rules, beliefs, values, or whatever; it cannot go on solely in the decontextualized head of an individual; the need for it only appears in the open meeting with an other. Such a form of nonrelativism may not satisfy the unreconstructed epistemologist, for it still seems to leave us, at this moment in history, reasoning relative to wherever we are "placed" in our culture, relative to where it is "placed" in relation to others, and where they are "placed" in relation to the rest of the cosmos. Thus it does not provide an Archimedean point for reason, only a guarantee of the possibility of the slow, historical slog of error-correction. This, it seems to me, is the best we can claim. Who can *realistically* ask for more?

REFERENCES

Arendt, H. (1958). *The Human Condition*. New York: Doubleday Anchor Books. Orig. Pub.

Bakhtin, M. M. (1981). *The Dialogical Imagination*. Edited by M. Holquist, trans. by C. Emerson and M. Holquist. Austin, Tx: University of Texas Press.

Cavell, S. (1969). *Must We Mean What We Say?*. London: Cambridge University Press.

Garfinkel, H. (1967). *Studies in Ethnomethodology*. Englewood Cliffs: Prentice-Hall.

Geertz, C. (1973). *Local Knowledge: Further Essays in Interpretative Anthropology*. New York: Basic Books.

Geertz, C. (1976). From the native's point of view: on the nature of anthropological understanding. In K. H. Basso and H. A. Selby (Eds.). *Meaning in Anthropology*. Albuquerque: University of New Mexico Press.

Gergen, K. J. (1985). The social constructionist movement in modern psychology. *American Psychologist, 40*. 266–275.

Giddens, A. (1980). *The Constitution of Society*. Cambridge: Polity Press.

Helder, F. (1958). *The Psychology of Interpersonal Relations*. New York: Wiley.

Koch, S. (1964). Psychology and emerging conceptions of knowledge and unitary. T. W. Wann (Ed.) *Behaviourism and Phenomenology*. Chicago: University of Chicago Press.

Macmurray, J. (1961). *Persons in Relation*. London: Faber and Faber.

Mead, G. H. (1934). *Mind, Self and Society*. Chicago: University of Chicago Press.

Merleau-Ponty, M. (1962). *Phenomenology of Perception* (trans. C. Smith). London: Routledge and Kegan Paul.

Rorty, R. (1980). *Philosophy and the Mirror of Nature*. Oxford: Blackwell.

Schutz, A. (1964). *Collected Papers II: Studies in Social Theory*. The Hague: Martinus Nijhoff.

Shotter, J. (1974). The development of personal powers. In M. P. M. Richards (Ed.) *The Integration of a Child into a Social World*. Cambridge: Cambridge University Press.

Shotter, J. (1975). *Images of Man in Psychological Research*. London: Methuen.

Shotter, J. (1984). *Social Accountability and Selfhood*. Oxford: Blackwell.

Shotter, J. (1986). A sense of place: Vico and the social production of social identities. *British Journal of Social Psychology, 25*. 199–211.

Shotter, J. (1989). Vygotsky's psychology: joint activity in a developmental zone. *New Ideas in Psychology, 7.* 185–204.

Shotter, J. (1991). A poetics of relational forms: the sociality of everyday social life. *Cultural Dynamics, 4,* 379–396.

Taylor, C. (1987). Overcoming epistemology. *In* K. Bayner, J. Bohman, and T. McCarthy (Eds.) *After Philosophy: End or Transformation?* Cambridge, MA: MIT Press.

Taylor, C. (1989). *Sources of the Self: the Making of the Modern Identity.* Cambridge, MA: Harvard University Press.

Verene, D. P. (1981). *Vico's Science of the Imagination.* Ithaca and London: Cornell University Press.

Vico, G. (1948). The New Science of Giambattista Vico. *Ed. and trans T. G. Bergin and M. H. Fisch.* Ithaca, N.Y.: Cornell University Press.

Vygotsky, L. S. (1962). *Thought and Language.* Cambridge, MA: MIT Press.

Vygotsky, L. S. (1966). Development of the higher mental functions. In A. N. Leont'ev, A. R. Luria and A. Smirnov (Eds.) *Psychological Research in the USSR.* Moscow: Progress Publishers.

Vygotsky, L. S. (1987). *Thinking and Speech.* In *The Collected Works of L. S. Vygotsky: Vol. 1* Edited by R. W. Rieber and A. S. Carton, and translated by N. Minick. New York: Plenum Press.

Wittgenstein, L. (1953). *Philosophical Investigations.* Oxford: Blackwell.

Wittgenstein, L. (1969). *On Certainty.* Oxford: Blackwell.

Wittgenstein, L. (1980). *Remarks on the Philosophy of Psychology.* Vols. 1 and 2. Oxford: Blackwell.

Wittgenstein, L. (1981). *Zettel.* (2nd. Ed.) G. E. M. Anscombe and G. H. V. Wright (Eds.). Oxford: Blackwell.

15 MORAL PHILOSOPHY AND SOCIAL SCIENCE: A CRITIQUE OF CONSTRUCTIONIST REASON

W. Gerrod Parrott

How might the social sciences contribute to our understanding of the moral dimension of life? John Shotter's paper seems intended to answer this question by example. Rather than merely writing about social science's potential in the moral domain, Shotter has skipped the preliminary speculation and gone off and done some social science for us. In my commentary I want to assess how successful this attempt has been, not only in terms of the correctness of this particular account, but also in terms of the type of account of which this paper is a token.

To do this, it is first necessary to provide some of the preliminary speculation myself—only this way will there be a framework within which to evaluate Professor Shotter's theory. I shall begin, therefore, by considering the ways in which the social sciences might illuminate the moral aspects of life.

SOCIAL SCIENCE AND MORAL PHILOSOPHY

One way for the social sciences to address ethics is to do what the philosophers do, but to do it in a manner that is informed by some of the theoretical assumptions of one or another school of social science. That is, social scientists can do philosophy, just as anyone else can; what would incline one to call such cogitation "social science" rather than (or in addition to) "moral philosophy" would be its incorporation of the perspectives of social science. To qualify as moral philosophy, however, the philosophical efforts of social scientists must address the problems traditionally of concern to moral philosophers, or at least provide a principled account of why they do not. These problems include the nature of ethical truth, its relation to the nonmoral facts on which it depends, whether or how one can specify the principles or rules that moral people should live by, whether people are actually better off for living in a moral fashion, practical guidance about how we ought to behave, and so forth.

One does not see much social science fitting this description. One may easily find it *implicit* in the work of social scientists; for example, Steven Tipton's interviews with psychotherapists suggest that radical moral relativism, subjectivism, and expressive individualism underlie the approach used by many therapists (Bellah, Madsen, Sullivan, Swidler, and Tipton, 1985, Chap. 5). Yet, these moral philosophies rarely are worked out systematically by the social scientists who use them (although they do sometimes find their way into the philosophical literature, because social science influences culture generally and thereby its philosophers). Social scientists are usually not trained to do this sort of theoretical work, but, rather, some sort of empirical work. Theoretical psychologists are an exception here, but their interests have tended to be outside the ethical domain.

Why the reluctance to engage in moral philosophy? The principal reason would seem to rest in the social scientist's conception of what science is about. Moral philosophy necessarily has a prescriptive, nonempirical quality about it. (Even those philosophies that reject its prescriptive quality—such as skepticism and subjectivism—seem to have little content other than arguments against prescriptivism.) Science, on the other hand, is supposed (at least by most social scientists) to be descriptive and empirical. Thus, even the most theoretically sophisticated social scientists, those who willingly and capably grapple with the philosophy of science and the hermeneutics of discourse, tend to consider ethics out-of-bounds.

The great irony in this fact, of course, is that the social sciences historically originated in moral philosophy. From the invention of philosophy with Socrates to the emergence of the social sciences in the second half of the nineteenth century, the subject of moral philosophy included not only ethics but also government, religion, interpersonal relationships, social dynamics, and human nature. A typical course in moral philosophy in an American college around 1800 included readings in the philosophy of mind, rhetoric, ethics, natural law, government, politics, and political economy (Bryson, 1932). Only in the late nineteenth century did the social sciences begin to emerge as independent disciplines. The reasons for this emergence were many and complex, but, as Haskell argues in his book *The Emergence of Professional Social Science,* they certainly included (1) doubt triggered by historical criticism of the Bible and Darwin's theory of evolution and (2) incentives for professionalism inherent in urban-industrial society. With the emergence of the social sciences there was a shift in the type of explanation offered for human action, from explanations based on the free will of autonomous individuals to explanations based on a set of interdependent forces that determine an individual's behavior outside of his or her will (Haskell, 1977). Whereas the former view may tend to exaggerate individual responsibility, the latter view tends to depict individuals as puppets pulled by strings of instinct and social forces.

Accompanying this transformation in the study of ethics and social science was a transformation in the social identity of those scholars doing the studying. Whereas the desired product of the early nineteenth-century college was the "man of learning," the research university of the twentieth century desired to produce the "scientist." This new identity had its disadvantages. To the extent that social scientists now wrote for their professional colleagues, used their professional jargon, and were evaluated and given status by their professional peers, they tended to withdraw from the culture at large (Bellah et al., 1985; Haskell, 1977). Specialization increased as the social sciences carved up the domain formerly called moral philosophy. Inasmuch as ethics requires a broader perspective than that spanned by any of the social sciences, social scientists feel unqualified to span the range of issues necessary to do the subject justice.

In summary, there are a number of reasons why social scientists fail to exercise their right to do moral philosophy. They tend to see their task as being empirical and descriptive. Their training does not equip them to combine the perspectives that inhere in good moral philosophy. They do not view themselves as authorized to try to persuade others to adopt the philosophy they hold. The philosophy they hold has often been either so deterministic or so relativistic that individual moral action ceases to have the importance that it once had.

These are the social scientists' reasons for avoiding moral philosophy, but many of these reasons are historical, cultural, and probabilistic—they do not apply to all actual social scientists (although they do apply to many), and even their successful application seems contingent, not necessary. One may still ask, then, whether it is conceivable that the social sciences may contribute to moral philosophy. The answer, I believe, is yes. I can think of three ways in which contributions might be made, although in the first of these cases the contributors may be found only in those Possible Worlds that are very nearly Ideal Worlds.

The first type of contribution is to those realms of moral philosophy that are ethereal, that is, nonempirical. I have in mind here two types of ether: faith and logic. Contemporary moral philosophers may balk at including faith as part of their discipline, but this only shows that the discipline of philosophy has not been immune to the forces that encouraged professionalism and specialization in the social sciences! Faith (and religion) was certainly a part of moral philosophy prior to our own century, and, in many of the greatest works, ethics and religion meld. A work such as Kierkegaard's (1846/1946) *Concluding Unscientific Postscript* is without doubt about ethics, without doubt philosophical, and contains arguments for the necessity of faith (the famous "leap" thereof). There is a natural discord between ethics based on faith and ethics based on empirical research; it was noted at the birth of the social sciences. There is an account by John W. Burgess, who began teaching history and political science at Amherst College in the 1870s, of the difference between his approach and that of his senior colleagues, who

> regarded the college as a place for discipline, not as a place for research. To them the truth had already been found. It was contained in the Bible, and it was the business of the college to give the preliminary training for acquiring and disseminating it. Research implied doubt. It implied that there was a great deal of truth still to be found, and it implied that the truth thought to have been already found was approximate and in continual need of revision and readjustment. Still more briefly expressed, they regarded research as more or less heretical. (Burgess, 1934, pp. 147–148, quoted by Haskell, 1977, pp. 46–47)

The second type of ether is that of logic. There are aspects of moral philosophy to which empirical data are simply irrelevant. For example, entire sections of Kant's (1785/1959) *Foundations of the Metaphysics of Morals* consist of logical arguments that are not open to empirical falsification. If they are wrong, it is because they are incoherent (as some of them are), not because they are inconsistent with some empirical finding. The arguments have the structure of syllogisms in which the premises are hypothetical propositions; conceptual analysis and the search for logical contradiction are the basis for determining the validity of Kant's conclusions (Wolff, 1973).

Social science, construed as an empirical endeavor, is clearly irrelevant to these aspects of moral philosophy. This conclusion is what I take to be one of the points made by Robinson (Chapter 7, this volume). Yet, inasmuch as not all of social science is empirical, not all of social science is irrelevant. It is conceivable that some aspects of social science are both nonempirical and relevant to the moral dimension of life, and therefore that social science could make contributions to even the most ethereal realms of moral philosophy. It is possible that the theory of social constructionism is such an aspect, and thus that Shotter's own paper may fall into this realm.

There is a second, potentially more empirically based manner in which social science could contribute to moral philosophy. It stems from the fact that not all moral philosophy is ethereal. Most systems of ethics are based on certain beliefs about human nature. Aristotle, for example, couches his ethical theory in the *Nicomachean Ethics* not only in considerations of what is right but also in considerations of what people are like and of what they are capable. Aristotle's account combines logical arguments with astute observations about human nature. It is often remarked that Aristotle's ethical theory is based on his psychology (Fortenbaugh, 1975; Robinson, 1989). Aristotle's investigation of emotions led to his development of a bipartite psychology that distinguishes logical and alogical portions of the soul, and this conclusion influences his prescription for the development of good character. His observation that reason develops relatively late in childhood informs his thinking about moral education and also about the possibility of virtuous action in the absence of deliberation. Observations (as they were) about slaves and women influence his conclusions about their moral status. Observations on the effects of verbal persuasion on hunger, thirst, love, and hate influence the ethical aspects of his classification of emotions and nonrational appetites. The tradition of naturalistic philosophy that follows from Aristotle bases standards of value in what are believed to be the basic needs and capacities of humans—in short, in a conception of human nature. In principle, the empirical findings of social science could be used as a source of information about human nature. Such a contribution is more tangential than the type described earlier, and it will be of little use to an idealistic philosophy, but it nevertheless appears to be a real and useful contribution to moral philosophy proper. Shotter's paper, if it does not qualify as the first type of contribution (and I do not think it does), might be construed as this type instead.

Both of these two types of contribution to moral philosophy require a certain degree of optimism to be taken seriously. In the case of those areas of ethics that fall within the domains of faith or logic, one must be optimistic to assume that social science can produce theory capable of adding to the Great Debate. In the case of using empirical findings to modify our view of human nature, one must also be a bit optimistic to assume that economic generalizations, sociological data, or the findings of the psychology laboratory could ever discover anything that Aristotle, Kant, or Bentham (or their grandmothers) did not already know. For this reason it is prudent to establish a third way in which social science can contribute to our understanding of the moral dimension.

Rather than try to contribute to moral philosophy per se, the social sciences might abandon any attempt at prescriptive ethics and instead limit themselves to "descriptive ethics." Social science might attempt to inform us about ethics by investigating how actual people treat moral issues in their everyday lives. This approach asks what moral beliefs people actually hold rather than what beliefs they ought to hold; it studies what social forces influence people's moral actions rather than what criteria ought to be influential; it investigates the ways in which people go about applying their general moral principles under the difficult conditions of actual life, in which events are ambiguous and in which principles conflict. This way of addressing the moral dimension of life plays more to the traditional strengths of the social sciences, whose empirically oriented practitioners have long been inhibited from moral prescription by Hume's (1740/1896) famous observation that "as this *ought,* or *ought not,* expresses some new relation or affirmation, 'tis necessary that it shou'd be observ'd and explain'd;

and at the same time that a reason should be given, for what seems altogether inconceivable, how this new relation can be a deduction from others, which are entirely different from it" (*A Treatise of Human Nature,* Book III, Part I, Sec. I).

An example or two of this approach will help establish the ways in which empirical investigation can illuminate the moral dimension of life. A superb example is provided by the book *Habits of the Heart,* by Bellah et al. (1985). Much like Tocqueville, they engaged a spectrum of American citizens in conversation about values and ethics in an attempt to learn about the American character, the cultural traditions and practices that shape it, and the language that is used to express it. Their essays explore the tensions between American tradition of individualism and the more communal traditions of republican civics and Christian religion. They describe changes that have occurred since Tocqueville's time, such as the extent to which the modern moral vocabulary has become more exclusively focused on private goals and rewards and less on public duty. Another example would be the work of Sabini and Silver (1982, represented by Sabini in Chapter 6, this volume). Their research includes both conceptual analysis of everyday moral language and empirical investigation. Their aim is to clarify the assumptions and considerations that influence moral thought and action in everyday life. Both of these examples certainly differ from moral philosophy, but both do inform us about the moral domain of life in interesting and important ways.

This discussion has developed a theme of our conference, the ways in which a social scientist could conceivably contribute to our understanding of the moral. It suggests that there are at least three ways in which such a contribution might occur: the production of moral philosophy informed by the theory of the social sciences; the contribution to naturalistic moral philosophy of observations and conclusions about human nature; and the observation, description, and analysis of the ways in which actual moral actors go about trying to apply ethics in real life. It is in this context that I wish to frame my comments on John Shotter's paper.

SHOTTER'S SOCIAL CONSTRUCTIONISM

John Shotter, despite his modesty in claiming to create only an unsystematic toolbox, seems to be striving for something much more ambitious: setting forth the foundations of nothing less than an entirely "new enterprise," to use his own description. Shotter begins by arguing that our sense of self is not something that is preestablished or self-contained. Rather, it is constructed from social relationships and institutions that are historically and culturally contingent. The social constructionist program, as I understand it, is to make explicit these contexts so as to better understand both the selves that we are and the possible selves that we have not become. The goal of Shotter's essay, I believe, is to provide a theory of the social self that is capable of explaining the moral worlds people inhabit. Shotter envisions his theory not as systematic, but rather as a collection of analytic techniques, a "toolbox" that can be used to articulate the sources of our moral natures. Shotter wishes to propose a form of reasoning, not a set of answers.

Shotter's theory borrows from three sources: the developmental psychology of Lev Vygotsky, the counter-Enlightenment relativism of Giambattista Vico, and the historical approach to self-identity of Charles Taylor. Following Vygotsky, Shotter begins with the infant and asks what is necessary for the infant to become a responsible person. The answer, Shotter argues, is that the infant must develop a social identity, because responsible behavior requires a sense of who one is in relation to other people. But certain mental capacities are required to accept responsibility—how does the infant acquire them? To answer this question Shotter again adopts the Vygotskian solution, that the origins of higher mental functions are social in nature, resulting from the internalization of activities that are initially stimulated by others in social interactions. This process is explored at some length by Shotter in his analysis of "joint action." Shotter argues that joint action develops moral conceptions of duties and rights: His example is of a speaker's right to expect of a listener the duty of taking the speaker seriously. A competent social actor will sense his or her position in the social order and will respond accordingly; he or she will also sense momentary changes in social position and will participate in the processes by which such positioning is negotiated between competing actors.

But how do such institutionalized patterns of social interchange become established in the first place? To address this issue, Shotter turns to Vico's idea—well, let us call it a "poetic image"—that humans began as preliterate, nonconceptual, and nonlogical communicators who developed a "sensory topic" upon realizing that all members of their group were having the same experience during a moment of mass fear. The inarticulate feelings of this "sensory topic" were then gradually transformed into the external symbolic forms that compose our social reality.

For Shotter, there are profound implications to the conclusion that the bases of social reality are as vague as these inarticulate feelings. The entire Enlightenment project of understanding reality with a grand epistemological theory is doomed, because reality will not fit any such theory. Instead, we are struck with a reality that is vague, uncertain, and confusing. For this reason Shotter thinks it is also necessary to abandon the goal of formulating general ethical principles. Instead, he proposes that we must try to understand the ethical by considering "intermediate cases" and "zones of tension" in which people display their use of "psychological instruments" and "embodied prostheses" such as "joint action" and "sensory topics," through which people construct their activities. Any such understanding must face the fact that social forms are provisional and subjective, vague and mysterious; to the extent that we experience life as grounded in absolute truth, it seems that we are merely revealing our strong motivation to deceive ourselves that it is otherwise.

THE CRITIQUE

John Shotter has provided us with a detailed statement of a social constructionist approach to the moral world. Strong themes of skepticism and of counter-Enlightenment thought color his essay. Acutely aware of the skeptical arguments against ultimate truth or meaning, he set forth to describe the best that can realistically be hoped for in knowing. With Vico, he rejects the concept of a timeless absolute Natural Law that can be true for all people anywhere. In my preceding summary of his paper, I hope that a number of virtues became evident: the cumulative structure of the arguments, its creativity in synthesizing a variety of sources, its sheer ambitiousness and scope. I now wish to address what I believe to be its shortcomings. In the sections that follow, I discuss some ways in which the paper fails as moral philosophy, some ambiguities in the constructionist account, and what I think is a fatal logical error inherent in this sort of constructionist position.

Ethics in the Ether

At the beginning of this essay I described three ways in which social science could contribute to understanding of the moral dimension. Shotter's endeavor might seem to be an attempt at the first, a nonempirical statement of moral philosophy informed by insight gained from the study of the social world. Shotter's paper is certainly nonempirical, but attempting to read it as a statement of the logic of moral philosophy leads to difficulty. The problem is that relatively little of the paper deals directly with moral matters per se. The paper contains a great deal of theory about how children are enculturated, but little that addresses moral development as a special topic. Shotter appears to believe that the moral dimension is not particularly different from any other social dimension, that the moral and spiritual ideas to which we aspire are simply components of our sense of self. He discusses the origins of the self as if any conclusions about the self in general would clearly hold true for one's sense of morality, but this assumption is not defended and it never becomes clear to what extent Shotter's conclusions about the self in general will be true of the moral sense in particular.

Judging from the examples Shotter has chosen to illustrate his points, one must wonder whether consideration of the moral dimension really entered into his theorizing much at all. There are only a few concrete examples in the entire essay, and none of them strikes one as being about what most of us mean by the moral dimension of life. His principal example of moral rights and duties involves the obligations inherent in being a first-person speaker, a second-person listener, or a third-person observer: first-persons have a right to speak and be taken seriously, second-persons the duty to listen, and so forth. Although I do appreciate that there are duties and obligations present in social roles, and although it is true that authors such as Goffman (1959) have used the word "moral" in connection with some of them, I must point out that *"Thou shalt not interrupt!"* is not a central example of morality! Even though this paper has frequent references to the "practical–moral life," there seems little direct evidence that the moral life had a part in shaping this theory.

There are several substantive points to be made about the paucity and noncentral nature of the examples in Shotter's paper. One is that it makes it nearly impossible for the theory to do two things that all theories must: be evaluated and be applied. Even someone as famous for abstraction as Kant, following his proof of the validity of the Categorical Imperative in the *Foundations of the Metaphysics of Morals,* proceeds to provide four worked-out examples of the application of this principle. Shotter's theory is intended to be "unsystematic, an 'analytic toolbox', . . . a form of reasoning, . . . attuned not to abstract universals or generalities, but concerned with the irremediably 'local,' and particular character of truth, argument, and validity." One would think that such an account would at least be presented in the concrete particulars of everyday life and be grounded in the specific details of actual experience. Yet, this account of the local lacks the references to the local that would make such reasoning ring true, and in this way fails to present the very advantages that it claims for itself.

When I characterized the elements of logic and faith in moral philosophy as "ethereal," I hardly meant that such philosophizing should itself float off into the ether, unconnected to concrete life. When we look at the moral dimension of everyday life, we see that people passionately debate the justice of war, the fairness of policy, the obligations of friendship. Moral philosophy needs to be grounded in the real stuff of actual ethics, both because that is its source and because its traditional function is to guide people in how to live. When the British moralists went about their inquiry into the moral realm, they adopted "the level of the plain man, and even the 'honest farmer,' not that of the saint in his cell nor that of the philosopher in his closet, and his experience is treated as supplying the material for further examination" (Selby-Bigge, 1897, p. xvii). There was always, in these thinkers, an effort to bring their generalizations to the test by applying them to the particular and the everyday. The language of Shaftesbury, Hutcheson, Butler, Price, and the rest had a simplicity and clarity that allows one to test their ideas against one's own experience, and to readily recognize errors when they occur. This feature, of course, was also true of Aristotle, and of John Dewey, and it characterizes the work of those modern "social scientists" such as Sabini and Silver (1982) and Bellah et al. (1985), who ground reasoning about moral action in observations about people's moral talk and in specific examples of moral choices.

For this reason, Shotter's paper is probably not best considered as moral philosophy per se, the first category. For similar reasons, it cannot be considered to be an analysis of the ways in which actual actors go about trying to apply ethics in real life, the third category of contribution. It is probably best regarded as an instance of the second category, an offering of insights about human nature and the social realm that may be of use in creating moral philosophies.

Constructionist Conundrums

In examining Shotter's theory, there are of course a number of places where one could raise objections or wish for clarification. It is possible to quibble with the definition of "objective" that Shotter uses when maintaining that moral reality does not have an objective existence. As Sabini and Silver (1982) have pointed out, there exist many senses of "objective," and in some of them it is quite plausible to state that moral facts exist objectively. In particular, one can state that, for the members of a given culture, it is true that moral beliefs are objective in the sense that people *treat* them as if they are objective, and act correspondingly. Thus, if people's actions "construct" reality as per the idea of joint action, then they can construct an objective reality.

Shotter argues that intermediate cases are the ones needed to reveal the nature of our skills and show that people do not operate with general moral rules, but, appeals to chaos theory notwithstanding, I could imagine making exactly the opposite conclusion from this fact. Is it not the case that intermediate cases are precisely the ones that give people trouble in real life, and might this not suggest that people in fact operate using moral rules?

Finally, Shotter makes such good use of Vico's counter-Enlightenment arguments that it seems almost unsportsmanlike to point out that this Neapolitan philosopher had some ideas that strain credibility a bit. We are asked to believe that humans began as preliterate, nonconceptual, and nonlogical communicators. When these creatures all experienced the same inarticulate emotion simultaneously they are supposed to have developed a "sensory topic," a sort of primordial beetle-in-a-box, as it were. Through means unspecified, these sensory topics allowed people to somehow bootstrap their communications to form external symbolic forms. Like most of the early counter-Enlightenment thinkers, Vico's thought contains elements that anticipate the Romantics a century ahead of time. Without further support, I am afraid that Vico's account strikes me as like much Romantic thought: fanciful, intuitive, and incredible.

The Central Fallacy

I have not gone into much detail in describing any of these quibbles because they do not seem significant in the face of what appears to be a serious, central inconsistency in the constructionist account: The arguments advanced in support of social constructionism are so powerful that they are usable against construc-tionism itself. The theory of social constructionism asserts that there can be certainty that we cannot believe anything with certainty. The theory claims that there is mystery and vagueness at the heart of our epistemological and moral worlds; but the theory claims to be exempt from this vagueness. Herein lies the central contradiction of the theory. If social constructionism is correct about the uncertainty of the world, to be consistent it would have to be uncertain about its own validity. Shotter seems quite certain about its validity, and thereby appears to be inconsistent with his theory.

This argument is hardly new, of course—we all learned it in our freshmen philosophy courses, but sometimes those freshmen-year arguments are just the right ones. This particular one has a long history in connection with skepticism, and its applicability in the present case derives from the skeptical epistemology that underlies many of the social constructionist arguments. To illustrate the connection, a brief review is in order.

The ancient skeptics (of the Academic and especially Pyrrhonian schools, as described by Cicero and Sextus) attacked the dogmatist Stoics and Epicureans on the grounds that there were no infallible tests of truth. In doing so they had to be careful not to be dogmatic themselves in stating that nothing could be known. Instead, they carefully *suspended judgment* on every issue. Their arguments for this conclusion were systematized in lists of tropes that sound quite consonant with some of the arguments used two millennia later by Shotter against the "epistemological project" of the Enlightenment. The tropes included assertions that: (1) the same thing appears different to people in different relative positions and to people from different cultures, (2) any proposition must be supported by another proposition, which leads to an infinite regress, and (3) dogmatists take unproved assumptions as their starting point in order to avoid this infinite regress (De Lacy, 1973). Yet, from these tropes the skeptics concluded that they should suspend their judgment, not that they could have certainty about the ultimate vagueness of the world. They described their philosophy as a purge that elimi-nates everything, including itself (Popkin, 1967).

It is interesting to examine the manner in which the skeptics were criticized in ancient times. One criticism was that the skeptical arguments made action impos-sible, since action requires a decision and decision is impossible when judgment is suspended. The skeptical reply, interestingly, was to accept peacefully the world of appearances and the customs of the society they found themselves in. More to the present point is the criticism that skepticism is self-contradictory, which was usually stated in the following form: a person claiming that nothing is known must admit that he or she cannot be sure that even this fact is known, and therefore must admit that perhaps something *can* be known (or else commit a logical inconsistency) (De Lacy, 1973). This criticism is what inclined the ancient skeptics to insist that the correct attitude was one of suspended judgment, not of certainty of vagueness.

Concluding Unconstructionist Postscript

There remains hope for universal moral principles, and even for social science's participation in finding them. Shotter at one point appears to endorse some recent arguments of Charles Taylor to the effect that some elements of ethics can be defended as universally true. Taylor's approach is to avoid the type of deductive argumentation that is based on premises that are universally and necessarily true (Nussbaum, 1990). He proposes a different sort of argument, one that, to me, seems pragmatic and almost quasi-experimental. Taylor tries to show that one ethical belief is superior to another by examining historical times in which each belief was held. To the extent that one belief appears to have prevented difficulties and promoted understanding superior to the other belief, the former is judged superior to the latter. Taylor's technique remains sketchily developed at present, but it seems to have potential for yielding a set of moral principles that is considerably less arbitrary than any that Shotter's account would allow (Nussbaum, 1990). Also, it would be a good deal less depressing: On Shotter's account—reminiscent of another modern skeptic, Albert Camus—we have the choice either of being aware of the vague emptiness at the core of all beliefs or of being fools. With Taylor there seem more grounds for preferring certain moral beliefs over others.

In a similar vein, it may be noted that Martha Nussbaum (1988) has recently interpreted Aristotle as developing an ethics that is both universal and nevertheless compatible with the constructionist view that there is no way of seeing the world that is entirely free of cultural and historical bias. Nussbaum depicts Aristotle's system of virtues as being derived from spheres of human experience that are universal. Courage, for example, is the virtue that is exhibited in the face of fear of important damages; generosity is the virtue displayed when managing one's personal property with respect to others; mildness of temper is the virtuous attitude displayed toward slights and damages. Aristotle's virtues can be seen as being derived from universals in the human condition, not from the specific "psychological instruments" of an ancient Greek gentleman. In Nussbaum's effort we see another attempt to defend objective, universal, nonrelativistic ethics from the arguments of skeptics.

And, supposing that the skeptics come back with more of the doubt-inducing rejoinders that they are famous for, we should always keep in mind that not all skeptics abandon the moral philosophies that they believe to be groundless. Kierkegaard, recall, was a brilliant skeptic, demolishing the Hegelian approach as he did; but he then took on his ethical and religious beliefs as a "leap of faith." *A fortiori,* he argued that he was all the better off for having done so. So, one way or another, it seems that the social sciences' deconstruction of the moral domain may lead to a moral reconstruction.

REFERENCES

Bellah, R. N., Madsen, R., Sullivan, W. M., Swidler, A., and Tipton, S. M. (1985). *Habits of the heart.* Berkeley: University of California Press.

Bryson, G. (1932). The emergence of the social sciences from moral philosophy. *The International Journal of Ethics, 42,* 304–323.

Burgess, J. W. (1934). *Reminiscences of an American scholar: The beginnings of Columbia University.* Morningside Heights, NY: Columbia University Press.

De Lacy, P. (1973). Skepticism in antiquity. In P. P. Wiener (Ed.), *Dictionary of the history of ideas,* Vol. 4, pp. 234–240. New York: Charles Scribner's Sons.

Fortenbaugh, W. W. (1975). *Aristotle on emotion.* New York: Barnes & Noble.

Goffman, E. (1959). *The presentation of self in everyday life.* Garden City, NY: Doubleday.

Haskell, T. L. (1977). *The emergence of professional social science.* Urbana: University of Illinois Press.

Hume, D. (1896). *A treatise of human nature,* Book III. Oxford, England: Oxford University Press. [Original work published in 1740.]

Kant, I. (1959). *Foundations of the metaphysics of morals,* translated by L. W. Beck. Indianapolis, IN: Bobbs-Merrill. [Original work published in 1785.]

Kierkegaard, S. (1946). Concluding unscientific postscript to the "philosophical fragments," translated by D. F. Swenson, L. M. Swenson, and W. Lowrie. In R. Bretall (Ed.), *A Kierkegaard anthology,* pp. 190–258. Princeton, NJ: Princeton University Press. [Original work published in 1846.]

Nussbaum, M. C. (1988). Non-relative virtues: An Aristotelian approach. In P. A. French, T. E. Uehling, Jr., and H. K. Wettstein (Eds.), *Midwest studies in philosophy volume XIII: Ethical theory: Character and virtue,* pp. 32–53. Notre Dame, IN: University of Notre Dame Press.

Nussbaum, M. (1990, April 9). Our pasts, ourselves. *The New Republic, 202,* 27–34.

Popkin, R. H. (1967). Skepticism. In P. Edwards (Ed.), *The encyclopedia of philosophy,* Vol. 7, pp. 449–461. New York: Macmillan.

Robinson, D. N. (1989). *Aristotle's psychology.* New York: Columbia University Press.

Sabini, J., and Silver, M. (1982). *Moralities of everyday life.* New York: Oxford University Press.

Selby-Bigge, L. A. (1897). *British moralists,* Vol. 1. Oxford, England: Oxford University Press.

Wolff, R. P. (1973). *The autonomy of reason.* New York: Harper & Row.

16 EPILOGUE

EDITOR'S NOTE

Symposiasts had the opportunity, after receiving the essays in this volume, to meet for two days to discuss points of disagreement. All of the remarks were recorded and transcribed and yielded about 500 typed pages of unedited text. Entire sentences and fragments of sentences were often inaudible, and yet other and numerous passages were incorrectly heard by the diligent nonspecialists who finally had the task of typing from the tapes. Nonetheless, the thick if cluttered record of these colloquies did provide many interesting and illuminating passages.

This Epilogue is divided into selections from the discussions and debates and selections from the summary statements each participant prepared for the final session, but including only those summaries not easily extracted from the discussions themselves. In stitching it together in intelligible form, it became necessary in some instances to relocate comments within the flow of conversations and (more rarely) to alter some of the wording. Every effort was expended to preserve fully the spirit and the letter of the separate statements, but with due regard paid to readers of a later day.

GENERAL DISCUSSIONS

George Howard

This is the story of the psychologist who was brought in because a mother was concerned about an overly aggressive child. The psychologist goes into the backyard as the boy is playing. Pretty soon the boy walks over and picks something up and the psychologist sees that it is a worm. The boy looks at the worm for awhile and, all of a sudden, breaks it in two. The psychologist is hurriedly scribbling notes about this worm-breaking. Thinking aloud, as children do, the boy is then overheard to say, "Now you won't be so lonely; there are two of you."

The psychologist in this story has a psychological world which has moral implications for worm-breaking behavior, generally speaking. But the child was in a different world. So, there is a sense in which you have to know the world that the child is in and the meaning of the action in that world before you can ever make any moral judgments about it. I would claim that probably the only way in which we can make statements about the morality of an act or the person doing it is by knowing the language world that that person is in while they are doing it. It sounds as if this is very relativistic, but it isn't. The psychologist listened to the little boy and then he understood.

John Shotter

The thing that I wanted to explore with Joseph Rychlak is his notion of mediation. Now I was unclear in your paper as to the degree to which this notion of mediation is central.

Joseph Rychlak

According to Vygotsky, at least as I understand him, "Speech cannot be discovered without thinking." One of his translators and editors, Alex Kazulin, refers to the predominance of sense over meaning, of sentence over word, and of context over sentence. Well, meaning stands for socialized discourse. This represents an interface between one individual and others, the means by which incommunicable thinking is made comprehensible to others. To me, this is a predicational and mediational model. It assumes one has the capacity to conceptualize. But I am not an expert on Vygotsky.

George Howard

I want to come back to something that Rom Harré said about whatever is person-sustaining and I want to paint two scenarios. A little critter who develops a person-sustaining world, who becomes a loving human being. Another little critter who, because of a hateful family and environment, develops a person-destructive attitude. What I'm trying to get at is where shoulds and goods and bads come from ultimately. What makes person-sustaining good and the converse bad?

Rom Harré

I don't think anything makes person-sustaining good and a person-destructive attitude bad as such. Rather, at some point we have to find what we take to be the paradigm cases through which such concepts are introduced into our world. Now I think all the attempts to provide paradigm cases for introducing moral concepts for our actions lead us to an enormous variety of irreconcilable differences. If you base your moral philosophy on the idea that the paradigm here is going to be actions, the situation is hopeless. It seems to me that the only way that we can even begin to look at what would be universal is precisely the notion of person-sustaining practices. On this view, the paradigm cases involve not actions, but discursive practices that either do or do not sustain the person, or whatever it is that is the subject of moral worth.

Insofar as actions sustain or destroy persons, they come under moral consideration. But if you ask what is the root of all of this, I would argue that the proper paradigm cases are given in terms of persons, not in terms of their actions.

Kenneth Gergen

You are giving us conversation in a sense as the paradigm case and I'm interested in this and intrigued by the possibility that you can look at conversation and see, as you said, universals "secreted" by it, *moral* universals. But I don't see that you can do this without assuming some particular standpoint which already embodies a set of moral assumptions. I mean one can look at conversation as a form of co-option where I'm simply trying to get you to be like me, an attempt to dominate or to compete.

There are many metaphors of conversation and, depending on the particular metaphor adopted, one may find "secreted" in conversation various sorts of universals. But I don't see how one can legitimate any particular interpretative status or justify its discovery of particularly moral universals. That is, why should we accept those as being moral? Why honor those as being anything except historical flags?

Rom Harré

What interests me here are the necessary conditions for conversation in general. What I'm picking up on is this line of thought which states that we are having to generate a transcendental argument to show what these necessary conditions are. How do these conditions count as moral? Answer: Only if the conditions duplicate the conditions required for the possibility of persons in the first place.

In the final step of the argument we consider what is it that is a necessary condition for something to be a person? Well, of course, it would have to be a being who can engage in conversational practices. So we tie the knot. Now these knots are all internal relations. This is philosophy we are doing. We are looking at internal relations within a conceptual structure.

Maury Silver

How do you get morality? It seems to me you get morality in two different ways and they are weighted. One is just an insult or a comment. That bastard. One of the most common ways of the moral thought isn't what Dan Robinson believes; it is something like going to Fred and saying I have a tremendous problem. I don't know what to do. I do this occasionally. Once every four years. I talk morally about every ten seconds. What happens when you tell funny stories? We call it gossip. Gossip is presented as idle, as fun, as having no purpose. But it has a lot of functions. Because the good story has to have a point. Such stories first of all allow for some moral articulation.

A major part of morality is stories. The wrong stories. That is why I was so delighted to see Jerome Bruner's paper which refers to the sorts of long stories that we used to tell each other as merchant seamen; stories that articulated what was owed, what wasn't owed; stories of what a "real man" is, of the manliness of merchant seamen, etc. During such hours you would never think the seamen were talking morally, but they were.

Daniel Robinson

I think if the constructionist position on morality is going to replace or success-fully challenge any one of the competing alternatives it is going to have to show that the attachment of serious persons to these theories was grounded in some sort of a mistake. It will have to show, for example, that competing theories misrecorded the actual facts of the world or failed to appreciate that their moral content is really a "secretion of language." To the extent constructionism is ambiguous to actual persons who have long regarded themselves as moral agents, it will not be enough for the constructionist to suggest to them that they somehow are caught up in a kind of trick of language.

The moral realm is one that becomes possible only on the assumption that actions of a certain kind could have been otherwise and were not determined by the causal laws of nature. Kant argued that creatures capable of such actions occupy the "intelligible realm" in which explanations are grounded in reasons, not causes. I think many of the narrative approaches to understanding human moral conduct are designed to render this conduct intelligible in just this Kantian sense.

What it is about an action that makes it right or wrong? Kant was not ignorant of anthropology. But he was fully persuaded that you do not make progress in moral philosophy by consulting the habits of various cultures, tribes, or persons. There has to be something external to such practices that provides grounds for evaluation. What is finally external to all such practices is the principles they instantiate. So there are indeed moral actions in the sense that certain activities do instantiate or materialize or give body and bulk to principles or maxims. It is the maxim finally that disposes of the case in moral terms.

Maury Silver

I was pleased that we actually joined on one point and a very important one; viz., that the notion of character is central to understanding the moral domain. That may also relate to Rom Harré's notion of person-sustaining actions as the basis for morality. If you focus on the notion of character I think you will have to focus on not only what you want to call "moral," but on other things that are more broadly aesthetic. Consider the person who is generous not because he thinks he ought to be but because he is glad-handed. He likes to do it. It is a pleasure for him.

Daniel Robinson

But Aristotle would not regard that as generosity. If it were simply an impulse it would not qualify as magnanimity. It has to be principled to be a virtue. It has to be natural in the sense that you have so cultivated the habit of virtue that you no longer have to deliberate on such things. That's a little bit different from being "naturally" glad-handed.

Maury Silver

What would happen if by luck of birth I was a very generous person. I gave my toys away to others, etc. I'm just a person you would recommend to anyone else as a fine, generous person who enjoys, takes pleasure in giving things to others, seeing their pleasure, etc., and this is all quite spontaneous.

Daniel Robinson

"Generous" would be the wrong word to apply. This would be very much like saying that he is "commendably tall." When Aristotle discusses magnanimity in his ethical works he doesn't quite know where to place it. He says rather than calling it a distinct virtue, it is best to regard it as underlying all of the virtues. What he means by this, I think, is that it is not enough to be fair, for example, in a grudging or resentful way. Rather, it is the disposition to bring a generous sentiment to bear on the exercise of all the virtues.

Jerome Bruner

Mohammed Ali gave us a justification for trying to get the World Boxing Championship from Leon Spinks. His observation was that Leon was just too ugly to be world champion!

There is something in this aesthetic quality but it is not the same as morality, and I wonder if the linguistic analysis is causing some blurs when it shouldn't be blurry. If you are a lawyer and your client has been convicted and you are at the sentencing hearing, there are things that you can suggest to try to mitigate his sentence. My client is a good citizen. He has this great record and he did this thing only one time. But you can't say, "Your Honor, look at this face. Surely, twenty years should be reduced to ten."

Maury Silver

When you listen to gossip and other sorts of accounts the value of the talk is not only aesthetic (about, e.g., beauty and ugliness) but about qualities such as generosity, etc. But there are trade-offs between the two, as we see in the example of Ali and Spinks. John Sabini and I believe that both aesthetic talk and moral talk are similar in many ways and that both are different from pragmatic talk.

Now we don't know how theoretically to explain the interchangeable or trade-off nature of these things. But I don't claim here that when people talk they actually propose such trade-offs. Character, for example, seems to be the center of moral talk, but character-talk is broader than moral talk. It is the center of moral talk. Evaluations of character include things that we would not call moral because they are beyond the will.

Daniel Robinson

There are eras and cultures in which such conflations are common. Recall the poor victim in certain ancient Greek religious rites, the *pharmakos*. It was common on days selected for religious ceremony to choose the ugliest member of the community, the *pharmakos*, and to wine and dine that person; to treat him as royalty and then summarily to stone him to death.

The rationale for this ghastly practice was straightforward. It was that the fates would not have picked on such a person to look and be this way unless there was something about him that warranted such disfiguring ugliness. Now, anyone who takes morality seriously must find such a practice reprehensible. But from the mere fact that the *pharmakos* was singled out for a form of abuse that civilized persons would deplore, nothing follows except perhaps the need for a quick remedy. One is not required to "respect" such a practice.

Fathali Moghaddam

I'm getting that kind of feeling right now that this social constructionism we have is one for a nice person! I've been wondering about what kind of a social constructionist psychology would evolve in a very different cultural system. For example, let's take Iran. If I wanted to gather a council and see how the world is constructed by different people in Iran, first of all, I would have to acknowledge the fact that much of this construction is carried out by a very small number of people and is propagated in a way that is conspiratorial. That is, the accounts that I would get of these various constructions would all be very much influenced by what certain persons wanted me to hear. I would have to go into this scene with my own set of correct ideas. Otherwise, I would come out with a lot of strange stories that would reflect what certain groups would want me to hear and understand.

Now if I went into this scene with my correct notions of what I should be hearing then I would have some set of rules by which to evaluate what I was told. Let me give a specific example. Let's take somebody, a friend of mine who just before I left Iran had been captured for some reason. The official account was that this person was involved in some kind of drug-related incident. Now you can take that account as it stands and you can interview people and they will tell you in that neighborhood where this person lived that yes, it is true, this person was a drug runner. Then you can take that account and say okay, this is one account of the construction of this incident of this drug runner and you might interview other people and they will say that he had political beliefs that were different from the ruling regime. Now you would have another construction of the story. And, you could go on and probably gather many different accounts of this one incident. Somewhere along the line you would have to come to a conclusion about what you thought the correct version was. In the end you would have to come out with some kind of a notion of the incident. Was it correct or not? Should he have been hanged or not? Was it a politically motivated hanging? All these questions arise because you began with the understanding that there is a conspiracy behind the various accounts. If you don't begin with that assumption you are going to come out with a lot of strange stories, none of which match. The overriding story will be the one the regime wants you to believe.

So I'm wondering whether or not we can have a social constructionism that is not of the nice person. It seems to me that without the categories of right and wrong to begin with, we are going to end up uncritically endorsing the system of the nice person who is invariably produced by that person's own story.

The nice person model assumes people are going to tell us the truth. That is what I'm worried about. The second concern pertains to the accounts that they give, the constructions that they present us with. I would like to see some kind of acknowledgment that these constructions are often derived from particular sources and these sources are in many cases conspiratorial. That they are trying to strengthen a certain type of society. When we are discussing accounts, I still come back to the point that in many cases the accounts will not reflect action as it really happens. People not only fail to give accounts accurately but in many cases they try to give an incorrect account. So I worry about the acceptance of these accounts and also the whole notion that we can accept what people tell us to be their constructions.

Maury Silver

Let me address Ali Moghaddam's concerns. Indeed, it is interesting that much gossip, even among nice, friendly people and regimes, is filled with horrible lies and exaggerations. But we've been interested in such issues and the function and meaning of envy or in what sorts of defenses that are seen as compelling in the defense. So, if I want to show that your friend deserved to be deported, what sort of evidence would I rely on so that other people would say, oh, yes, of course. Now this does not mean that the evidence is true. As a social constructionist— and not a historian or anthropologist—what I study are the sorts of categories of the envious or angry person. I don't really care about the accuracy or truth of the constructions. Of course, sometimes I do care. Sometimes I'm really interested in why people committed a violent act and the relation between the act and the justification offered.

Now in your case in a police state, the techniques that any historian or anthropologist uses presupposes conceptual techniques for finding the truth; techniques are "protected," as it were. How is an outsider to construe such a society? Consider applying the usual techniques to an Indian village in which lying about everyone else is routine. The fact is that most endeavors come upon ambiguity and we can't finally decide. We don't have enough information. We can't ask the right questions. Someone may kill us. If we do ask the right questions, people are afraid to answer.

Fathali Moghaddam

So what you are endorsing is this view that you can only work within a society where people are "nice."

Kenneth Gergen

Regarding Dan Robinson's comments, I don't think you can justify or adjudicate among those or try to deal with the problems of competing claims or values by falling back on yet another value system or some value system that happens to come out of your culture. You say that to deal with that problem in the first place would require falling back on something like a view of some sort of universal.

Daniel Robinson

I was responding to you when I asked earlier what the basis was for insisting that tolerance was owed to other and different cultures. I thought I found in your work a plea for tolerance and I want to know why one should be tolerant.

Kenneth Gergen

You shouldn't, necessarily, at least if tolerance falls back on claims about moral absolute. Any claim of "should" is always a possible "shouldn't." There is always yet some other principle, some other generalization, some other universal law that will allow us to do otherwise.

Daniel Robinson

But then why do you make this plea for tolerance and on what do you base it? If it is not should, what is it?

Kenneth Gergen

Well, it is a plea for tolerance but it is not based on any "moral foundation." It is saying well, look, here is a conversation we can have, come join it. I don't have any grounds for it.

Daniel Robinson

You have one ground for it, don't you, Ken? Because if you are registering a plea, then indeed you are leaving open the possibility that something I might otherwise do, I now won't do in response to your plea and therefore you are giving me some proprietorship over the various courses of action I might take. Through the rational discourse itself, you are assuming that indeed I could do otherwise.

Kenneth Gergen

No, I don't think so. I think the problem that you and Maury Silver have hit on calls for some greater set of moral principles for us to carry out these kinds of activities I've discussed. I think there is no justification for saying that because one can carry out the games they know something about the principles or rules on which the games are grounded.

Jerome Bruner

Once you take a look at mankind under law, which is where he always is, you'll find that there are constraints against certain sets of behavior. And the first thing you'll find about law is that law is a highly specialized set of slots so to speak. What it does is to set up a very firm set of rules but not the usual sort of rules about what kinds of behavior bring down the law on the actor. When you bring down the law you do something very specialized. You have an instance of joint coercive action by the community against the individual. Now how do you determine whether somebody fits into one of the categories calling for such coercive restraint? How do you decide whether an action fits?

I won't go over the arguments again that neither the rationalist's conception that somehow we can decide by rational means or that we know such things intuitively, nor that you can decide it by empirical means. It is enough to say that when you judge the fitness of an act the emphasis is upon the rhetoric of immorality rather than the rhetoric of rights. When it is judged as immoral, it turns out to be within a story of a kind that is recognizably in the same pedigree as a story that priorly was judged to be immoral. Now this is very interesting. Don't take it as just an accident that things are still judged as they were in the past. It is absolutely the basis of every known legal system that has ever been looked at. And the Anglo-American system makes it very specific and it is called *stare decisis:* When you make a decision now, you relate it to a decision that was made before and show the manner in which it was like the decision that was made before. So one of the main constraints about being moral is, that in carrying out your hermeneutics, you are fulfilling the decision which says, things will not be arbitrary. If you knew the way this place ran or has run, you'll know how it runs now. But you have to know how this place runs. You have to know its particular rules. In our own political regime, so devoted to the rights of the individual, there is no mention in the whole Constitution about any other repository of morality, except the individual. This tells us, in a manner of speaking, how this place is run.

I then raise the question of the foundational basis whereby one judges a priori that there are certain things worth preserving; for example, life and limb, property, happiness. I think that in some sense there are constraints on the kind of legal system that one can build in any culture; that there are certain kinds of things which are given in the nature of human nature. For example, there is no way in which the autonomy of the person can be denied. There are a few, a very few abstract notions that come into virtually every constitutional system.

Now let me come to another example of what I mean. We've been taking a look at the way in which shopping malls come to govern themselves; about who puts on big advertising at the time of sales, how much, who is trusted, etc. Now what's interesting about the status of law as a concept is that by a priori consider-ations one knows that the only way in which some things are going to be suffered is by virtue of an apparatus called law. This is an extraordinarily powerful constitutive device. The settling of disputes precedes the specific content of any law. It is this kind of thing that I speak of as being among the universal or among the foundational bases of law and morality. It is what makes possible "morality" and the operation of law as a constraint on the bad guys.

But on the other hand this can only work at such times when it is possible to have the kind of law that is governed by meaning; that is to say by joint meaning, in which I take your individuality to be sacrosanct and inviolable. I cannot maintain the rule of law by shared meaning when the community becomes too diverse. There is always the balance between law or morality which is backed by coercion and law or morality which is backed by shared meaning.

So you can see that I'm stuck with not being able to answer Daniel O'Con-nell's critique. But the fact of the matter is I know that there are some constraints on what constitutes morality. I'm not convinced by the example of his spirited defense of his brother, because I would want to know the pedigree stories that had to do with the way in which he threatened those other kids. So even that example is not intuitively obvious to me.

Daniel O'Connell

One thing that I would comment on that I failed to put into my response is that in general this society we have is one in which the majority of the people are law abiding. I think in a way we neglect those people when we emphasize that the law is made for those who violate the law. The law is made very much for those who support the law and it provides those people with a boundary within which to work, and I think that somehow got lost.

I would also like to address the concept of stories and narratives in this connection which brings me to a more general comment about vocabulary. I'm having serious trouble, because even within constructivism everybody means something different by "story." What is a story?

Robert George

Regarding my own essay, let me just say a few words by way of amplification. I clearly wrote the paper from within a tradition, the natural law tradition. And quite appropriately Nancy Much responded to me by writing out of a different tradition instead of simply trying to take a contrary viewpoint from which to criticize me. In Alistaire MacIntyre's terms I'm certainly not a first-language reader or speaker in Nancy Much's tradition, and I take it that she's not in the one that I'm working in.

The way I approach morality, I take it to be fundamentally a matter of practical reasoning, a fundamentally practical business. Law is practical science as well. Although it's a funny kind of practical science, it bears an interesting relationship to morality. The goal of the law giver, it seems to me, is fundamentally to translate the moral law into what one has called human law, positive law. Why? Well, I think in order to render to some extent technical judgments about what is the best way to live. It will enable us—enable our culture, most of whose members don't have the luxury of being moral philosophers—to resolve some things and to enable us to work out our excuses and coordinate our behavior. It enables us to do this in ways that don't require us to enter into full-blown moral analysis on every occasion. And where disputes arise or where things are unclear we rely on technical experts like lawyers and judges to work things out. That means that human law is made in the sense that natural law is not.

To understand the law of any particular culture or to understand the extent to which a culture has achieved the rule of law it is necessary to adopt the practical viewpoint of someone who, for whatever reasons, accepts the fundamental terms of social relations of that culture; to adopt what has been called "the internal point of view." It doesn't mean you have to agree. It doesn't mean you have to be someone who approves of the Aztec rituals. But if you're going to understand Aztec law you've got to look at it from the point of view of an Aztec. You have to adopt that internal point of view and understand the point of what he's doing. Well, ultimately he's trying to save the son who will in fact die if he doesn't remove this other poor fellow's heart.

Despite the fact that the tradition from which I operate makes claims to universality it has always acknowledged a certain kind of relativity in moral judgment although a limited one. And that's clearest in the sense in which, according to the tradition, new moral precepts can arise in particular circumstances simply by a fact of a law having been made or a custom having arisen. Driving on the left instead of the right or the right instead of the left (depending where Rom Harré is this semester) is illustrative. In the absence of some law or custom on that matter, we are all going to be under an obligation to drive safely and with care for others, but not under any moral obligation to drive, say on the left, at all times. But a law, having been put in place by due authority, or a custom having arisen, one now is under that obligation.

In a Japanese home we give insult to enter without removing one's shoes. One is under an obligation to do that. When I enter Dan Robinson's house, I don't remove my shoes and he takes no insult. I'm not under any obligation. Nevertheless, natural law tradition has held that there are certain moral norms that are absolute and there's no thought that they only hold within Western societies or developed societies. But they hold in all places. Now, it's an independent question, of course, it's always an independent question of moral consequence in itself whether one ought to do anything in particular, intervene or interfere with the immoral practices of somebody else or some other tradition or practices one judges to be immoral. The reasons for action that may be relevant there will have to be deliberated upon. They will not necessarily be the same reasons that lead us to conclude that the practice is wicked.

Nancy Much

My essay in reply to Robert George was actually a playful attempt to look at constructionism as it might represent a type of morality. At the same time it was an attempt to illuminate some of the controversies and questions in unclear areas that seem to exist in constructionism. I focused on what seemed to be Robert George's presuppositions about rationality and free choice, and I then looked at how this particular view of constructionism would look at the idea of rationality; what place rationality has and how it's defined, and the same with the issue of freedom or free choice.

Rationality has to do in part with the relation of reason to conceptual structures. I contend that all rationality is imbedded in such structures, these being culturally and linguistically derived. My claim is not that reality is thus constituted, but that knowledge structures are; and that in particular we don't have direct access to things like natural law. We only have indirect access to it through culturally constituted knowledge structures. This is the reason, by the way, why tolerance is recommended at least in many cases. It's because ultimately we don't know. We can see reality only through our own knowledge structure which has some kind of bias.

The problem that I find with an absolutist position is that if you have only one possibility—only one possible view of reality—the choices that you can make are naturally constrained by that view and to that extent precisely you do not have freedom of choice. So rationality, the epitome of rationality, in this particular theory, becomes a sword so sharp that it cuts its own ground.

On the other hand, since this discursively constructive world, which is what I call the relative world, is the world that we exist in and live in socially, it has to be taken seriously and it has its own reality in some sense. And a sense of respect and reverence for that world is required while at the same time we are seeing through it. Its transparency is also required. If you fail to do either you are going to run into intense kinds of pain that will bring you back to reality in one direction or another; bring you back to practicality. I think we have a point of agreement—the idea that morality is practical, and that the constraint on things like cultural construction is also practical. The constructionism at issue suggests that morality, including moral rationality and free will, may not be something that we just have by virtue of being born as human beings. Actually they are high-level fields that have to be cultivated and trained for in a rather strenuous fashion. Now the moral impetus behind that is one's own pain which one wants to free oneself from suffering; plus the realization that the subject is somehow in a symbiotic relationship with others so that others' pain is one's own pain as well, and one wants to liberate others from suffering at the same time. And the way to do that is to cultivate the intellect but first free oneself, and then others from a primitive belief about reality.

It turns out that there were two aspects to this morality: First freeing oneself and then accumulating fields to work for the benefit of others. First you must have the discernment to see through discursive processes and therefore or thereby know situations, understand situations. The intelligence or the wisdom is said to be in the situation and not located particularly in the person. The situation speaks for itself. Your job is to discern it.

I'd like to comment briefly on Ali Moghaddam's concerns. The kind of constructionism actually recommends that you ought to approach every situation in the same way that you ought to approach a hypothetical Ayatollah. That is, with suspicion! In other words, you ought to be watching for the discursive processes that are going on to create reality a certain way and to negotiate it in a certain way. You are to be on top of that idea to see what is going on so that you're not taken in by somebody else's view of reality; or, for that matter, by the one you bring in with you. The possibility for choice, in fact, is the awareness of different possibilities and different ways of looking at things and different ways of doing things.

James Lamiell

I would ask Ken Gergen and Nancy Much how they have succeeded in liberating themselves from some of the binds they have drawn attention to in their essays. Yesterday we—the executive council of our College here at Georgetown—met and the topic of discussion was multicultural diversity at the University. And of course, the topic of discussion there was in very many respects the same as the one here, or at least overlapping. And we were all sitting around this table talking about how we were going to liberate ourselves, the University, the College of Arts and Sciences and various departments within it, from a Western cultural bias. And the question comes up, how we're going to come up with a good culturally diverse curriculum. What would prevent someone from saying, well this program that you've designed for cultural diversity is itself just the mere product of twenty or so faculty members who are already steeped in this Western culture. Thus, any program that we could come up with would offer no means for judging it as better than any other program that someone might come up with or perhaps no reason to judge it as better than coming up with no program at all—in which case it would be time to adjourn the meeting! You and Nancy Much speak about the necessity of transcending one's own culture or the limits of our own acculturation. And I want to know how is it that both of you who have grown up in the Western culture have succeeded in doing it. It can't just be that growing up in a Western culture makes it impossible for us to do this because if that were the case then it wouldn't be possible for you even to recognize alternatives, let alone defend them.

Nancy Much

First of all, your focus on what you see as the individualism of my position perhaps misses the idea that in this particular philosophical context there isn't the same subject–object, self-and-others dichotomy that exists in the West. You see, it's that itself that is dissolved. That's quite a Western point, you see.

Robert George

I wanted to respond to a couple of Ken Gergen's points. First, I think that if some sort of relativism is in fact, for want of a better word, true, then that can't be assumed in advance against my position but has to be shown. I think that the way to show it is to show some internal inconsistency or other problem or implausibility in my position. Now, the other thing is I think that you are at risk of falling into the problem that MacIntyre identifies with liberalism, although I can see your position in certain respects is not one that falls under his definition. It would not be a liberal position because you've rejected individualism and so forth. Yet you seem to want to find a tradition-independent viewpoint from which to criticize the various traditions. But you seem to be relying on a tradition that has kind of spun off of the Western tradition. It's hard to see how at the end of the day you wouldn't be vulnerable to the kind of retorsive argument that Jerry Parrott develops in his paper against John Shotter.

The other matter pertains to individualism. I think I want to distinguish, as Jim Lamiell does, between individualism and individuality. I think that the West is right. That tradition is right to hold for individuality. I think it would be a mistake to fall into individualism but I don't think there's anything in my position that would commit me to individualism. Among what I develop as reasons for action are considerations that foster communication and empathetic and sympathetic relations with other people. I think Aristotle's dialectic of friendship is really unsurpassed and I don't think that anything that we have from another culture or from criticism of our culture is a reason to displace it. If you think that we ought to give up a position that we hold, whether Nancy Much should give hers up or I should give mine up, because you think there are reasons why we ought to give them up, those reasons are debatable. And we can enter into dialogue to try to sort the whole thing out together. None of that is radically individualistic despite the fact that, in a certain significant sense, the activity is happening in our individual heads. You have what you think is a good reason to reject the position that I've taken and you're trying to communicate that to me and I just might conclude that you're right. But if so, it will be the fruit of this dialogue and debate.

Kenneth Gergen

I would say there is something quite different if we're undertaking a dialogue in which I believe myself to be representing a whole series of conversations and I'm only the local manifestation of a large array of conversations, rather than my trying to show that your reasoning powers are faulty and should be changed.

Robert George

That's not what you're trying to show. Presumably we're not playing a dominance game where one of us is aiming simply to achieve a relation of power over the other. We're trying to get at the truth of the matter. You are proposing that I give up my beliefs because you think there are good reasons for me to do it. And you are inviting me to enter into a conversation so that ultimately we can understand whether or not there are in fact good reasons to do it. We might in the end disagree. We might in the end agree. But whatever happens I think there's no good reason to think, unless we have independent evidence to think, that really what this is about in the case of Ken and Robbie is an attempt to establish dominance.

Kenneth Gergen

I don't think it's a matter of dominance, but I don't think it's a matter of truth and I would say that if it's a matter of truth, we'll never manage it. We'll never end up agreeing. Let's suspend the notion of truth.

James Lamiell

You seem to be pretty settled in the position that the moment one allows some notion of individuality or individualism (which are very different to me but not to you), to enter into the discussion, it is finally going to be a matter of dominance or imperialism. I'm sure that's not true though I haven't had a chance to work out that yet.

Kenneth Gergen

I don't want to say that's necessarily true either.

James Lamiell

I would hope that the working out of just that point may be an important element in achieving such an emergent view from these discussions which Dan Robinson was hoping for last night. I have some ideas on the matter and I think that we might make some real progress in that direction but I don't want to take that up too far now. I was raising some questions before about Nancy Much's paper concerning how one liberates oneself from the fact of having been raised in this culture. You said the answers are written on specific pages in her essay. And I thought, well how silly of me. I had read the pages. Why didn't I realize that? So I went back to see what I wrote down and what I find first of all is an assertion on one of the specific pages concerning what she is pleased to regard is the deluding processes of mind. Lurking behind that is some appeal to a universal principal which she is pleased to believe she knows about right now, but that we don't. This would be very interesting to see how it got worked out. On another page we are invited to believe that moral intellect and moral skill do not develop spontaneously. Training and cultivation are required. I expect that a full fleshing out of that point of view would lead us back to Aristotle. On yet another fundamental point, moral capacity is here described as not something an individual possesses natively merely by virtue of being born a human being with normal capacities. Yet, it is natively present only in the embryonic form of an impetus toward compassion. Something very similar to that can be found in Alfred Adler.

Robert George

I have another set of comments to address to the constructionists, tied to what has been said by others; a kind of final foundationalist challenge.

For something to be affirmed or denied, the proposition to be affirmed or denied has to be understood. To be understood it has to be intelligible. If it is a practical proposal, its intelligibility will depend on its having a point. So we can take examples that have arisen, practical proposals made by Ken Gergen and John Shotter. John Shotter proposes that we expand the conversation. Here is a practical proposal directed at doing something. I submit this proposal is only intelligible, therefore understandable, therefore to be affirmed or denied if it has a practical point. There is a point to it that I can grasp. There is a reason for it.

Take by implication Ken Gergen's proposal that there was something bad (I don't want to import moralistic language in here Ken, but I must to some extent) about bombing Nagasaki and Hiroshima. The judgment puts it in moralistic terms by saying it was wrong to do. It seems to me that that proposal, to not bomb innocent civilians, even in a case of war, only makes sense if there is a practical point to it.

Now the natural law tradition would supply reasons that would be practical and a practical point for both Ken Gergen's and John Shotter's propositions. Take

Ken's for example. The proposal would be that among the reasons for action that required no further reasons for their intelligibility are just protecting or preserving or sparing innocent human lives. That is a reason for action. Now the trouble is of course that it competes with other reasons. There are sometimes reasons to kill, competing with the reason not to kill. But it seems to me without some reasons for action, ultimate reasons for action to provide the intelligible point of these types of proposals, we would just have no reason to affirm or deny them because we couldn't understand them in the first place.

Kenneth Gergen

I don't see this as a foundational question in the sense of how it is that understanding can take place, or in the sense that understanding only can take place if you see the consequences. I may not want to accept that as the criterion for what understanding would be about. The practical consequences may only be one vehicle by which understanding can be achieved. Then too you and I probably would not share the same principles about what understanding means.

There is yet another area where I think we probably would disagree with which makes the questions problematic. You argue in your paper that decisions are made on the basis of reasons and that reasons can form decisions. But the whole view of the individual psychological function is what I find problematic. For me, reasons are not of that sort of thing. We go on acting from moment to moment to moment. If we're asked to provide reasons, well, we can often do so. Often not. But if we do, we are going to just dip into the cultural repository of "reasons." And we're going to use the ones that are moralistic and legitimate under the circumstances. You can only take those off the shelf that make sense within the culture. It is not a matter of looking into yourself and being able to identify, aha, there is the reason, now I know why I did it or why it is worth doing. I don't see any sense being made of that notion.

Robert George

I would add a few words about "reasons for action." Free choice presupposes a possible set of reasons for action. You need more than one motive for action in order to have any traditions for free choice. The possibilities for profound toleration are grounded in the fact that there is a plurality of reasons for action. There are many different rational motives. You can't act on all of them. There are different things to do. Not in one lifetime. Not in a lifetime of a whole civilization or of all mankind can they be done. Most of the decisions we face, it seems to me, are decisions among a range of rationally grounded possibilities, you could have reasons to do that aren't held out by any conclusive reasons or second-order reasons, moral reasons. But, you've got to make a choice. You've got to do something. Now the choice that you make is rationally grounded. The freedom is made possible, it seems to me, by that range of choices. And I would not at all, I can understand the desire to rid oneself from suffering, that seems to me to constitute a reason for action. I can understand compassion for others. Although, I think compassion is conceived as an emotion. Nevertheless, it's an emotion that's tied to an understanding of the value of another, of the work of another. And friendship or sociability, as everyone within the tradition back to Aristotle and Plato understands, constitutes a reason for action.

I would simply say that in a certain sense, the Western tradition is more catholic in visaging a much larger range of possible reasons for action and a good deal more room for freedom.

Rom Harré

It seems to me that right from the start we haven't been clear about what we meant with respect to the main popular issue. I do not for a moment suppose that individual people once manufactured, are not capable of individual action and cognition. The constructionist view is that persons are artifacts that are made. Now, there may be things about the manufacturing process that lead to some kind of autonomous individuals or the feeling that we evidently are. But one must not confuse social causation with social phenomena. I think what Ken is doing is continually pressing for us to accept the idea of a social production or social causation of, say, the answer to the question that Nancy Much poses about how you get to some other position. Ken doesn't want us to be able to get there.

John Shotter

Rom, you talk about a policy really. It seems to me that what Nancy Much wants is also a form of policy. But, I think in actual fact, these are policies to keep the enterprise going. It may be a good idea to call social constructionism a movement, not a position. And I think it is correct to call it a movement. I think one of the problems that we're having tying Ken Gergen down is our failure to grasp the character of what it is to have a set of attitudes or policies towards coping with the world where you don't end up in static positions.

George Howard

Let me put my cards on the table. My feet are rooted in the clay of the Western intellectual traditions that celebrate free will. And my feet are also rooted in the clay of science. And I make no claim that knowledge gained from either of those perspectives is superior to any other form of knowledge.

Determinism to me means things happen because they are caused. Now, good

reasons can be causes of behavior. The opposite of that is a causality or random-
ness or something like "things just happen," spontaneously, miraculously or
whatever.

What I would say is that for most of us, certainly those of us who claim to be
scientists, one should be very close to the determinism pole. The second dimension, I would call self-determination or free will on one end and complete
mechanism or complete nonagentic determination of behavior on the other. And I
am somewhere in the middle. I believe there is a component to self-determination
in human action. But, I would be foolhardy to say that our biological inheritance
and also transient physiological states don't influence the way we think and the
way we act. Environments, social environments, all of those factors are nonagentic in the sense that they push us or tend us towards certain actions. So,
when I look at human beings, I see them as being somewhat self-determined and
somewhat caused.

As Miller Maynard said, "Stories are habitations, we live in it through stories. They conjure worlds. We do not know the world other than in the story
world. Stories inform life. They hold us together. They keep us apart. We inhabit
the great stories of our culture." What Ken Gergen and John Shotter are often
saying is that, it's not just us telling the story of our race and place. We as a
collective are negotiating the story of our race and place.

Fathali Moghaddam

I'm just going to pick up on one point in George Howard's essay and elaborate on
it; viz., the whole notion of narrative. The point I want to focus on is his
insistence that he is not going to make any claims about having stories that are
better than other stories or any answers that are better than other answers.

Now, he makes this explicit claim that I would suggest that implicitly he has
already given us certain notions about what he thinks is better than other stories.
Let me take an example. In his written discourse he discusses the notion that
gays, Blacks, minorities have been victimized. Now, he says that within the
internal framework that he gives, this victimization is clear and he wants us to
accept this. But what if we look at this issue from another point of view and
suggest to him that they have not been victimized; that affirmative action is
working gloriously, etc. Now, somewhere along the line, we've got to make
some kind of a judgment as to who is more correct. Otherwise, we're going to be
shouting across borders at each other. Now, we can go on shouting across borders
at each other if the groups that we belong to don't interact or if the world that we
live in is homogeneous in terms of culture. But neither of these is the case. First
of all, the groups that we belong to do interact. There is multiculture. So, there is
no way in which we can have a just and moral psychology in a kind of static
world because that static world does not exist, nor is it homogeneous.

With respect to the kinds of narratives that George Howard is collecting, I come back to my point about the "nice people" model in psychology and its limitations. In a word, this world is not a simple one in which people actually are motivated to tell us the truth. In most or even all societies, people are motivated, particularly those in power, to tell us what is not true. So, the accounts they give us must be looked at and criticized from a particular moral standpoint. And it's only by assuming certain universals that we can treat other people in a fair way. When coming across people who are not nice, who are not going to tell us the truth, we have to look finally at actions, not narratives.

Jerome Bruner

The particular dimension that I'd like to introduce into social constructionism is developmental dimension, but developmental right across the board, not just child development. How does one at a practical level, in terms of practical reason and practical knowledge, capture the character of something which is inchoate, which is radically incomplete, which is ongoing, but which nonetheless requires responding to and dealing with? When I first started work of this kind in the 1970s, the problem for me grew out of very practical issues having to do with how at first was it that a mother understood the character of her child's abilities and what the child was doing at any one point in time such that she could intervene in an intelligible and instructive way into that process? And why did we as investigators, when we were looking over the videotapes, pick out of this great flow of events, certain events which for some reason we thought to be crucial?

Now, I took what later on I came to call a point of common reference to indicate something very important socially. These seem to me to be worth emphasizing. I don't know how it works internally. But, there are points at which you can begin to recognize common feelings, shared circumstances which can work as the standards which, when you want to talk about what is going on, you can use as a basis for more explicit formulations.

So, what I wanted to try to understand was not just mothers in their negotiations with their children, but our own practical reasoning as investigators as to why we selected the aspects and topics that we did. What was it that made us come to think they were important?

If we are trying to understand practical reasoning, there's no point in making theories of practical reasoning. Practical reasoning is not done by holding to certain theoretical principles and then trying to find different ways for applying different particular circumstances. It seems to me that reasoning is not done that way.

Regarding Joseph Rychlak's notion of mediation and the directive function of mediators, I would want to go a step further and to suggest that long before words take on new names they should be looked at as some kind of prosthetic instrument through which we can both act and see. A child learns to see through his speech as much as through his eyes. And long before words have meanings they should be thought of as means, as an instrument, a device both for having an effect on other people as well as having an effect upon oneself; for giving shape to both one's actions and one's perceptions. I've emphasized this sort of pros-thetic aspect through the instrument of a reflexive language as being prior to any later production of whole interlinguistic systems of meaning.

John Shotter

It is said that we on the social constructionist side want to do negotiating and that there doesn't seem to be an end of it. Here I would like to offer a bit of Wittgenstein who says that giving grounds, justifying the evidence does come to an end, but the end is not certain propositions striking us immediately as true. It's not a kind of seeing on our part. It's our acting which lies at the bottom of the language game.

Yes, we are after a new culture in which elite groups do not, ahead of time, set down principles which the others have got to see as indeed true. It's a new place for academics, who, along with others, are going to be prepared to work it out as we go along. I think that's the difference.

Robert George

My recollection of this quotation from Wittgenstein is that, in context, it's not— he's not there talking about ethical judgments. Right?

John Shotter

Right.

Robert George

It seems that you want to harness this basic idea that at the end of the chain of reasoning isn't any reason, but our acting. Not propositions, but our acting, and this in the service of the cause of getting rid of elite groups who control things. Now speaking in terms of practical reasoning and, ultimately, morality—if the bottom of it all is just our acting, which is, itself, unconstrained by reasons, isn't that just the recipe for the rule of the strong?

John Shotter

Well, why is it unconstrained by reasons?

Robert George

Well, because I thought at the end of it all we can't get a justification in terms of a publicly accessible reason. It is our acting, so we choose to act. Now, acting for a reason gives us, at the end of it all, a reason and not an action.

John Shotter

As a psychologist, I've still got to say, why is it that some reasons work? Why do they come to an end? What do they tune into? How do they, so to speak, strike people—that is, these are the reasons that, us being us, we can't object to them and still be the kind of people that we are. They strike into our identity somewhere.

Rom Harré

I want to just refine the individuality–individualism distinction just a tiny bit more, because I think there are two different implications drawn from it, and they have not been very clearly distinguished. One is the question of how does my value arise? And the other is where does my responsibility come from?

It seems to me that my value arises from the community to which I belong, so that it is the community's value which diffuses to provide me with value. So clearly it is not from the instrument through which I construct individual value, because my individual value arises through the value of the community. In that sense, I am not an adherent of individualism. On the other hand, if you turn it the other way and ask from what or to what does my responsibility arise, then it seems to me that my responsibility is not diffused through the community, but pertains to me as created by me, as an individual and a responsible being.

So I think we must keep these two issues clear, and be aware of the two aspects of where the moral qualities of a person come from, lest we get too crude a notion of individualism. So Dan Robinson's argument, which I fully share, about the location of responsibility does not, it seems to me, entail the conclusion about the location of value.

Now, in my view, the individualism I object to arises when institutions are the arenas for the private or individual construction of value. That's the element in individualism I dislike. On the other hand, I do think that it's right to say that my responsibility can't be sloughed off onto the institution. The responsibility for my acts is mine. Again, you have to split the notion in two. I can't go along with individualism if it contains or if it is the conjunction of those two theories about value and responsibility. I am very happy to go along with it when it's a matter of responsibility. I am not happy to go along with it when it's a matter of value.

Joseph Rychlak

I'm struggling to understand what you're saying here, particularly as it concerns this notion of joint action, and the allegedly extrapersonal origins of personal value. I think it has much to do with the term Nancy Much used, *symbiosis*. Let me read two passages from Daniel Stern:

> Only when infants can sense that others distinct from themselves can hold or entertain a mental state that is similar to one they sense themselves to be holding is the sharing of subjective experience or intersubjectivity possible. The infant must arrive at a theory, not only of separate minds, but of interfaceable separate minds.

Or again,

> These observations lead one to infer that, by nine months, infants have some sense that they can have a particular attentional focus; that mother can also have a particular attentional focus; that these two mental states can be similar or not; and that if they are not, they can be brought into alignment and shared.

My point in offering these passages is that agentic powers seem to be present and necessary at the very outset.

SUMMARY STATEMENTS

Kenneth Gergen

Without moral discourse there wouldn't be any moral issue. There wouldn't be any moral problems. That is, the discourse which frames problems as moral is constitutive of morality. There isn't a problem about morality outside of that array of discursive devices.

However, that talk, that discourse operates, I would argue, as a kind of cultural resource. That is, it is talk upon which we can draw in daily activities or in writings about war, for example, which could have suasive appeal. That is, it has some rhetorical value. It can have some impact on the course of human affairs. So it operates then as a kind of cultural resource, a repository of things that can be said on certain occasions for certain pragmatic effects.

Now, in that sense it is only one discourse among many that can be used on those occasions. And it has to be looked at in comparison with other forms of discourse which will create the world or constitute the world in different ways. So one can contrast that discourse, for example, let's say with a scientific discourse which will not yield the same solution to a problem.

One can argue, then, that indeed for many of the problems that we face from day to day, moral discourse sits there as one repository among a variety of others that could be used pragmatically just for getting on in life.

Now, I view constructionist discourse, the development of this literature, as yet another discourse. I mean, it's simply another set of talks that we're having, another set of conversations, another set of terms. I, myself, don't see that these are synonymous with moral discourse. That is, they do not in themselves make any claims to morality. It is simply one discourse among others for getting things done, for getting on in social or academic life. Though constructionism doesn't make moral claims, it can be extended in moral directions so that there could be a meeting between those two endeavors, and I think that's not an unuseful meeting. But that's not part of what I'm doing.

Now, my own sense is that what constructionism does is to raise questions about moral discourse and about its comparative effects and implication for social life. That is, it asks what are the gains and losses in using moral discourse and, for those who would like life to be of a certain kind, is moral discourse the best way to proceed to generate those kinds of life patterns that you would be satisfied with. Whether or not you call them moral is irrelevant to this argument.

So the question then becomes: Is there something in the constructionist view which would lend itself to what we might call moral ends without claiming that they're moral? That is, which might lend itself to the kind of life patterns that we might prefer even without the moral foundationalism.

I would claim that constructionism is opening a space for relational analysis— that is, for attempting to carve out a vocabulary, a set of concepts, new cultural resources that try to look at everything in relationship—knowledge not as something in one's head, but in relationship; emotions not as private possessions, but in relationship; language as being jointly produced by people in relationship; symbiotic relationships between people, so that there is always the concentration on the between.

James Lamiell

A major aspect of the social constructionist view, at least in Ken Gergen's account, involves what he called a de-ontologizing of persons; that persons are no longer the units of discourse; that we are now going to talk about social units and social interactions as the irreducible units of social discourse.

His misgivings about any system that leads us into a discussion of individuals become bifurcated in his paper. He first discusses the limitations of so-called modernism under the view of which the individual turns out to be, really, just a machine, the holder of the residues of causal factors emanating from the environment. Any action on this account or the behavior of the individual is seen to be determined finally by forces or factors outside of the individual. Since, in this system, the individual cannot be regarded as having any autonomy or free will, moral discourse on this view simply dries up.

The other individual-centered view about which Professor Gergen expressed misgivings was romanticism, the view that there is a kind of deep inner self, an autonomous moral self, a moral agent. The limitations of this view have primarily to do, on his view, with the fact that it has led to the articulation of merely abstract and very general moral principles, empty of specific content and, therefore, not in and of themselves useful in guiding us in any concrete instance. So that, for example, the directive "Thou shalt not kill" is not going to help us in any concrete instance because it's too vague, it's too abstract, it's too empty of content and its usefulness must only be worked out then within the interpersonal milieu. In this same essay he also points to the dangers of moral discourse. In a nutshell, this has to do with the idea that moral discourse can actually have a downside. If two people enter into a debate about what is right and what is wrong, it is too easy for that debate then to become a question of dominance.

My own view is that a system that de-ontologizes persons cannot finally have anything consequential to say in the moral domain. We simply must be prepared to talk about individual human beings as, in some respects, autonomous agents and the authors of their own actions under circumstances where it would have been possible for them to do otherwise. And without some way of talking about this possibility, there simply is no moral discourse.

When he goes on to say that the expansion in the range of complicity does not go far enough, the question I raise is what would going far enough mean. What would prevent us, on the social constructionist view, from concluding that the victims of crime, people killed and people injured in examples he has offered, were not themselves also responsible for the crime, or bore some complicity in the crime, on the grounds that, after all, if they had not been there, if they had not been part of the entire social interpersonal constellation under which such crimes are committed, the crimes would not have occurred?

Joseph Rychlak

It strikes me that social constructionism is getting at the issue of what we are really to do as psychologists. There is almost a moral imperative in what we ought do in the profession. There is also a moral suasion in social constructionism in the sense that they are very much interested in minorities and feminist issues.

My problem with social constructionism is the nature of the organism we're out to describe because I think of myself as a psychologist, and my duty, my responsibility is to discover how the individual works. Can an organism that simply mediates between inputs and outputs be more than that? Do we not have to construe the organism as an evaluating organism as well? To my way of thinking, predication is also involved with oppositionality so that, fundamentally, as persons you are not merely responding to inputs, are not merely machines, but are and must be taking positions. This kind of evaluating organism also renders judgments in terms of preferences, likes, dislikes, and so on. It is on this basis that we can begin to build a moral theory.

Now, of course, social constructionism is not concerned with that because there is this fear—which I think is a sort of ideological fear—that if you do that, you validate the person, and then all those bad things that have happened as a result of that selfishness are somehow vindicated. I'm not convinced, though, that that has to be the philosophical outcome.

As for the future of constructionism, I don't know, it's up in the air. Just off the top of my head, I would say there's no future; it doesn't answer my questions.

Rom Harré

I think it's quite good to be in a minority. May I remind you that, in 1780, the majority thought that when things were burned and got heavier, that was because they lost a substance which had the peculiar property called levity, but by 1810 the future belonged to the oxygenists. So I'm looking to the twenty-first century, where I'm quite sure that constructionists will belong to the right-thinking people!

But it puzzles me about how a chap who is as intelligent as Ken Gergen could put forward this thesis of his. I think I have come to see what it is at the root of all these difficulties. I think it can be explained if you look at the gesture made by forming a circle with thumb and forefinger. For most of us, that gesture is, "dead right," "well done." Don't do it in Greece; it's the rudest gesture you could possibly produce.

A distinction that hasn't yet taken root over here, but arose originally in the discussions of a group of people in Europe who tried to found a science they were pleased to call human ethology, is between "act" and "action." I think somewhere with that distinction, we can begin to get a grip on what's been going on over the last couple of days. Now, in performing an action, one does something that is, in a very general sense, intended by the human being. It is something which is done intentionally. The *act,* however, is what it means in this or that cultural milieu. Thus, killing is an *action* which people do intentionally, and murder is an *act* which locates the action and therefore the "killer" in this or that or the other moral discourse. If it's the moral discourse of war, killing is not murder. If it's the moral discourse of Saturday events in a shopping mall, that's another matter, or murder! So we can see how Ken Gergen can be culturally multiple, but one has to learn that the conditions for his being so is his being morally aware. Now it seems to me quite clear that, if we're talking about cultural multiplicity, then we're talking about acts. I've just demonstrated a case where the intention or action is subject to cultural multiplicity. So this is how it can be that, by cultural transformation, we can find ourselves meaning something different by what we did or will do. But the action is quite different. The action rests upon the possibility of discourse—the condition for the possibility of discourse.

But there couldn't be discourses unless there were persons. So that if Ken Gergen's version of relativism is arguing that there could be discourses without persons, Ken is simply shooting himself in the foot, or sawing off the branch he's standing on. The possibility of discourse rests upon two mountains—one is the existence of persons and the other is the possibility of certain language games which must occur within any discursive practice. It is an old Wittgenstein idea that you determine the boundaries of a discursive practice or discourse in general from within, not from any outside considerations. Now, if persons are what it is that makes discourse possible, John Shotter and I and other social constructionists want to say that persons are discursively constructed, so they are, themselves, the product of the very thing which they themselves produce. But, of course, the queer thing about this is that these constructs are, themselves, individual moral agents. So what we've done is produce the very conditions for morality in the course of discursively producing ourselves. Now, person-producing discourse is joint action, and there I am entirely with John Shotter and Ken Gergen. There could be no such thing as a person as an atom; the individual source of an atomic, meaningful act. Persons produce *joint* actions.

The final twist to tie it all up together is that I believe that the notion of action, of discursively meaningful joint action is, itself, tied up with personhood. To have the concept of person is already to have the idea of joint action. So the transcendental condition for the possibility of everything we've been doing is that we should be individual persons.

Daniel Robinson

On so difficult a set of issues, I would be more comfortable merely summarizing, in actuarial fashion, the central propositions that would ground my understandings of persons and cultures.

First, I take "person" as referring to any potential cultural participant. The qualification "potential" secures personhood, not only for sleeping persons and hermits, but for children and other symbol-using animals entering into cultural life in various and nontrivial ways as participants. The definition of symbol here is broad and not confined to language.

Second, the realization of this potential for cultural participation is achieved solely by, through, and within cultures. There are no self-made persons.

Third, there can be selves without persons, but not vice versa. This is important, but need not be explored further here. I will say only that only a being with agentic and self-conscious powers can be acculturated, for acculturation involves both focus and selection.

Fourth, once made, persons are then, to different degrees, self-refining, in that (a) persons are never complete and (b) culture itself is defined, in part, in terms of a respect for its own creations—these including persons centrally.

Fifth, as per four, culture's respect for its own creations, liberty, and expressions of personal autonomy are not merely possible within cultures, but stand as necessary attributes of them.

Sixth, as per five, cultures cannot then be neutral as regards various modes and principles of political organization and jurisprudence.

Seventh, as per one through six, it follows that the establishment and maintenance of cultures entail that, as regards the moral dimensions of life, some answers are simply wrong answers, some practices are morally wrong, and some participants are absolutely blameworthy.

Maury Silver

People in a culture feel that attributional terms (such as "envious," "unfair," etc.) are all objective; as real as desks or floors; the sort of thing that anyone should know. Yet, at the same time, people construct the rules that create, for example, envious persons and the stories that permit moral judgments to be made. So you have a very interesting junction; the rules for society are both objective (to the naive members of that society) but socially constructed. Because of this, there are interesting consequences. One is that, although to us our moral system looks rocklike, nothing in fact guarantees moral coherence within the domain of social practices. The coherence is produced by *moralists,* by those who reflect upon the morality of their society and seek to develop rules and principles. Secondly, because the assumption is that moral attributes are objective, all sorts of trouble is created when one tries to tie practices to principles. Consider only experiments on social influence. When people don't help victims, for example, they still invariably claim afterwards (or before the fact) that, "Of course, one should help those in distress."

With John Shotter, we are interested in how joint action, combined with this assumption of an objective moral universe, involves the social construction of judgments that may be puzzling, shocking, and surprising even to the people who are constructing them.

Jerome Bruner

I thought that perhaps the best role that I could play is rather as an anthropologist of ideas. I wish I could be some other identity and change easily, but I can't. I'm a Western anthropologist of ideas, and I've discovered that there are two species of constructionists. One of them I want to call full of character, full of courage, having constructionism as a program and an aim, trying to elucidate it to find what possible ramifications it might have in the realm of morals. And then there's the other species, amongst whom I include myself, who are rather weak in the spirit, lacking somehow in character, who use constructivism as a tool, not expecting that its application will somehow change either the flavor of science as such, or the way in which the humanities conceive of their way of looking at man. Let me be specific.

If I take an example of a constructivist in the humanities, I would take the historian as my prime example who says, "Look, there is no such thing as history out there. History is always in the mind of the historian who produces it." We should recognize that, when you put together history, you have your point of view. Try to see others' points of views. See whether you can come up with a picture of the thing. Constructionism is not the object. It's kind of a bloody bore along the way. The fact of the matter is there is nothing out there of a kind that you can put your finger on. So let us do our best with this.

The strong version constructionists tend to push the view of constructionism as somehow replacing all views in order to save our souls. This worries me. But I have very strongly the feeling that, in the end, if the characterless types like me on this particular side would own up to what we're doing, I think we could have a good battle with the constructionists on the other side.

Daniel O'Connell

I would like to emphasize that it is the moral agent, ultimately, that we must deal with; not ourselves as moral agents so much as that poor old "man-in-the-street," who is the moral agent who is the subject of our discourse, and one of whom, of course, we are.

I think the phenomenology of this discourse and the introspective aspects have gone begging. How do people really use stories? Ali Moghaddam has tried to get at that and some of the rest of us too. I wish to repeat that I don't think any story line has the moral potency within itself, nor are possibilities, freedom of options as yet morality.

Morality needs more than just plain old options. Puppy dogs and snails have options. We have more than that, and that's what we're trying to get at, and possibly never get at it. I would, therefore, end with a plea for a sort of modesty—not agnosticism, but modesty. Now, I have calculated the amount of "I don't knows" that we have expressed during this period of time. It had to be very, very roughly calculated, but if you take as a minimum expression of hesitation phenomena the filled pauses or "uhs," "ums" or that sort of stuff, we spend a minimum of 15 full minutes uh-ah-umming. If you add the other hesitation phenomena, it adds up to a minimum of a full half hour. That's what we're really doing, wallowing in our uncertainties, and I think we should continue to wallow joyfully.

Robert George

I should say that I consider myself a moralist and my position in these matters to be moralistic. I am sympathetic to positivism broadly construed as the effort to describe social phenomena accurately and to every extent possible without importing evaluative judgments into the descriptions. I think that extent is limited, however.

I see the constructionism of Harré and possibly Sabini and Silver and Bruner to be "positivist" constructionism, the sort of constructionism that itself is compatible with—at least to the extent that I understand it—a range of different positions on moral questions, including fundamental moral questions or meta-ethical questions. I see the constructionism of Gergen and, I think, although I'm less clear, Shotter to be moralistic and to represent a competing view to the view that I take and to the range of other possible views on meta-ethical questions and normative ethics.

I think that the positivist-constructionist position could be very valuable in social science in helping us to flesh out precisely how cultures form persons, put people in the position of being autonomous actors who, through their autonomous action, help to shape the culture. And with those tools, I think that we can have more and more accurate descriptive anthropologies, sociologies, psychologies of those positive moralities, notoriously inconsistent with one another, that one finds across cultures. So I feel not the slightest threat to the positions that I have been defending as a moralist from the positivist social constructionists.

But I do feel a threat—and I put that forward as a something positive—from the Shotter–Gergen school of moralistic constructionism, and would ask them to provide me with reasons for why I should change the views of moral issues that I hold. I feel myself under a burden or obligation to them to provide reasons for them to abandon moralistic constructionism.

Nancy Much

Many of us seem to use the same words in rather different ways, words like person and self and culture, social order, law, and so on. It so happened that I found the paper that I was asked to comment upon used rather different language to talk about persons and morality and the social order than the language I, myself, would have proposed to talk about these same things.

I was interested in using, as a model of the constructionist philosophy, the notion that was developed within the context of Buddhism in India. Sometimes constructivist positions are thought to be incapable of generating morality, and this is an instance in which a specific kind of morality was indeed generated by a highly developed constructivist philosophy and psychology.

The main idea of this particular prescription, shall we say, this particular philosophical system focuses on appreciating how discursive processes create a world of reality. There may be a kind of reality, for example, such as natural law, that is independent of the reality that's discursively created. The point is, however, that we don't have access to that world independent of our discursive constructions except through those very discursive constructions. We never have direct access to reality—capital "R"—through our language, which is always a culturally constructed knowledge system of some kind or another, and which can only really index or point to that which is independent of it. It cannot directly access or describe it.

In other words, our discursive reasoning is always imbedded in culturally constructed knowledge structures which are relative realities. This isn't relative in the sense of relativism, and particularly not in the sense of moral relativism, which this approach does not necessarily lead to.

This view suggests, however, that the ultimate skill of discursive rationality has, so to speak, cut through its own ground. In other words, to see through its own discursive processes, to make discursive processes of the world transparent. In this way a kind of moral prescriptivity turns out to be attached to this particular system, and it has to do with the idea of defeating false consciousness defined as the over-reification of one's own discursive productions and the discursive productions of others.

In this system, that seeing through the discursive process is the beginning of moral intelligence, and the precondition for moral intelligence is to realize how discursive processes operate to construct alternative versions of the relative reality. The problem of human existence—it is very basic—is suffering. The causes of suffering are two. Number one, primitive beliefs about reality. This means the over-reification of our discursive constructions, naive realism if you like. The second cause being conflicting emotions which means that we fail to appreciate what is actually required for the cultivation of one's self and others in a given situation. So this provides, in a sense, a way for judging or evaluating societies, cultures, institutions, groups of any kind. How you know something is wrong with a group is that it generates pain and suffering. Now, suffering here is a technical term, and it doesn't just mean pain. Not all pain is bad.

Illusions created by discursive processes are both unreal and real at the same time. They are unreal in that they are contingent; they are constructed; they are independent of us. And they are real in that they are the reality in which we happen to live and operate and so which we have to respect and revere, in a sense, because they constitute the world in which we have possibilities for acting altogether. So the idea is, really, to see through illusion and, at the same time, treat it with reverence because it's the only contact with reality that we actually have.

The second part of the morality has to do with compassion, which means the realization that one is in a symbiotic relationship to others. This is the impetus for morality of the institute or the system. But the intention or images of self isn't enough. Moral action requires more. It requires the development of certain resources and skills—virtues one could say—that enable one to intervene in situations in such a way as to cultivate, rather than to destroy, one's self and others.

George Howard

The relativism that we've been talking about arises from the fact that none of us has direct access to reality. We're telling stories about reality. And the way in which one values that story is a function of where it gets us, what we can do with it, what its fruits are in a very long-term sense. To the extent that it is a compelling story, then it isn't just a waste of our time. Compatibly with what Joseph Rychlak has proposed, we can say that, in fact, we now understand our own humanity better because of that predicational story about what it is to be a human being.

I want to say that I find it difficult to understand considerations such as justice and/or morality unless there are persons, and that these persons are capable of some degree of self-determination. If there aren't persons, if they aren't capable of some degree of self-determination, I haven't a clue as to how one can think about dimensions like morality and justice.

What I have tried to do is to take the notion of human beings, to assume that they are agents with some ability to self-determine their actions, when, in fact, they might have done otherwise, within the cultures that they are currently existing in and trying to make sense about the world.

I would like to hope—and it is only a hope—that in that process of each of us trying to understand humans from our own living perspective, given the constraints of the system—whether it's the legal system, the scientific system, the philosophical system—within which we work that we will do our best. And in time, all of us will come to an understanding, or at least a better understanding, of human beings.

Finally, I would like to just say when one gets to issues of excellence or virtue or guilt or failure or blameworthiness, I take the MacIntyre position of saying all of those determinations are only possible within the system in which you are working. I cannot be held blameworthy from the system which I don't know. To the extent that anything I do or any of us do is seen as virtuous, it's because it is the proper practice within that system, that community in which we have identified ourselves. But again echoing Nancy Much, no community has divine access to the truth, to reality. Every community has a way of speaking, a way of using language to try to describe reality as best it can come to know it. Thus, the accounts are all ideologies in the way Jerry Bruner intends the term to be understood.

Fathali Moghaddam

Let me begin by telling you a story from another culture. This story is about an ostrich. In the Farsi language, the word for ostrich is a short word which literally translated into English means camel bird. The story goes like this:

They told the ostrich, "We would like you to fly and take a message." And the ostrich said, "I can't do that. I'm a camel." And they think to themselves and, "Okay, would you take some baggage for us if we could put it on you?" He said, "No, no, I can't do that. I'm a bird."

My problem at the moment with social constructionism is that it is acting very much like the ostrich. On the one hand, we say, "Okay, could you please bring us some data that we can deal with in a sort of objective way?" And they say, "Oh, no, no, no, we're not that kind of enterprise." On the other hand, we say, "Oh, you're not the positivist sort. Then perhaps we could have some clear ideological stance so that we know what is right and wrong." And they say, "Oh, no, no, no, we're not that kind of thing," and they fall back in the other camp.

Now, what I would like to do is to encourage what has been termed the moralistic constructionist and to push them along a little bit so that they go to that position where there's explicit ideology, explicit in the sense that we go beyond this position that we can't tell right from wrong because, well, right and wrong really only make sense within your cultural framework. Once you come out of that, then there's another cultural framework that could say what you are saying is right is actually wrong.

Well, this kind of thinking only works—as I tried to point out in my title—in a world that is either static, where there are no social interactions between cultural groups, or in a world which is completely homogeneous. If you have Salman Rushdie coming to Britain and then you have the Ayatollah saying this man must die, there has to be some way in which we can analyze these constructions of reality and make a decision of which of them is correct.

It is not enough for social constructionists to take the old positivist approach and say, "Oh, well, we are really outside all this. We're not going to make any decisions about what is right or wrong. We are apolitical." That kind of position doesn't serve our purpose, which is actually to try to achieve a just world.

What I would like to see is constructionism move along a little faster, in the sense that the ideology of constructionism must become explicit and there must be some explicit stands. Without these and without the explicit presentation of some kind of moral order, we are going to be back in that position where we're always standing outside of these very touchy decisions, and never coming to grips with what is really just and moral in the world.

John Shotter

I seem to remember a saying of Einstein's where he said it's not the task of science to give the taste of soup. And I do not think it's the task of the social constructionist, even of a moralistic kind, to provide everybody else with sure-fire moralities for the sure-fire decisions. I would like to emphasize that I am interested just in ordinary, naive, everyday, practical acting and reasoning of a moral kind and how to understand it. I don't think it can be understood in terms of providing abstract theories stated in terms of principles and laws, etc.

How does one perceive in a way which, quite literally, respects the being of the other? What actually does it mean to respect the being of the other? Now, I don't know. I think, in fact, that is one of the themes of investigation that we've got to conduct. What actually is a form of investigation which respects the being of the other?

Now, the diagram that was missing from my paper had to do with joint action, and it was a diagram that went like this. To say there was interaction between a first and second person, and to say the very general character of that interaction was such that it constructed a situation such that there was an inside and an outside to that situation. The outside was the third person. This created an "us"; this created a "them." And, of course, we can draw many such other embeddings for this kind of situation. But here we've got, quite literally, situated action. Here's a situation in which joint action is going on.

As I said at the time, this gave rise to two properties, but it gave rise to unintended consequences. We still had intentionality in the sense that quite literally there was a content for this situation and only certain actions fit. So already there was, so to speak, among the people involved in this action, a sense of what was fitting or not in that situation.

As far as social accountability was concerned, this joint action situation gave rise to unintended consequences which actually were still open to interpretation. But—and here, literally, is a moralistic aspect to the whole process—to the extent that any situation is still open to yet further determination, it is necessary to keep in existence, to institute the ways of interpretation, the ways of making sense, and to keep them going through history. Here, then, is a combination both of morality and power. That's why I said it was moralistic. We see that there are certain dominant ways of talking.

We've got ways of talking and ways of talking can therefore lend formal structure to circumstances. Our ways of talking must be grounded or rooted in circumstances. There may be a whole multiplicity of different ways of talking but they are all of a kind permitted by circumstances which remain open to yet further lendings or givings of structure and form.

I accept the two constructionisms cited by Robert George. I would suggest that the moralistic version (and I accept the accusation) is simply the commitment to open up the conversation to yet more voices.

Jerry Parrott

Well, to those of you who are here as newcomers or spectators, I hope that at least one thing is clear, now that we've succeeded in shrinking our seven hours of talk down to merely two. It was a good conference. What people were saying this morning wasn't quite the same thing they were saying on Friday. That's not true of all conferences I've been to, and so I think that's at least one measure in which we have succeeded. We have influenced each other and bent our views a little bit.

The theme of the conference, social science and the moral dimension, is one that is a strange question which leads you to ask, "Does social science have anything to tell us about the moral dimension in the first place?" We had to start off by showing that. And I think it's clear from the comments this morning that people have sketched out at least two main routes to try to do that.

One of them is to place emphasis on the second half of the term social science. That is, to emphasize that it's a science, and to thereby take advantage of social science's ability to describe and observe. A number of our speakers, I think, featured that as their new contribution to understanding the moral dimension. That is, there is not only this branch of prescriptive ethics, moral philosophy that exists, but there is also the everyday social world that we live in. Part of what social science can do is to describe how ethics can apply to everyday life, how it is capable of bringing about moral actions, negotiating moral realities in particular situations.

You can do this mostly within a single culture the way, say, Maury Silver has been doing; or you can take a look at the anthropological approach, what Nancy Much and George Howard presented us with; or you can talk about the theory of how all this goes on; or you can go about looking at the particular moral accounts, moral stories, and so forth that Jerry Bruner has been doing. This all seems to be one way social science can go about explaining the moral dimension and informing us about it.

One thing that's interesting about it is that it doesn't threaten Robert George, as he told us this morning, and the reason it doesn't threaten him is because, for the most part, it doesn't try to be prescriptive; it's descriptive. It's social science, a science.

The other routes would be to involve something a little bit more in the way of deciding what it is people ought to be doing in the first place, which involves departing from the strictly scientific (in some sense). You can do that in a couple of different ways. You can attempt actually to develop a systematic and internally consistent set of principles; that is, a moral philosophy. But another way is to take advantage of at least some versions of naturalistic moral philosophies which prescribe ethical maxims, not solely based on reasoning, but on some view of what human nature is like. To the extent that social science can inform us about human nature, it would influence our views of what people are capable of.

John Shotter's account is at once descriptive of everyday life—I think it certainly tries to be—but also, as I think he acknowledges, it has a prescriptive element as well. The worry that I've expressed about it is not in these terms. In fact, one thing that I think John Shotter's paper does is highlight something that came out as the theme of the conference; viz., that people sometimes talk about social constructionism as if it were this new discipline on the block, a very young discipline. It doesn't come across that way at all. It has been around for a while. It's not just a single theory; it's obviously more of a "movement" hosting a large number of different perspectives here being represented under one name. It already has to its credit quite a range of theories and techniques that have been developed under it. It's a fairly mature field.

All of that is impressive. The reservation I need to express about it is the extent to which it seems to require some version of moral relativism and, therefore, a certain skepticism that puts it in danger of doing one of two things. One is being inconsistent—that is, being certain that you can't be certain. This is problematic epistemologically. The other possibility is that it ends up not being able to say anything by being so consistent in its uncertainties. This is what Ali Moghaddam was getting at by the camel-bird problem. It's got to be careful to avoid becoming a theoretical ostrich.

But one most promising note that seems to come out of this weekend's meeting is the idea that, by continuing the theory-making and the cross-cultural observations and so forth, we can continue to get a better view of how people at different historical times and in different cultures come to flourish—or fail to. That seems to me to be a positive contribution to our understanding of what has been called here "the moral dimension."

INDEX

73799

DATE DUE